Early Warning and Conflict Resolution

Edited by

Kumar Rupesinghe
Senior Research Fellow
International Peace Research Institute, Oslo

and

Michiko Kuroda
Management Analysis Officer
The United Nations, New York

St. Martin's Press

First published in Great Britain 1992 by
THE MACMILLAN PRESS LTD
Houndmills, Basingstoke, Hampshire RG21 2XS
and London
Companies and representatives
throughout the world

This book is published in association with the International Peace
Research Institute, Oslo.

A catalogue record for this book is available from the British Library.

ISBN 0–333–56952–0

Printed in Great Britain by
Antony Rowe Ltd , Chippenham, Wiltshire

First published in the United States of America 1992 by
Scholarly and Reference Division,
ST. MARTIN'S PRESS, INC.,
175 Fifth Avenue,
New York, N.Y. 10010

ISBN 0–312–08564–8

Library of Congress Cataloging-in-Publication Data
Early warning and conflict resolution / edited by Kumar Rupesinghe and
Michiko Kuroda.
p.   cm.
Includes bibliographical references and index.
ISBN 0–312–08564–8
1. Pacific settlement of international disputes.   2. Conflict
management.   3. United Nations   I. Rupesinghe, Kumar.   II. Kuroda,
Michiko.
JX4473 . E23   1992
327 . 1 . 72—dc20   92–11321
                                                          CIP

Contents

Preface

Three years ago, a new commission devoted to internal conflicts and their resolution (ICON) was established within the International Peace Research Association (IPRA) in response to the growing recognition that internal conflicts within existing state boundaries would become the dominant form of conflict. ICON has become a loose network of scholars working in the area of internal conflict and governance pursuing an inter-disciplinary, global approach to conflicts and their transformation. ICON aims to stimulate and support scholarly work on early warning and conflict prevention, and holistic studies on conflict transformation. The present three volumes, and others planned for the future, are intended to contribute to the field, not least by encouraging scholars from regions of conflict to contribute to the discussion.

Acknowledgements

We would like to thank the various donors who financed the preparation and publication of these three volumes, containing contributions by nearly 50 scholars from many regions of the world who met at IPRA's XIII General Conference in Groningen in the Netherlands, from 3-7 July 1990. Without our donors' support, these publications would never have materialized. Particular thanks to Jan Ryssennars of the Netherlands Organization for International Development Cooperation (NOVIB), to Halle Jørn Hanssen and Ann Bauer of the Norwegian Ministry of Foreign Affairs, and Werner Lottje of the Evangelical Church in Germany, to Jan Erichsen of Kirkens Nødhjelp, and to Hiroshi Fuse, President of the Institute of Peace and Justice of the Risho Kosei-Kai.

Our special gratitude to Belinda Holdsworth of Macmillan Press Ltd who encouraged us to proceed with publication, and to Macmillan's obliging cooperation throughout the editorial process.

The editors would also like to thank Beth Steiner and Per Olav Maurstad for helping to organize the Groningen conference participation, and Arild Engelsen Ruud, Morten Løtveit, and Jan Helge Hordnes for careful pre-editing of the papers included in this volume, and for their painstaking work with references. Jan Helge Hordnes did particularly fine work in getting all the manuscripts into camera-ready form. Susan Høivik has given much of her spare time in language editing; Erik Ivås typed some of the manuscripts. I would like to thank Tord Høivik, my colleague and friend, for carefully reading the manuscripts and offering many suggestions for improvements. And my thanks also to more than 40 referees who provided valuable suggestions and criticisms at an early stage.

The International Peace Research Institute (PRIO) provided an excellent scholarly environment for the pursuit of this work. Finally a special debt of gratitude to our families and friends, who patiently bore with us throughout the many evenings and vacations which were devoted to this work.

Oslo, March 1992   Kumar Rupesinghe

Notes on the Contributors

Gregg Beyer
Gregg Beyer is currently the Director of Asylum at the U.S. Immigration and Naturalization Service. From 1988-1990, he was Senior Policy Analyst in the Office of Refugees, Asylum and Parole, at INS Headquarters. He is a 1966 graduate 'with Honors' in Political Science from UCLA, and received his Master's Public Administration from the J. F. Kennedy School of Government at Harvard in 1969. He has over 23 years experience in directing and managing 2 years in the Peace Corps in Thailand, 4 years directing an anti-poverty social service agency in California, and 11 years with the UNHCR.

Jürgen Dedring
Born on May 7, 1939 in Essen, Germany. Studied political science, history and sociology in Germany and in the United States. Degrees: Diplom-Politologe (Berlin 1965); A,M, and Ph.D. (Harvard University). Since 1972 at the United Nations. Joined in 1987 the new Office for Research and the Collection of Information where he is responsible inter alia for matters relating to early warning. Several publications on peace research, multilateralism, conflict resolution and early warning.

Helen Fein
Helen Fein is Executive Director of the Institute for the Study of Genocide and currently (1991) is a Visiting Scholar at the Human Rights Programme at Harvard Law School. She is known for her work on collective violence, the Holocaust, and genocide and recently did a comprehensive review essay on social-scientific theory on genocide for *Current Sociology*, (Spring 1990). She is the author of *Accounting for Genocide: National Responses and Jewish Victimization During the Holocaust*, 1979, the recipient of the 1979 Sorokin Award of the American Sociological Association.

Leon Gordenker
Leon Gordenker is Research Associate of the centre of International Studies and Professor Emeritus at Princeton University, and Adjunct Professor of the International Organization at the Graduate Institute of International Studies at Geneva. A long-time student of international organization, he has written many books and articles, among which are (with P.R. Baehr), *The United Nations in the 1990s* (in press) and *Refugees in International Politics*, 1988.

Michiko Kuroda, b. 1959 is a Management Analysis Officer of the United Nations at the UN headquarters in New York; until recently she was a Research Officer for the Joint Inspection Unit at the United Nations in Geneva; she holds a BA and an MA in International Relations; she has been involved in the publication of several JIU studies, including reports on early warning.

Hugh Miall
Hugh Miall is currently a Research Coordinator, Oxford Research Group. He received BA in Modern History, Oxford, and PhD from the University of Lancaster in Peace and Conflict Research. Previously worked with Earth Resources Research on energy policy issues (1979-85) and with the Open University Systems Group (1977-9). Author of *Nuclear Weapons: Who's in Charge?*, Macmillan, *Energy Efficient futures: Opening the Solar Option* (ERR), *The Peacemakers: Peaceful Settlement of Conflicts Since 1945*, Macmillan, (with Oliver Ramsbotham), *Beyond Deterrence: Britain, Germany and the new European Security Debate*, Macmillan. Secretary of the Conflict Research Society. Current research interests: conflict resolution, resource and environmental conflicts, European security issues.

Kinhide Mushakoji
Kinhide Mushakoji was born on October 1929 in Brussels. Presently Professor at the Faculty of International Studies of Meiji Gakuin University from 1969 to 1976, and Vice Rector for Programme of the United Nations University from 1976 to 1989. The President of the International Science Association from 1985 to 1988. He is the author of, inter alia, *Global Issues and Interparadigmatic Dialogue Essays on Multipolar Politics*, Torino, 1988, *Chikyuka Jidai no Kukuksai kankaku* (Internationalism in a Global Age), Tokyo, 1980, etc.

Gangapersand Ramcharan

B.G. Ramcharan is a national of Guyana. He was educated at the London School of Economics and Political Science, from which he holds a Ph.D. degree in international law. He is also a Barrister-at-Law of Lincoln's Inn. He served in the United Nations Centre for Human Rights for Fourteen years and then joined the Offices of the Secretary-General in New York, where he is currently chief of the Secretary-General's Drafting Service. He is the author of several books, including, The International Law and Practice of Early-Warning and Preventive Diplomacy (1991). His main interests are in international law, human rights, diplomacy and peacemaking.

Kumar Rupesinghe, b. 1943, Ph.D. in Sociology, City University, London, BA, honours, London School of Economics; Senior Researcher at the International Peace Research Institute, Oslo (PRIO); Secretary General of International Alert, 1992-; Chair of the International Peace Research Association's Commission on Internal Conflicts and their Resolution, (ICON); Coordinator of the United Nations University program on governance and conflict resolution. He has published and edited many articles and books in the field which include: *Conflict Resolution in Uganda*, James Curry Ltd., London, 1989, and *Ethnic Conflicts and Human Rights, a comparative perspective*, United Nations University, 1989.

Stephen Ryan

Stephen Ryan is Lecturer in Peace Studies at Magee College, University of Ulster. He received BA in International Relations from the University of Keele and PHD from the London School of Economics. His doctorate was a study of third party involvement in the Cyprus conflict between 1974 and 1983. He is the author of *Ethnic Conflict and International Relations* (1990) and of several articles on the relationship between ethnic conflict and interstate politics. He is now working on the role of peace-building initiatives in the resolution and transformation of inter-communal conflicts.

Hans Thoolen
Former Executive Secretary of the International Commission of
Jurists in Geneva and first Director of the Netherlands' Institute
of Human Rights. Since 1986 the head of UNHCR's Centre for
Documen-tation on Refugees (CDR).

Peter Walker is currently head of the Disaster Policy
Department at the League of Red Cross and Red Crescent
Societies in Geneva. He has previously worked as a Field
Director for various NGOs on disaster response and development
programs in the Sahel and Horn of Africa; he holds a BSC in
Environmental Sciences and a Ph.D. in Geography from the
University of Sheffield, England; current research interests are
on Disaster Vulnerability Analysis and Indigenous Knowledge.

Introduction

Kumar Rupesinghe

On the threshold of the 21th century, our societies are under-going major changes, on the move from one world order to another. Surely now is the time to ask whether the next phase in human civilization might see an end to war and violence. The demise of the Cold War – might that not provide a welcome opportunity for a serious and consistent approach to conflict prevention and early warning?

As long as the Cold War held sway, proposals for early warning were always controversial. Varying interpretations of national sovereignty stood in the way of building an effective system, as did resource ability and technical problems in data gathering. Early warning and conflict prevention seemed largely a pastime of a few intellectuals. Today, however, the concept is no longer taboo in international circles: development agencies, humanitarian agencies and governments alike have come to recognize the importance of conflict prevention.

The 20th century has truly been the bloodiest, most violent in all human civilization. We are all too aware of the death and destruction caused by two world wars and the countless interstate wars of this century. Less well known may be the staggering numbers of peoples killed by their own governments – the genocides, democides and ethnocides committed by the state against its own people. At the same time, there are paradoxes. At the time of writing, we may note few interstate wars in the world. Although the possibility of such wars always exists, most wars in recent years have taken place within a given nation-state. And yet, the international system persists in defining 'global security' largely in terms of interstate wars! Most recent and ongoing conflicts have centred on issues of ethnicity and self-determination, although they are not restricted to that. New conflict may be a result of many factors: ideological conflicts seem to have declined, whilst wars and conflicts over such issues as governance, democracy, environment and racism have increased in salience. Casualty figures and the refugee flows tell their own story. Over 18 million refugees are victims of such conflicts. Even more tellingly, there is a growing number of over 20 million who are defined as 'internally displaced' persons – unable to leave their country, and protected by no-one.

There are powerful reasons for the escalation of violence and war in many parts of the world. Indeed, the process of democratization itself may provoke ethnic and nationality conflicts. In redefining citizenship or in adopting unitary constitutions, majorities may alienate minorities. The greatest danger to the democratic process may lie in uncontrolled ethnic passions and violence. Furthermore, there is the sense of deprivation and poverty experienced by many millions of people. Many of the young today feel economically deprived, as well as alienated from a democratic process which seems to ignore their well-being. Frustrations may find a ready home in the appeal to ethnic and religious extremism. Moreover, the overriding impact of modernization and consumerism itself may evoke strong counter-tendencies towards nationalism and ethnicity. To compound all this, there is a massive proliferation of arms throughout the world. This involves not only the dangers of nuclear proliferation, but the equally but often unnoticed proliferation of small arms which can be bought and sold freely by merchants of death in so many parts of the world.

On the positive side, an important dividend of the close of the Cold War is that many old conflicts which had been fuelled by proxy wars may now be coming to an end. Examples are recent peace efforts in Cambodia, in Angola, in Mozambique and several other war-torn situations.

The challenge before us, then, is whether we can grasp this chance, and act to prevent violent conflicts from occurring. Can we halt the flow of refugees and create a climate of lasting peace and security? The answer will depend on how the international community chooses to address the issue of internal conflicts and civil wars, and whether we can create modalities for their timely resolution. Many of the old conflicts will disappear – but new ones are likely to appear with equal force. This point was brought home forcefully when, just as we were on the point of celebrating the end of the Cold War, the Iraqi invasion of Kuwait brought home to many the fragility and weakness of the international system. The world found itself even less prepared to stop the escalation of violence and war in Yugoslavia, a country once hailed as a model of a multi-ethnic democracy; the eruption of violence in Liberia; or in Somalia – and of course the extraordinary violence and ethnic and social unrest emerging in the former Soviet Union. Neither was the world prepared for the spate of new nations now claiming recognition and independent statehood. The question of self-determination was merely seen as a problem of decolonization: nobody was prepared for the new claims now being placed on the agenda.

A major weakness of the international system has been its inability to prevent or intervene in many of the internal wars that have plagued peace and security throughout the world. Civil wars – whether in the Horn of Africa, or in Mozambique, Angola, Sri Lanka, or Cambodia – rarely came to the attention of the UN Security Council. Now, preventing such civil wars, and developing a capability for warning and prevention, has become of urgent importance. Research on conflict formation and their maturation has revealed the many lacunae in the field. A significant problem has been the inability of the international system to give early warnings as a basis for preventive action. Even if such warnings do exist in the information world, this information is not transmitted as required to appropriate bodies. We know that early warning and early intervention are still the weak links in the chain. We also know that once a conflict matures there is a mismatch between the event and forms of intervention. Intervention, whether in the form of fact-finding or mediation, generally comes too late. Bloodshed has already begun, rancour and bitterness have developed, and both sides have already militarized the conflict. We know that parties to conflict can rarely find legitimate frameworks to discuss these issues. We also know that negotiations are not a matter for amateurs, but require the use of organizations with an insti-tutional memory. The process from early warning to conflict transformation calls for different types of intervention along the way. The problem is not only to reduce the duration of the conflict but also to reduce the mismatch between conflict escalation and intervention. This is why the UN and other organizations need to prepare a major contingency approach for conflict prevention.

Discussion on early warning is bound to be controversial, particularly when interpretations differ concerning sovereignty and forms of intervention. Many ideas about sovereignty are now being modified, and we can note a healthy debate as to the proper limits and extent of outside intervention. There is widespread agreement that gross and persistent violations of human rights need to be monitored, and that non-compliance should be met with universal condemnation and sanctions. Whilst there is agreement on the universality of human rights, there is as yet no agreement as to acceptable forms of intervention. This is bound to be a thorny issue, but there is no doubt that in the new dynamic situation, standard-setting is necessary. Instead of a universal formula which can be applied to all situations, we are likely to see a case-by-case approach which over the years can develop a consistent set of standards for timely intervention. There have already been some commendable examples, such as the UN intervention in El Salvador, in Cambodia, in Afghanistan and in Nicaragua. The forms and modalities of intervention will need to be addressed if the United Nations is to play a role in peace-making and peace building in the future.

The United Nations is rightly placed and has within its mandate the possibility to address this issue once and for all. At the moment, the UN would seem to have several options: traditional peace-keeping, or large-scale collective enforcement action as in Korea and more recently in Kuwait. Another proposal, put forward by Brian Urquhart, is a UN force to police ceasefires, where he suggests that a third strategy of international military operation is needed, somewhere between peace-keeping and large-scale enforcement. The aim would be to put an end to random violence and to provide a reasonable degree of peace and order so that humanitarian relief work could proceed and a conciliation process commence. Following Brian Urquhart's proposal has come another proposal, from Sadruddin Aga Khan, for UN Guards to contain civil conflict. The Guards Contingent formula was designed to meet the complex issue of humanitarian, security and political challenges concerning the refugee crisis in Iraq.

What is still needed is to address the issue of preventing large-scale conflicts and bloodshed. The very dynamics of conflicts are such that we need to have on hand an enlarged political 'package' in which many initiatives can have a consistent place. This is why the international community needs to provide a new framework to address these issues. Such a mechanism will in turn require early and timely intervention. Creating such framework may provide a basis for negotiating territorial grievances within an international setting. Further, guarantees for minorities may also be secured by providing comparative knowledge, as well as constitutional provisions and other mechanisms tried out elsewhere. Given timely warning and early enough alert information, the United Nations and Secretary-General should be able to provide their good offices to facilitate frameworks in which disputes can be resolved in a peaceful manner. There must be a quick and effective procedure for bringing impending violent situations to the attention of the Security Council. Fact-finding missions, if dispatched quickly, can accomplish a lot. Providing fora where the parties can identify the issues is another possibility – as are sending skilled peace-makers to talk with the parties, and providing competent negotiators as technical assistants. The point is to draw up a comprehensive contingency plan for entire regions of conflict. A contingency approach requires that due note is taken of the growing competence of regional bodies, which may prove better equipped to deal with conflicts at an early stage. The Conference on Security and Comfidence Building in Europe (CSCE) process in Europe is at present developing mechanisms for conflict resolution, and during its short history shown a willingness to provide for mediation and conflict resolution. The CSCE may in the end provide for standard setting with regard to minority protection, human rights violations and early intervention in conflicts. Other regional bodies, such as the Organisation of African Unity (OAU), or sub-regional bodies in different continents have shown a greater capability in taking an interest in inter-state and internal conflicts.

In the pursuit of peace-making initiatives, the UN can benefit from closer cooperation with non-governmental organizations (NGOs) in the field. Better understanding is required of the role that NGOs can play in early-warning information, and research, and in collaborating with the many organizations dealing with negotiations and conflict resolution. NGOs have a comparative advantage when it comes to early warning and conflict prevention. Human Rights organizations such as Amnesty International have already developed a global network of monitoring; and many others have developed global information systems, specializing in single-country situations or in thematic issues such as censorship or torture. There is a growing body of NGOs working on conflict resolution, ranging from mediation to developing negotiating skills. Also more and more global humanitarian organizations are in the forefront of victim protection. We need a better understanding of the comparative advantages of each type of organization; coalitions should be built up around issues. The current discussion on the role of the United Nations requires that informal coalitions be formed to address these issues at the highest level. In these ways, perhaps the 21 century may see a less violent and more peaceful world.

The contributions in this volume, then, are intended to address some of the conceptual and practical problems involved in early warning and conflict prevention. They are a result of a conference organized under the auspices of the Commission on Internal Conflict Resolution (ICON), a body organized under the International Peace Research Association (IPRA). The papers represent different approaches and different vantage points, but their common denominator is that they all seek to arrive at consensus as to the minimum requirements for early warning work.

Leon Gordenker suggests that the very popularity of the early warning idea and its manifold potential may obscure the need for conceptual clarity. He argues that the concept requires further elaboration and experimentation before it can be treated as practical. A distinction must be made between forecasting and early warning: by early warning we mean the ability to predict a given trend early enough for there to be a timely response.

Another useful distinction made by several of the authors is that between early warning as contingency planning for refugee flows, and early warning for conflict prevention. Contingency planning for refugee flows refers to the use of information to evoke active responses from organizations who need an effective early response system to meet a situation of mass exodus. The response system is primarily based on the work of the UNHCR and related humanitarian organizations. Another use of the concept however is linked to a conflict resolution perspective, where the concern is the ability to forecast potential conflict, so as to provide room for timely and more effective action. We must keep these two perspectives analytically distinct. Early warning must aim not only at contingency planning for victims, but also at victim prevention.

Several authors argue for human rights standards as an appropriate measure to monitor country-specific situations. *Gregg A. Beyer,* in his case study of the Issaks in Somalia, provides a telling example of the failure of human rights monitoring and early warning. Studying unsuccessful early warnings and ineffective intervention may be useful in avoiding mistakes and strengthening mechanisms. Beyer draws attention to the large gaps and lapses that still exist within human rights monitoring, where reporting is frequently episodic, incidental and fragmented. While arguing for the development of human rights indicators, he also points out that there is no agency to coordinate the information already received, and suggests cross-cutting alliances between the human rights community, the refugee community and various non-governmental entities and their governmental counterparts.

Helen Fein provides an innovative study on how to identify states which have a pattern of violations with the potential for escalation to mass murder and genocide. She uses life integrity rights as a basis for analysing violations in 50 states and 6 occupied regions. Her findings strengthen arguments for the use of human rights indicators. On the basis of the violations and their systematic nature she classifies states according to their propensity for genocide, and provides a scale ranging from Epidemic Genocide, Danger or Disaster Level, Calculated Killings, and to Bad and Good governments. An interesting observation based on her study is of course the neglect of early warning signals and the neutral attitude of bystanders. A conclusive finding is the lack of international responses to such violations, which helps to reinforce the power and audacity of the perpetrators.

Jürgen Dedring argues for a comprehensive early-warning operation using indicators which could capture the key dimensions of internal conflicts. He suggests the need to develop early-warning indicators for internal conflicts within states and stresses the importance of monitoring. Today, there is no longer a closed system; given the end of the Cold War, societies will become increasingly open, with modern communications systems facilitating monitoring and recording of information. However, such information handling requires systematization. According to Dedring, early-warning indicators should include the characteristics and behaviour of governments, classified according to levels of instability, incompetence and oppression. Further he refers to the issue of human rights violations, noting the need to develop standard formats for registering such violations and the importance of developing effective information exchange. The resurgence of ethnicity, nationalism and minority questions will become a major source of conflicts in the future.

Hans Thoolen's concerns are those of the practitioner, focusing on the massive explosion of information and how information as a raw material can be efficiently managed and organized. Computerized information systems have developed exponentially over the past decade, with thousands of data-bases now available. Telecommunications have improved equally: the combination of electronic data and high speed transmission holds out great promise for early warning, as this will permit the rapid transfer of large amounts of data at relatively low cost. Further, Thoolen notes that the political and international climate is more favourable towards early warning work, if only because traditional notions of sovereignty are being redefined. On the other hand, even if the United Nations has the authority to intervene, it requires a capable and competent policy on information exchange. Co-ordination must be not only at the decision-making level: needed are common approaches, protocols and standards which are compatible with each other. The lack of resources in the UN can even be turned into a positive factor by developing a division of labour within the UN, and with the proliferation of non-governmental networks and documentation centres.

Several contributions discuss the role of the United Nations in early warning. *Gangapersand Ramcharan* rightly places the issue of early warning within the larger perspectives of the United Nations – particularly in the way the organization defines its role, and who defines its role for the future. The answer will depend on many things, including the future of the early warning system at the UN, which he holds should be situated within the context of a much-needed grand strategy for the organization. Ramcharan identifies as one of the central problems in developing an integrated early warning system the fact that there is no central forum where the constituency for early warning can marshal its resources and stimulate policies and strategies. There is no general forum where member states, NGOs and the Secretariat can come together in a creative manner to encourage growth of early warning and preventive arrangements.

Compared to peacekeeping, early warning is still new within the UN; there should be a gradual, step-by-step approach. He also stresses that the UN cannot undertake the work of early warning and conflict resolution alone: rather the UN should draw on specialized networks drawn from different constituencies – from governmental representatives, non-governmental organizations, research institutions and think-tanks, and from the UN Secretariat. He calls for an annual consultative meeting of the representatives of different early warning networks not only to identify potential sources of conflict but also to develop preventive strategies.

Michiko Kuroda, in reviewing the various bodies and agencies within the UN, demonstrates the extent of specialization and competence which each has evolved in early warning work. However, what is unfortunate is that these efforts are fragmented, with lack of cooperation and coordination – a point made by many in the current volume. She suggests that one possible answer to this could be the special role which is to be played by high-power coordinator for humanitarian assistance. The problem emphasized by Thoolen and Gordenker, however, is that whereas there is a need for coordination at the top, what needs to be done is to integrate work at the bottom level through the adoption of common computer policies, protocols, and standards for the collection and exchange of information. Kuroda underlines the strengths of the UN, particularly in the vast network of field officers at the country level. They represent a potential capable of providing an excellent information source. On the other hand, this raises important policy issues, such as whether field officers should be required to exchange information on the human rights situation in a given country. Kuroda concludes by stressing the importance of a managerial approach to early warnings within the UN system.

Stephen Ryan addresses a highly relevant issue in discussing the role of the United Nations and the resolution of ethnic conflicts. He reviews the evolution of the UN and traces its strengths and weakneses particularly in responding to ethnic and internal conflicts, and asks how the UN can respond constructively to such conflicts. This question is important when states are themselves parties to such conflicts or are unable to respond constructively. Although the UN in its evolution has been primarily an organization of states, it has over the years developed an increasing willingess to involve itself in internal conflicts. These initiatives have been many sided, but significant breakthroughs have been achieved by the quiet diplomacy and good offices of the Secretary-General and his immediate aides. Ryan concludes that a successful strategy for dealing with ethnic conflict will have to involve a mixture of four strategies: peace-keeping, peace-making, peace building and minority protection. These approaches, he argues, must be seen as complementary to each other.

The UN has established a good record in peace-keeping operations. Ryan correctly points out that the organization is uniquely placed in view of the current international situation to set new standards and approaches and build competance in peace-making, peace building and minority protection. Minority protection will have to be seriously addressed and remedies sought for building a better and more effective system of protection and security. Further Ryan argues that the UN should co-operate with a variety of non-governmental networks engaged in conflict resolution. He emphasis the importance of training in skills for conflict resolution at the local level. Finally, Ryan's essay confirms once again the basic point: what is required is a contingency approach to conflicts emphasizing the preventive aspects and focusing on the need for frameworks for peace making and peace building.

The essay by *Kinhide Mushakoji* is a reflection on the emergence of a new world order and provides a wider discussion on conflicts and global governance. The issues which confront the global system are wide-ranging: the technocratic state system is no longer able to solve these problems, which range from global ecology to local identities. Technocratic rationality has become a prisoner of its own unilinear means and rationality. Technocratic rationality fails to discern the countervailing tendencies and movements which are in opposition to rational global management, and this produces a crisis of governability. As the different institutions and regimes in the international system, especially the United Nations, have to deal with all the above processes, they must therefore avoid becoming an instrument of techno-cratic globalism – regardless of how universal that claim may appear. Global mediation should not involve technocratic globalism: rather it should enable various social movements to participate freely in the governance process.

Mushakoji's main point of departure is that governance today cannot be guaranteed by the mere creation of institutions and regimes. Of vital importance is the growing contradiction between two opposing trends, one aiming at global governance and the other aiming at a governance approach rooted in local realities. The concept of civil society must be enlarged to provide space for new identity groups and social movements of the future. What is needed are institutions and regimes, from the local to the global levels. Global governance must be firmly based on the realities of local governance, with respect for all the diverse cultural communities within their own space. The new world order then is a process whereby conflicts between human groups can be transformed into a creative process. An important point, Mushakoji reminds us, is that technocratic concepts regarding crisis management must be replaced by more flexible approaches involving conflict transformation from within the self-organized processes. In this perspective conflicts are seen as part of the process of social transformation.

On the basis of a larger study, *Hugh Miall* examines the factors which influenced whether conflicts were peacefully resolved during the post war period. He compares settlements in both armed and peaceful conflicts, in order to identify the conditions for peaceful resolution of conflicts. His study differentiates clearly between internal and international conflicts. The international system is more competent and capable of resolving international conflicts, whereas only few cases of internal conflicts have been resolved through the use of the international system. The study also confirms the fact that conflicts over interests were easier to resolve peacefully than conflicts over values such as identity and ethnic conflicts and internal struggles for power. The international system has not been designed to cope with internal conflicts and is inadequately equipped to do so. Neither the UN or the regional organizations operate a functioning dispute settlement regime. The study confirms that early third-party intervention can assist peaceful resolution, and points to the need to develop regimes for dispute settlement appropriate to conflict at different levels.

Peter J.C. Walker explores the importance of building local knowledge and capabilities as a capable response system to famine. This important essay focuses on a related area of early warning – famine preparedness – where many findings may be relevant to early warning and conflict resolution as well. Walker's main conclusion is that the most effective famine early warning system can be developed by involving the local population in information gathering. A famine is not a catastrophic event which suddenly renders its victims helpless and dependent on outside aid for survival. A famine is a result of a process which goes through a whole series of stages: early warning means the ability to observe – in time – how the various stages in the process may develop. Measures must be taken to identify the early stages, so that famine relief strategies can build upon local coping mechanisms and work in partnership with the affected peoples, rather than as an imposed outside system. The lessons which Walker draws are of great interest to conflict early warnings.

NGOs in particular can learn much from the approaches and methodologies which have been used quite effectively. With regard to information gathering, Walker stresses that the communities who are affected must be closely involved in information gathering, analysis and prognosis of early warning information. It is the local communities who are able to observe close at hand the complex and contradictory processes underway in their societies, it is they who understand local languages and the cultural symbols associated with their society. Gathering and understanding information is not a linear process: it must be evolutionary and participatory. The vulnerable need to be trained and provided with skills for developing their own information systems. Walker again stresses that there is no point in investing in a warning system if no-one heeds the information. Local capacity-building therefore must go hand in hand with developing a capable national, regional and international response system. The system should not create a single message, but rather a network of messages, moving out and targeted to an ever-widening audience. The message must state clearly what the threat is, and what action the receiver of the message is being urged to take.

The limited space of the present volume has unfortunately not allowed us to focus enough on the extraordinary development of the non-governmental sector, at the country, regional and international levels. The progress of this 'third system' is truly astounding and heartening. Today's non-governmental networks – particularly in the field of conflict prevention – span many areas such as human rights, documentation and monitoring to conflict prevention, conflict resolution and transformation. In addition there are the humanitarian agencies and the refugee agencies, all of whom can play a leading role. What is necessary is to evolve a clear understanding of their strengths and weaknesses, and develop forms of cooperation. Humanitarian agencies who are in the frontline of victim protection have come to realise that there will have to be a better early warning capability and better coordination to enable timely response to humanitarian disasters. They have themselves through their work come to realise the cost effectiveness of conflict prevention. Unfortunately conflict prevention is still at an early phase of development. It is still war and violence which catches the headlines. But there is a growing and expanding awareness that more scholarly work needs to be done on the preventive aspects of conflict and violence. Many agencies and governments are beginning to realise the cost effectiveness of conflict prevention, if only to avoid the mindless violence and destruction which accompany internal strife. The United Nations itself is now more open and ready to discuss timely intervention, and has recently stressed the importance of preventive diplomacy and peace making. There is still a long way to go between perception and the art of the possible. We need to build new institutions and mechanisms which will transform the many phases leading to violence and large-scale violence. The end of the Cold War has meant that at least the horrors of a nuclear holocaust may be replaced by stable agreements on arms reductions and the limits being imposed on nuclear proliferation. Similar standard setting and work needs to be developed, to provide for the peaceful transformation of conflicts. This remains an open agenda for the new world order.

1

Early Warning:
Conceptual and Practical Issues

Leon Gordenker

1. INTRODUCTION

Large-scale movements of forced migrants[1] during the late 1970s and the following decade inspired a keen interest and a number of inquiries into the possibilities of systematic early warning. (Beyer, 1990; Clark, 1989; Drüke, 1990; Gordenker, 1986, 1989a, b; Kanninen, 1990). This notion has appeared to offer clear advantages, especially to administrators and policy-makers who deal with forced migrations. They have encouraged some of the basic explanations and have seen its elevation to a serious part of the program of the United Nations. To them, it appeared to promise additional time to prepare for the tasks ahead and even to take preventive action. Early warning, however, could equally apply to resolution of international conflicts that cause human disaster.

The very popularity of the early-warning idea and its manifold potential perhaps tend to obscure the need for conceptual clarity about what is really meant. This becomes all the more necessary if the idea is to be brought to practical application. Specific operationalization clearly needs development. This could best be done by a group of experts from several disciplines. It would be a costly, time-consuming effort, but essential to definitive testing of the potential of early warning. This paper will concentrate on the concept of early warning as it has been elaborated in connection with rural forced migration and makes suggestions about the practical potentials and limits of the idea.

1

It assumes that the interest in early warning has primarily humanitarian aims and that it does not merely further the control of human movement or sealing borders for some political end. It will emphasize the transnational aspects of early warning, rather than concentrating on the policies of any particular government.

Early warning as it is understood here consists of the use of informational data or indicators to forecast the movement of people who are forced to leave their customary dwelling places. (See further discussion, Gordenker, 1986: 170-71; Kanninen, 1990; United Nations Joint Inspection Unit, 1990). This definition neither specifies who develops the information nor the period of time covered. Moreover, it leaves aside the issue of who receives the forecast and what is done with it. These are issues that deserve careful attention if the concept of early warning is to become the basis of policy or action on behalf of forced migrants.

2. CAUSATIVE APPROACHES

In order to develop a practical system of early warning some assumptions about causation of forced migration are necessary. In the practical world of refugee affairs, causative hypotheses tend to be pushed aside as politically dangerous, irreparably vague, inapplicable in the short term or irrelevant to emergencies. Such arguments may simply mask other, not always contradictory, assumptions.

The political dangers that may be involved in early warning refer partly to the possibility that the forecasting agency may be criticized or repressed by a government or other organization that takes a forecast as injurious (Gordenker, 1989a). That has little directly to do with causation or with explicit reasoning about an early warning. Rather, it admits that an implicit analytical procedure correctly points to causes of forced migration and that the organizational parties involved prefer to avoid responsibility.

The claim of vagueness may simply reflect the failure to make assumptions explicit. If those who make forecasts and those who use them do not reach some mutual understanding about what they are undertaking, uncertainty will follow. As for the time period involved – short-term, middle-term, long-term –

that also depends on clarity about what sort of forecasting is undertaken and on the assumptions about causes of forced migration. Whether early warning is useful in a particular case is not a function of forecasting itself. It depends rather on the nature and timing of the warning and its reception by those given responsibility for response.

One set of causal approaches includes very general theories about the nature of society and social change. Classical liberal economic approaches to social organization suggest that migration depends on a cost-benefit equation. When marginal disutilities of staying put become too high, rational beings will move. This could be translated, for instance, into an assumption that when the market price of food becomes so high that many people begin to go hungry, they will seek to leave. Or if public services decline to the point of producing hardships, displacement will follow (Carruthers & Vining, 1982). Such an approach implies a long time frame with indicators mainly near the end when market prices become apparent. It relies on individual decisions but assumes that in some sense the market is shaped by non-economic, authoritative political or social externalities.

Another very general approach has to do with the systems of production and distribution. Various brands of Marxists suggest that imperialism, the nature of the capitalist system or changing relationships of production and distribution imply that individuals and groups may be forced by unemployment or social repression into migration. At a very abstract level, such causal theories resemble the cost-benefit analysis of the liberals, since both trace behaviour to economic causes. The time frame is long and the relationship between factors of production and distribution and forced migration appear deterministic. Exactly how specific forced migrations are related to the underlying factors in the causal chain is not charted in advance and probably would be visible only in retrospect.

A third approach reasons from certain classes of proximate causes, such as evident political, racial or religious persecution. This is the basis of the organized international approach to refugees and constitutes a basic element in the UN Convention on the Status of Refugees (United Nations Treaty Series). Two of its aspects have a direct bearing on the concept of early warning. Convention refugees include only those who are outside of their own country, so that formally the international mechanism for dealing with refugees does not take account of those persecuted people who could not reach shelter abroad. In addition, because it relies on a 'well-founded fear' of persecution at home as a test for extending refugee status, a subjective element forms a basis for decisions.

A related but broader causal scheme points to violations of human rights by governments or social forces as the fundamental factor in forced migration. The rights cover and go beyond political, racial and religious persecution to include the notion that if people do not enjoy minimal material and social rights they will feel forced to depart. Their deprivation may result either from deliberate governmental decisions or explicit social practices or from failure to act so as to produce a reasonable level of welfare. The time frame, obviously longer than the proximate causal reasoning of the existing international system, can be adapted for either very long or short time periods (Gordenker, 1987). The subjective element of the 'well-founded fear' is not necessary to the use of the human rights approach which employs legal standards and third-party observation in governments and inter-governmental organs. In addition, an impressive network of non-governmental organizations monitors observance of human rights.

3. DIMENSIONS OF EARLY WARNING

Whatever the causative approach, a set of behavioral dimensions has to be identified in order to establish a structure of thought to frame early warning. These dimensions include specification of a time frame, indicators of movement, and determination of the involvement of social institutions.

The time span of the indicators of early warning can be set out as long-term, medium-term and short-term. The precise length of these times probably must remain somewhat arbitrary as each incident of forced migration has particular characteristics. The time span depends partly on the type of early warning sought. If it has to do with proximate causes of immediate departure, then the time span must be short-term. If it has to do with the development of impulses to move deep within a social structure, then the perspective will be long-term, extending over years and even decades. The medium-term time frame therefore probably extends over months and includes readily discernible reasons for forced migration.

Indicators of movement may be grouped into three main sets: causes of forced departure; rate and character of movement; and direction of movement. The first is the most complex and the most difficult to measure. Nor is there any general agreement on how to turn a causal scheme into standard measurements. Nevertheless, for the sake of precision and informed judgement, such indicators should be further developed.

Recognizing causes of forced movement relates directly to the general approach used. As the existing international cooperation on the treatment of refugees offers one widely accepted set of causes and the international human rights standard a related and broader one, the latter appears to offer the best elaborated base for behavioral indicators (Gordenker, 1987; Kanninen, 1990). As the broad human rights standard, including provisions for refugees, can be used in all three time perspectives, it promises both flexibility and comparability among incidents for forced movement. Indicators of forced movements as a result of violations of the international human rights standard could be set out according to their time frame. Specific persecution, such as arbitrary arrest, imprisonment and general repression of members of specific political or social groups, are clearly visible and generally treated as recognizable proximate causes for movement in the short term. Guerilla activity, insurrection and international war should be included among the obvious proximate causes as well as, perhaps, long-term factors. They too arbitrarily deprive people of normal lives and reasonable expectations, even if they are not usually related to the human rights standard.

Because specific repression develops as a result of governmental decisions or failure to contain endemic social attitudes, a middle-term time perspective is appropriate. It would seek to identify the rates of development of reasons for forced migration and the growing intensity of reaction to them. Incompetent, malicious or otherwise faulty governmental programs would probably be grouped with these middle-term indicators. So would the gradual onset of guerilla warfare, insurrection or international warfare. All of them fall within the general framework of the human rights standard, which seeks to guarantee social integration of all people and a decent standard of living.

Violations of human rights may be encouraged by social attitudes and organization. These may include such factors as endemic racism, tribal or clan separation, caste systems and continuing political instability. Such long-term social factors directly relate to the application of general human rights standards, for they condition the ability of the societies involved to protect its members and meet a reasonable standard of human rights.

Once people begin a forced migration, for whatever cause, early warning should make clear with some precision a number of characteristics of the movement. The rate of movement derives from whether fast or slow transportation is being used: the range is between air travel and walking. Whether people are moving as individuals, small groups (such as families), large related groups or chaotic masses is also relevant to early warning. Their physical condition-whether they are sick, hungry, tired or well – also relates to the character of the forced migration. So, too, does the demographic composition of the forced migration, including the proportion of children, old people, young males, females and even levels of education and accustomed income.

The final set of indicators deals with the direction of movement. Forced migration is usually not confined to persons who cross state borders. A larger number is probably always left behind (Clark, 1989). Early warning should include notice of where the forced migrants aim to go, both within the borders of the state where they originate and outside. It should be able to indicate whether the migrants focus on particular target areas or are simply on the move in any possible direction away from danger.

4. USING EARLY WARNING

While a conceptual scheme for developing early warning of forced migration could be further developed along the lines indicated here, undertaking that technical task still leaves open the issues of how it is used. The most general purpose, it has been assumed here, is to further humanitarian service. That raises the specific questions of what is expected from early warning and who is expected to act on it (Gordenker, 1989a,b; Drüke, 1990; Kanninen, 1990; Pitterman, 1987).

Using existing structures of authority and service as a framework for determining the possible targets of early warning, four main types of units could be set out. These are: governments; intergovernmental organizations; transnational non-governmental organizations; and various non-official publics.

Early warning can be used by national governments in the near term to prepare policies and resources for the reception of forced migrants from other countries. It can be employed by subnational governmental units to put in place reception facilities and protection for newly-arrived forced migrants. Within national policies, both central and local governments could look ahead to more extended programs for forced migrants. Another use of early warning at the national level leads to assistance from and joint programs with intergovernmental organizations.

The involvement of intergovernmental organizations with forced migration has become increasingly clear in recent years (United Nations Joint Inspection Unit, 1990). The two obvious intergovernmental actors are the Office of the United Nations High Commissioner for Refugees (UNHCR) and the International Organization for Migration (IOM). Beyond that, the European Economic Community (EEC) and the World Food Program (WFP) have been major participants in humanitarian programs involving forced migration. A number of other organizations have also played varying roles and increasingly the World Bank and other development agencies have reacted to forced migrations. The United Nations and regional organizations concerned with the maintenance of peace or the promotion of human rights are also engaged by forced migrations. This network of interconnected organizations with an international perspective takes on important tasks in organizing member governmental responses to forced migration. Such organizations would be obvious consumers for early warning which could be employed both to anticipate the effects of forced migrations and even to avoid them by securing changes in the conditions which cause them.

Transnational non-governmental organizations come into contact with forced migrations in two primary ways (Lanphier, 1988). Some organizations, such as the British Refugee Council and the United States Committee on Refugees, undertake an advocacy role in national or international institutions, calling attention to forced migrations and urging responses to them. Other organizations serve as contractors to governments or intergovernmental organizations in assisting migrants. Some voluntary organizations function along both these main lines.

Beyond all of these institutions are groups of people of various definitions. Some of the activity of non-governmental groups mobilizes attitudinal and material support from either already defined publics or assemblies convened to address a particular incident of forced migration. Similar mobilizing effects may emanate from governments and intergovernmental organizations. Since early warning consists of information, it obviously could contribute to the formation of public attitudes and consequent actions.

As early warning is expected to begin a process of humanitarian response to forced migration, merely announcing a forecast of anticipated movement would seem too gross to be useful. Rather early warning should be directed to targets that could best use it for a specific situation. Consequently choices are required on the part of those who assemble early warnings. These choices essentially are political judgments about who will respond and how and why (Gordenker, 1989a,b). In some instances, it is conceivable that early warning would have negative results on the forced migrants or on the organizations receiving the data. In other instances, the warning agency would be heavily criticized. It can be taken for granted that governments will usually react defensively to outside criticism. So will social groups that violate the rights of others. Consequently, the form of an early warning and the degree of its public disclosure could have an important bearing on its results.

5. ORGANIZATIONAL CONCEPTS FOR EARLY WARNING

Although considerable discussion and thought has been devoted to early warning over the last decade, no reliable, functioning machinery to produce authoritative early warning of forced migration yet exists (Drüke, 1990; Tapinnen, 1990; United Nations Joint Inspection Unit, 1990). As forced migration almost inevitably involves governments and usually intergovernmental organization, not surprisingly the United Nations system has given some attention to the issue. It seems fairly clear, however, that neither generally accepted conceptual and organizational frameworks for early warning, nor a practical system under active management, has yet emerged. Nor is there any assurance that it ever will.

The conceptual basis of intergovernmental organization casts some doubt on whether in fact a reliable system could develop, whatever the policy decisions of the General Assembly. Assuming that indicators of forced migration were based on the human rights standard, the governments involved could be expected to throw up the same kind of dust blankets that characterize the behaviour of those criticized in the UN Commission on Human Rights (Franck, 1985). While the truth about human rights violations probably emerge eventually, obscurantist manoeuvres can succeed for long periods. The secretariat has often been doused with criticism. Moreover, anecdotal evidence accumulated over decades in the corridors of international organizations make it clear that senior officials shy away from confrontations with the representatives of governments. Those that do not, write their memoirs.

The nature of early warning of forced migration intrudes into the realm that governments usually describe as their domestic jurisdiction. While the promotion of human rights and the UN activities to diminish the effects of colonialism, as well as the new networks of field operations, have in fact resulted in a shrinking of this reserved area, the staffs of international organizations actively avoid accusations of intrusion. Moreover, the UNHCR, the organization most directly engaged in coping with forced migrations, has explicitly shunned any notion of early warning during all but the last three or so years of its 40-year existence. As a consequence, the international secretariats have few strong precedents on which to build a warning system.

Nevertheless, a majority of the UN General Assembly membership accepts in principle the utility of a centralized early warning function in the UN system (United Nations, 1989). The Secretary-General supports this idea and formulated the notions which led to responsibility for early warning being placed under the five-year-old Office for Research and the Collection of Information (ORCI). As a background to these developments were unprecedented refugee situations in the Horn of Africa, Afghanistan, Indochina and Sri Lanka and the very large movements of people out of eastern Europe and the Soviet Union after the massive political changes that accompanied the Gorbachev reforms.

The effort to create an early warning capacity in the UN system, however, began in a time of penury (Puchala, 1988, 1989). The leading financial contributors wanted zero-growth budgets. They also did their best to reduce expenditures on handling of refugees. As the governments that may be identified as involved in setting off forced migrations also adopt and contribute to the budgets of international organizations, creation of the necessary organization for early warning has been afflicted with considerable suspicion. Consequently, at the beginning of 1991, ORCI was not even equipped with suitable computer capacity, let alone a tested data base that was appropriate to the analysis that would lead to early warning (United Nations Joint Inspection Unit, 1990). Only a handful of busy officials was made available to improvise the system.

The notion that the UN system of organizations could be brought into a coordinated relationship so that their very large data-gathering resources might be used (United Nations Joint Inspection Unit, 1990) also involves conceptual difficulties. While the organizations associated with the United Nations have related general purposes, such as establishing the economic and social conditions for maintaining international peace or improving the human lot, they have quite different constituencies and relate to quite different parts of national governments. As a matter of course, they do not expect or accept instructions from the General Assembly (Williams, 1987). In some instances, their work began more than a century ago. They operate in every corner of the world. Consequently they have built up impressive data banks of various sorts and their officials may have a great deal of expertise on subject matters related to forced migrations, such as agricultural policy or labour conditions.

To take advantage of these resources, government representatives and senior organization officials often seek better coordination among these agencies. On the one hand, this is supposed to maximize the use of scarce resources by avoiding duplication. On the other, it is intended to create synergy. A substantial set of coordinating devices, such as the network of Resident Coordinators posted to more than 100 countries by the United Nations Development Program (UNDP), has been constructed. Yet while organizational coordination has been a constant theme in the General Assembly, in the Economic and Social Council and elsewhere in the system for more than 40 years, it is obvious that the system remains more a conceptual identification than a working reality (Kaufmann, 1990; Williams, 1987).

Nowhere is the lack of an operating concept more obvious than in the computerized data banks maintained by organizations in the UN system. Their computerization proceeded in fits and starts, beginning at different times and aimed at diverse purposes. The data banks are now notoriously disconnected and difficult to enter from outside. Consequently, either an early warning facility based in the UN system must develop its own dedicated data bank or await the construction of a coordinated system from the present disconnectedness.

If the conventional organizational concept of a centralized service which has steady support from connected agencies raises doubts, alternative approaches have not so far attracted support. These would involve either basing the system entirely in a non-governmental setting or combining non-official with official functions in some combination. Such alternative concepts would certainly not be immune from criticism on even deliberate hampering by governments. But they would be less susceptible to paralysis as a result of such criticism. As financial support would come partly from outside governments, they could conceivably continue after running afoul of one or several governments. Moreover, their disappearance would not involve the prestige of governments within a lofty multilateral structure.

Finally, the UN efforts to construct an early warning system implicitly assume that the best or most useful methods are known. As the entire subject is of recent origin and the conceptual framework of indicators can still generate doubts not tested by experience, an alternative procedural concept might still be applied. This is experimentation and pilot projects. Little systematic experimentation with early warning, either inside or outside of the UN system, has been reported[2] (United Nations, Joint Inspection Unit, 1990). The governmental procedures in the UN system have tended to overshadow the potential for development and experimentation in non-governmental organizations or in academic institutions.

6. CONCLUSIONS

Although the interest in early warning suggests that it is an idea of special relevance today, it remains a concept that requires further elaboration and experimentation before it can be treated as practical. Its further development depends especially on the choice of an appropriate, clear theoretical basis for understanding the causes of forced migration and on a scheme for using the results of analysis.

The centralized approach to early warning adopted by the General Assembly involves a number of serious political and management difficulties. The emergence and continuation of long-term support for UN services involves much uncertainty. As the international secretariats are both highly responsive to governmental pressure, dispose of restricted resources and serve enormously varied constituencies, attempts to create a high-grade, authoritative early-warning system may prove abortive. Or they may offer too easy a target for short-term advantages to bureaucratic free-booters or opposition based in national governments. Moreover, the difficulties with coordinating data resources within the UN system cannot be expected to be resolved easily or soon.

Beyond the conceptual and structural considerations, early warning involves a great deal of political judgement. The designation of ORCI as the bureaucratic centre of early warning in the UN system so far has meant that the Secretary-General ultimately becomes the early warner. This puts yet one more burden on an office that now has heavy tasks and slender political and material resources. The choice of the target for early warning, a crucial decision, might well be coloured more by political linkages than by humanitarian needs while still at a stage where worse could be prevented. In any case, the whole set of relationships among targets for early warning, the desired outcome, the degree of non-official involvement and the potentials and dangers of wide publicity is far from fully explored.

The same comment applies to more decentralized approaches to early warning. Aside from UNHCR and IOM, forced migration is not a central issue to any of the intergovernmental organizations. Their constituent members are states that have encouraged limited mandates and historically both UNHCR and IOM have operated under severe self-restraint with regard to early warning. National governmental organizations generally approach the matter as a domestic issue, defined by municipal law. Consequently, the least constrained organizations concerned with forced migration are non-governmental groups. They and especially constructed research agencies could perhaps become major developers of, and experimenters with, systematic early warning schemes.

NOTES

1. This term will be used to cover both refugees under the UN Convention on the Status of Refugees of 1951 and those persons who for reasons beyond the definition of the convention believe it imperative to flee from their normal homes. See further discussion in Gordenker (1987).

2. Akira Onishi and his colleagues at Soka University have been developing a model for monitoring displaced persons. (Akira Onishi, 1990). This model deals with a very broad set of economic indicators that were developed for other purposes and partly relies on expert opinion to track certain human rights violations.

REFERENCES

Beyer, Gregg A., 1990. 'Human Rights Monitoring and the Failure of Early Warning: A Practitioner's View', *International Journal of Refugee Law*, vol. 2, no. 1.

Carruthers, N. & R.A. Vining, 1982. 'International Migration: An Application of the Urban Location Choice Model', *World Politics*, vol. 35, no. 1.

Clark, L., 1989. *Early Warning of Refugee Flows*, Washington, D.C.: Refugee Policy Group, 1989.

Drüke, L., 1990. *Preventive Action for Refugee Producing Situations*, Frankfurt am Main: Peter Lang.

Franck, Thomas M., 1985. *Nation Against Nation*, New York: Oxford University Press.

Gordenker, L., 1986. 'Early Warning of Disastrous Population Movement', *International Migration Review*, vol. 20, no. 2.

Gordenker, L., 1987. *Refugees in International Politics*, New York: Columbia University Press.

Gordenker, L., 1989a. 'Early Warning of Refugee Incidents: Potentials and Obstacles', in Loescher, Gil & Monahan, Leila, eds, *Refugees and International Relations*, New York: Oxford University Press.

Gordenker, L., 1989b. 'Refugees in International Politics', in de Jong, D. & A. Voet, eds, *Refugees in the World: the European Community's Response*, Amsterdam and Utrecht: Dutch Refugee Council and Netherlands Institute of Human Rights.

Jonah, James O. C., 1989. 'The Monitoring of Factors Related to Possible Refugee Outflows and Comparable Emergencies', statement made to United Nations Commission on Human Rights, New York, February 17.

Kanninen, T., 1990. 'Early Warning of Forced Migration in the United Nations: Conceptual and Practical Issues', paper presented at Seminar on Development Strategies on Forced Migration in the Third World, The Hague, Institute of Social Studies, August 27-29.

Kaufmann, J. & N. Schrijver, 1990. *Changing Global Needs: Expanding Roles for the United Nations System*, Hanover, N.H.: Academic Council on the United Nations System.

Lanphier, C. M., 1988. 'Bureaucratization and Political Commitment: Challenges for NGO Refugee Assistance', in Bramwell, Anna C., ed, *Refugees in the Age of Total War*. London: Unwin Hyman.

Onishi, A., 1990. 'Model for Early Warning of Displaced Persons: FUGI Modelling System for Monitoring Early Warning of Displaced Persons', paper presented at the International Peace Research Association Conference, July 3-7, Groningen.

Pitterman, S., 1987. 'Determinants of International Refugee Policy: A Comparative Study of UNHCR Material Assistance to Refugees in Africa, 1963-1981', in Rogge, John R., ed., *Refugees: A Third World Dilemma*, Totawa, N.J.: Rowman & Littlefield.

Puchala, D. J. & R. A. Coate, 1988. *The State of the United Nations*, Hanover, N.J.: Academic Council on the United Nations System.

Puchala, D. J. & R.A. Coate, 1989. *The Challenge of Relevance: The United Nations in a Changing World Environment*, Hanover, N.H.: Academic Council on the United Nations System.United Nations, 1989.

UN General Assembly Resolution 44/164, adopted Dec. 15.

United Nations Joint Inspection Unit, 1989. 'The Coordination of Activities Related to Early Warning of Possible Refugee Flows'. UN Doc. JIU/REP/90/2. Geneva, July 1990.

United Nations Treaty Series, No. 2545, Vol. 189.Williams, Douglas, 1987. *The Specialized Agencies and the United Nations*, London: Hurst & Co.

Zolberg, Aristide, Astri Suhrke & Sergio Aguayo, 1986. 'International Factors in the Formation of Refugee Movements', *International Migration Review*, vol. 20, no. 2.

Zolberg, Aristide, Astri Suhrke & Sergio Aguayo, 1989. *Escape from Violence: Conflict and the Refugee Crisis in the Developing World*, New York: Oxford University Press.

2

Human Rights Monitoring: Lessons Learnt From the Case of the Issaks in Somalia[1]

Gregg A. Beyer[2]

1. THE CASE OF THE ISSAKS OF SOMALIA

The tragic situation of the Issaks of northern Somalia is about as close as one could come to a textbook case of human rights monitoring and the failure of early warning. Long-standing ethnic and economic tensions, exacerbated by the presence on previously Issak land of over 370,000 predominantly Ogadeni refugees from Ethiopia competing for scarce resources and influence, moved from accommodation to active enmity, culminating in open civil warfare between the Somali National Movement (SNM) and Somali government forces in May 1988 (United States Government Accounting Office, GAO, 1989, pp. 2-5). The Somali National Movement is a predominantly Issak rebel group reportedly formed in 1980, fighting against what it perceives as official discrimination by members of the non-Issak clans dominating the government (Immigration and Refugee Board Documentation Centre, 1989). Between May and July 1988, the northern cities of Burao and Hargeisa were almost completely levelled by Somali government shelling and aerial bombardment causing thousands of casualties among the civilian – mainly Issak – non-combatant population (GAO, 1989, p. 5). In addition, by one account, at least 5,000 unarmed civilian Issaks may have been 'purposely murdered by the Somali Armed Forces between May 1988 and March 1989.'[3] Another 600,000 Issaks may be internally displaced within Somalia, while some 350-450,000 are now refugees in Ethiopia and Djibouti (Burkhalter, 1989).

Since the events of May-July 1988, various governmental and non-governmental organizations (NGOs) have more formally recorded what human rights monitors and other observers had previously heard and had only publicly hinted at earlier:[4] that Issaks had been victims of human rights abuses since 1982, ranging from imprisonment and detention without charge or trial – during which many men were subjected to torture and beatings while women were repeatedly raped – to summary execution of suspected opposition guerrilla members or sympathizers (GAO, 1989, p. 3).[5] The US Government Accounting Office (GAO) reported that Issaks frequently had to pay large sums of money to the Somali military to obtain the release of their friends and relatives (GAO, 1989, p. 3). These and other abuses reportedly led to the radicalization of Issak students in 1984, which in turn led to increasingly severe repression of student demonstrations, ending in 1987 with a dusk-to-dawn curfew in the area. In late May 1988, the SNM attacked government officials in Hargeisa and Burao, two of the main cities in northern Somalia; the Somali Armed Forces responded with a massive show of force, in a brutal counterattack against the SNM and its predominantly Issak followers; civilian Issaks – accused collectively of supporting the SNM – were almost indiscriminately targeted for persecution (GAO, 1989, pp. 2-3).[6]

All this did not happen completely outside the range of international oversight and reporting. On the contrary, with the influx of the Ogadeni refugees from Ethiopia in the late 1970s, the international community had established itself in force in the area, represented by international organizations, national humanitarian and development activities, and non-governmental organizations working on refugee-related relief and development projects.

According to the United Nations High Commissioner for Refugees (UNHCR) – the international organization with lead responsibilities for legal protection and material assistance to Ogadeni refugees – since 1980 the international community has spent some 175 million US dollars on refugee-related projects in the area. UNHCR further reports that, at the height of this international effort, over twelve international and non-governmental organizations, involved directly in the implementation of these projects, were physically present in the area. This number has since declined, as most agencies pulled out in the face of continuing physical insecurity and the purported involvement of their erstwhile beneficiaries – the Ogadeni refugees – in the fray. Agencies from Austria (1), West Germany (1), the United Kingdom (4), the United States (5), and the Sudan (1) were among those involved at one time or another in project implementation; some even had sub-offices in Hargeisa, the site of many of the incidents involving Somali government forces and the Issaks.[7]

There can be no doubt that human rights abuses against the Issaks were noticed – either consciously or unconsciously – by the staff of many of these agencies, or that information concerning these abuses was included in reports sent to their own headquarters. In preparing this paper, the author contacted six humanitarian relief and/or development agencies which had operated in Somalia during that period. But none of them felt that human rights monitoring, *per se*, was in any way a formal part of its overall brief, or that it even should be part of their activities in any given country.

These agencies mentioned that their reports of tensions and violence in the area focused on human rights abuses only as indicators of the overall or regional context of their own operations. The agencies polled seemed to have had no clear idea about *how to monitor* human rights in any comprehensive manner nor *how to report* on abuses in any systematic way. All mentioned the 'non-political' and humanitarian character of their work in the country and the need 'to maintain good relations' with as many segments of the host country population as possible. They mentioned that even if they did monitor abuses and did wish to report more formally on them, they had little idea of *to whom* such reports should be sent, or *to what use* they might be put. By extension, it appears probable that for most of the agencies present on-site in Somalia, human rights monitoring was not an active part of their consciousness or of their sense of organizational responsibility.[8]

Yet, because of national sensitivities, governments accused of human rights violations sometimes barred human rights agencies, such as Human Rights Watch, from sending their own observers (Burkhalter, 1989, p. 2). Out of necessity, therefore, human rights groups interested in monitoring the situation of groups such as the Issaks have had to rely primarily on the unsystematic collection of observations by on-site 'non-political' humanitarian relief and development agencies, and on *ad hoc* briefings among their staff members. As a result, human rights reporting is frequently episodic, incidental, sporadic and spotty. The Canadian Immigration and Refugee Board's Documentation Centre, IRBDC, reports that a review of its data bank for the period 1980-1988 did not produce any substantial or substantive reporting on the increasing tensions between the government and the SNM, or on many of the systematic human rights abuses being perpetrated against the Issaks (IRBDC, 1989, p. 4). Similar results were reported by the Human Rights Internet as regards its search for pre-May 1988 published human rights reporting on the Issaks.[9]

Had systematic monitoring and reporting been done over time, the results could have been made available to international and national decision-making processes. Decision-makers might then have directed some of their foreign policy and financial resources specifically towards ameliorating these problems, thereby perhaps averting another flow of refugees.

If the international community is really interested in *averting* new flows of refugees, concerted international and national action is required. Deteriorating human rights situations must be identified early, and problems must be prevented from developing into human rights crises which could produce new flows of refugees. Action will have to be focused on several aspects of a situation, and implemented according to an agreed-upon integrated strategy. And if such action is to be effective, it must be coordinated by an organization with recognized lead responsibility over such activities.

In the case of the Issaks in Somalia, this did not happen. In addition, many of the Ogadeni refugees in the area – the recipients of continuing international humanitarian attention and assistance – reportedly actively assisted the Somali government forces in the 1988 repression of the Issaks (GAO, 1989, pp. 2-5). The situation of the Issaks in Somalia is not only a monumental human rights failure of the government of Somalia; it is also a failure on the part of the international community and of international organizations to cooperate in such a way as to avert new flows of refugees. The rhetoric of the mid-1980s, which called for a focus on the root causes of refugee movements and then for cooperative actions to address identified problems and thereby avert new flows, has not been followed by effective action.

2. THE UNITED NATIONS GROUP OF GOVERNMENTAL EXPERTS

For almost six years, a Group of Governmental Experts met under the auspices of United Nations General Assembly resolutions 36/148 (1981) and 37/121 (1982) to discuss international cooperation to avert new flows of refugees.[10] On 13 May 1986, its report and detailed recommendations were transmitted to the General Assembly for review (United Nations, 1986).

The main focus of these recommendations is on the use of existing international organs and their resources to *prevent* new flows of refugees by better targeting international attention on 'those projects that directly or indirectly could help avert new massive refugee flows...' (United Nations, 1986, para. 72). To achieve this, the report concluded that better planning and greater international and national coordination of efforts were required (United Nations, 1986, paras 63-4). In making its recommendations, the Group of Governmental Experts advocated better coordination not only of international action, but by implication, of direct national action also (United Nations, 1986, paras 58, 61, 66(e), 66(g)). Repeatedly, the report sought to limit the range of such actions and international coordination to those which are possible only in the context of international prohibitions against interference and intervention in the internal affairs of States (United Nations, 1986, paras 47-52).[11]

At the same time, the report refers to 'violations of human rights and fundamental freedoms, as defined in the Universal Declaration of Human Rights and other relevant international instruments [primarily the 1966 Covenants] ... (as) among the principal causes of massive flows of refugees' (United Nations, 1986, para. 35). At the same time, relevant international instruments reiterate 'the importance of maintaining and strengthening international peace founded upon freedom, equality, justice and respect for fundamental human rights ...'[12]

In considering actions necessary to avert new flows of refugees, the provisions of these two elements of international law and national responsibility may be in conflict. By frequent juxtaposing of references to the need for greater/better international cooperation on the one hand, and international prohibitions against interference in the domestic affairs of States on the other, the Group of Governmental Experts indirectly acknowledged this conflict, but left it unresolved. Actually to avert – a word which implies an active prevention – new flows of refugees, individual States and/or the international community as a whole may need to take action against a State which is seriously abusing the internationally-recognized fundamental human rights of its citizens. Such national and international actions may eventually include those which, almost by definition, would constitute non-physical interference in the internal affairs of the violating State. The question is not the compatibility of the two elements, but rather the relative primacy of one over the other in international law. It is difficult, if not impossible, for both elements of prevention and 'non-interference' to 'peacefully co-exist' when confronting situations such as Idi Amin's Uganda, Pol Pot's Kampuchea, Ayatollah Khomeini's Iran, or Nicolae Ceausescu's Romania.

One could argue that the purpose of internationally-recognized fundamental human rights standards is to circumscribe and constrain unbridled sovereign State action. 'Universal' human rights declarations identify general parameters of acceptable State action. States whose domestic actions go beyond these parameters could then be seen as violating international law and as threats to the maintenance of international peace and security. National governments individually, and collectively through the various forums and organs of the United Nations, have a moral and even quasi-legal responsibility to both note and react to such threats by State actions which violate these international parameters. In the context of systematically monitoring root causes and actively averting new flows of refugees, such non-physical 'interference' would be not only unavoidable, but even necessary.

In the case of the Issaks in Somalia, while the international community was preoccupied with assistance to Ogadeni refugees, another mass flow of refugees was developing, and eventually exploded in the events of May-July 1988. Few agencies seem to have directed either their attention or their resources to these incipient problems, and little effort seems to have been made to ameliorate, much less to prevent, a deteriorating human rights situation. Instead of improving conditions which could have led to the eventual voluntary return home of the Ogadeni refugees in Somalia, international assistance policies and programmes became an unwitting catalyst when one refugee situation helped beget another.

Clearly, international cooperation to avert new flows of refugees failed in the case of Somalia. Information on abuses could have been collected and reported; in general, it was not.[13] The main problem seems to be that international and national human rights monitors and policy decision-makers were compartmentalized by actual or self-defined, narrow institutional mandates; they were constrained by limited bureaucratic perspectives to a decision-making model that focused solely on the implementation of its own objectives. As such, they were unable to reach beyond these barriers in any concerted effort to address identified problems in the comprehensive and targeted way required to have an impact on them. Necessary bridges among governmental and non-governmental human rights monitors, and between these human rights monitors and institutional decision-makers, do not yet exist, either within the international community or in national settings such as the United States. Perhaps only national intelligence communities go about getting information in a systematic way that transcends narrowly-defined mandates. But obviously, their ends are not the same as those of policy-makers involved with humanitarian interventions. And even then, their intelligence reporting often requires inter-agency vetting and coordination, and their resultant actions are not always effective.

3. UNIFORM SYSTEMATIC HUMAN RIGHTS MONITORING AND RATING

Monitoring root causes may be difficult to coordinate with active explicit international cooperation to avert new flows of refugees, but clear possibilities exist within existing human and financial resources to make substantial improvements over the present. These possibilities require a new perspective on dealing with problems, rather than new or additional resources. Using this new perspective, the usual decision-making prisms (see Figure 1) would be reversed.

Instead of compartmentalized, agency-specific decision-making processes, which focus initially and primarily on the achievement of identified internal departmental or agency objectives (such as those dealing with foreign policy, human rights, economic assistance, or humanitarian assistance), and only secondarily on any particular situation, agency and inter-agency attention would begin with a focus on a specific human rights situation. Agency objectives and programmes would be formulated, implemented and coordinated in terms of an inter-agency situation-specific focus (see Figure 2).

Figure 1: *Decision-Making Prisms*

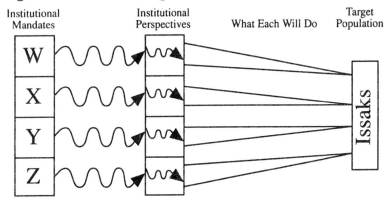

Under the former perspective, attention to a problem such as that involving the Issaks in Somalia is a by-product of inde-pendently determined, agency-specific decision-making in fur-therance of its own limited objectives. Using the latter perspec-tive, focus on a specific situation would require inter-agency attention and coordinated decision-making.

Given the experience of the past few years, in situations such as that of the Issaks in Somalia, one could question the commitment of national governments and the international com-munity as a whole to the concepts of monitoring root causes and averting new flows of refugees. The remainder of this article presents some ideas on the work needed, and the coordination required, to turn this rhetoric into reality. It addresses the collection of information, the collation and dissemination of information, and finally the use of this information in an early-warning process to avert new flows of refugees.

3.1. Collection of information: Monitoring root causes

Despite the many agencies and organizations involved in moni-toring human rights and reporting on abuses,[14] much of this collection is done according to self-defined mandates, using self-defined criteria and terms, and reporting primarily to internal or already-committed organizational constituents. Many human rights organizations already recognize that this situation is not conducive to the systematic collection of information and shared use of it. In response, several are beginning to coordinate their information gathering according to agreed-upon collection and retrieval standards. But bridges to decision-makers and into decision-making processes are vital, if this information is to be used and have an impact on resource allocations.

Figure 2: *Situation Specific Decision-making Process*

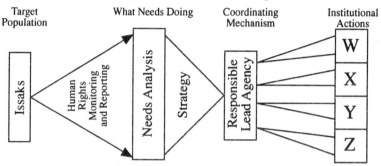

One such standardized system is that of HURIDOCS, the Human Rights Information and Documentation Systems, International. While other systems also exist, only HURIDOCS is reportedly attracting the international inter-agency support necessary for a system to eventually become something of a standard. HURIDOCS is involved with developing agreed-upon terminology and standard formats for collecting and disseminating bibliographic entries of interest to human rights monitoring (Thoolen, 1989). The Human Rights Internet in Cambridge, Massachusetts, which collaborates closely with HURIDOCS, also 'reviews, abstracts and indexes human rights literature, particularly that produced by non-governmental organizations (NGOs)'. In addition, HURIDOCS is actively promoting the development of standard formats for recording human rights 'events', that is, records of situations involving the violation of human rights. However, a distinction needs to be made between bibliographic activities and actual human rights fact-finding. HURIDOCS standards are particularly important for their facilitation of information searches and exchange, but there will always be a need for primary investigations and reporting by sources such as the media and implementing agencies present in or near to the sites of human rights violations.

Improving the collection and retrieval of human rights information is a necessary first step to a better system of international cooperation. Two other important aspects fundamental to monitoring root causes and averting new flows of refugees and displaced persons involve the development of a common identification of root causes and the formulation of an agreed-upon articulation of the human rights abuses, especially of those which might lead to persecution and refugee status according to the 1951 United Nations Convention relating to the Status of Refugees and its 1967 Protocol.[15]

While the 1948 Universal Declaration of Human Rights, and the 1966 International Covenants on Economic, Social and Cultural Rights and Civil and Political Rights, provide the basic definitions of fundamental human rights, the rights discussed are not yet organized into a system which would assist diverse agencies to systematically monitor and report on them within a comprehensive uniform framework. Without such a framework, each agency is likely to continue monitoring and reporting only on its 'own' human rights focus. While systematically collecting and disseminating information on a wide range of human rights abuses would be problematic for even the most well-established agencies, individual agency monitoring and reporting within a common framework would encourage both a broader spectrum and a clearer understanding of those human rights aspects that are left out. Developing the 'big picture' and an appreciation of the full pattern of abuse would thus be facilitated. Without this common framework, identifying gaps in the monitoring elements would be almost impossible.

A standard matrix of human rights and indicative levels of violations and abuse could be a useful contribution to the systematic assessment of human rights situations. Using a simple matrix, agencies could monitor various specific aspects of situations which may either lead to new flows of refugees or create conditions conducive to voluntary repatriation.

In discussions prior to the writing of this paper, the idea of a matrix – as an **idea** – received some initial support among human rights practitioners. However, almost no one was willing to try to construct it. Therefore, paraphrasing the adage whereby generalist-practitioners rush in where experts fear to tread, the present writer has made an initial attempt to collate the basic human rights enumerated in the Universal Declaration of Human Rights into one possible, indicative hierarchy of their fundamental importance to the prospect of potential refugee status,[16] and to identify various types of abuse or levels of violation which might be experienced under each (see Table 1).

The proposed matrix focuses on acts of discrimination and/or persecution which are examples of active abuse or violation perpetrated or targeted against an individual or group of individuals. Thus, for example, compulsion to join an association is included as one of the enumerated violations in the narrower focus of this matrix, while denial of the broader human right of freedom to form or join an association is not. Similarly, discriminatory denial of access to social services available to others is included as a violation in this matrix, while a government's inability and/or unwillingness to provide such services in general is not.

Broader formulations of these human rights would have to be included in a more general matrix than the one proposed here. Jack Donnelly and Rhoda E. Howard propose a 'short-list' of ten rights grouped into four categories: 'survival' rights; 'membership' rights; 'protection' rights; and 'empowerment' rights (Donnelly & Howard, 1988). For the purposes of monitoring root causes of potential Convention refugee status (that is, potential situations giving rise to a well-founded fear of persecution), the narrower focus of the matrix proposed in this present paper seems more appropriate and more manageable.

The proposed matrix is certainly not yet in its final form but the writer hopes that it will serve to inspire – or provoke – human rights experts to posit their own matrix for public scrutiny, comment and, eventually, consensus. One critic has already suggested the eventual need to include within any more definitive matrix some way to record the extent and/or the intensity of human rights abuses, beyond the more limited individual focus of the draft proposed in this paper.[17]

Once a draft matrix has been tentatively agreed upon – or at least accepted for purposes of discussions or coordination – it should be tested by various agencies involved in human rights monitoring and reporting. There is then a need to identify which agency or agencies (internationally and nationally) are to be responsible for monitoring and reporting on which specific box or boxes of the matrix. Exactly how to monitor human rights abuses and measure levels of violation requires urgent attention. For example, Michael Stohl and others propose a multidimensional perspective for such measuring which entails assessing the *scope* (that is, the level of harm), *intensity* (that is, the frequency), and *range* (that is, the size of the population targeted for abuse) of the abuse monitored (Stohl et al., 1986).

In assessing current mandates of existing human rights organizations, several different agencies or organizations may be involved in monitoring the same box, while other boxes may not be systematically monitored at all. Using the matrix, such gaps in monitoring the entire range of human rights situations in general could be identified. Also, the need for an overall coordinating apparatus to collate this information into a complete human rights picture of a particular situation would be illustrated.

3.2. Collation and dissemination

Once the above has been generally agreed upon, the agency or office must be identified which, internationally and within each national setting, is responsible for collating this information and disseminating it to relevant policy-makers and decision-makers. The Group of Governmental Experts recommended the establishment of a coordinating effort within the Office of the United Nations Secretary-General (United Nations, 1986, paras 70-1). Partly to this end, on 1 March 1987 the Secretary-General established the Office for Research and Collection of Information (ORCI) at United Nations Headquarters in New York, and named an Assistant Secretary-General as its head. The functions of ORCI include overseeing many aspects of this task, especially as these activities relate to monitoring and reporting on root causes and identifying potential refugee flows.[18]

In the United States, at least two attempts are being made systematically and regularly to monitor and report on human rights abuses around the world, and to make this reporting accessible to governmental and non-governmental policy-makers. In compliance with sections 116(d)(1) and 502(b) of the 1961 Foreign Assistance Act, as amended, reports on the human rights conditions in all countries that receive aid from the United States and all countries that are members of the United Nations are produced by the US government annually (US Department of State, 1989). These reports are compiled by the Bureau for Human Rights and Humanitarian Affairs of the US Department of State, based on reporting from US embassies and vetted through the Department's regional and functional bureaus.[19]

The main purpose of these reports is to provide the Congress with background information on human rights 'when considering assistance programs for specific foreign countries'.[20] According to Ambassador Richard Schifter, Assistant Secretary of State for Human Rights and Humanitarian Affairs:[21]

One of the very important consequences – perhaps unintended – of these legislative provisions (requiring annual human rights reporting by the Department of State) is that they have made human rights concerns an integral part of the State Department's daily reporting and daily decision-making. A human rights officer in an Embassy overseas who wants to write a good annual human rights report on the country in which he or she works must carefully monitor and observe human rights developments throughout the year on a daily basis.

However, the Human Rights Watch/Lawyers Committee for Human Rights' joint critique of these reports for 1988 notes that many of the US embassy human rights officers on whom this basic monitoring and reporting depends are often randomly selected, poorly trained by their predecessors and the Department, and inadequately supported by their ambassadors and the Bureau for Human Rights and Humanitarian Affairs within the Department of State (HRW/LCHR, 1989, p. 7). Furthermore, according to the same source, '(the) disparate quality of the reports illustrates the continuing intrusion of other foreign policy concerns in the reporting process...' (HRW/LCHR, 1989, p. 1). Another source notes that these annual reports, despite being initially perceived as vehicles for policy-making, produce little official US government response or policy adjustment.[22] In that view, these annual government-produced country human rights reports serve mainly to sensitize their preparers to the human rights situations in the countries concerned, and as a public informational document against which government actions can be assessed.[23]

Despite the existence of these two main human rights groups (as well as numerous other private human rights organizations of somewhat varying and often narrower foci), no national US apparatus for coordinating responses to the findings of these human rights monitors has yet been established, either within the Government or in the non-governmental sector. Several agencies inside and outside the government have mandates and staff which nominally could undertake this function. However, questions of organizational perspective, independence and turf seem so far to have prevented any meaningful discussion on the subject, let alone produced any general agreement on which agency could or should undertake the lead within the United States.

3.3. Uses of the information

Procedurally, national bureaucracies, both governmental and private, should act in such a way as to make maximum use of collected information. Seven main uses of such information can be identified, and are illustrated below using the United States as a model. Such arrangements would appear equally applicable and necessary for collective action within the international arena.

Identifying root causes
Developing baseline data specific to a particular situation through the creation of comprehensive integrated baseline reports on countries' respect for individual human rights and current abuses and/or levels of violation.

Monitoring root causes
Systematic reporting to identified government agencies and non-governmental organizations on improvements in, or deterioration of, the overall human rights situation in each country. Such agencies would include, at a minimum, those involved with human rights monitoring; foreign policy and diplomacy; economic assistance; representation of US views at international fora; US aid to international organizations; US refugee and asylum affairs; and non-governmental relief and development operations.

Early warning
Making predictions and preparations. Early identification of specific human rights abuses and the causes of any emerging human rights problem situation or situations.[24]

Averting new flows of refugees
Through coordinating 'preventive' responses. If a crisis appears to be developing, using the information as background to convene the appropriate agencies to discuss the options available and the actions (individual agency actions and actions integrated into a coordinated collective strategy) needed to have an impact on these problems.

Addressing new flows of refugees
By coordinating 'reactive' responses. If a human rights situation
develops into a crisis leading to either internal or external displacement of a country's nationals, using up-dated monitoring
and reporting as background to re-convene the appropriate
agencies to discuss options available and actions (individual
agency actions and actions integrated into a coordinated collective strategy) needed to ameliorate these problems and protect
and/or assist its victims.

For the United States, these responses could include,
amongst others: US government (USG) and/or NGO public
information activities, USG/NGO representations in appropriate
public and international fora, human rights representations,
foreign policy initiatives or diplomatic activities, allocation
or targeting of available economic assistance, additional or
earmarked USG allocations to international organizations, programming or re-programming refugee assistance and resettlement admissions policies and funding, and alerting or sensitizing
INS refugee and asylum adjudicators to specific situations;

Monitoring improvements of problem situations
As human rights situations improve, public recognition and/or
encouragement of further improvements should be considered,
and any agreed-upon position effected in an integrated and
coordinated inter-agency manner.

Adjusting policies accordingly
As situations improve, policies and procedures should be
adjusted accordingly.

4.   BRIDGING HUMAN RIGHTS MONITORING AND GOVERNMENT
     NGO ACTION

Each of the above activities requires detailed and reliable information gathered as a result of in-depth country monitoring and
objective reporting on human rights problems. Such monitoring
and reporting cannot or should not be left solely to either the
government or to NGOs. A bridge between the two main categories of information sources is urgently needed, as is the
identification of an appropriate locus for coordination of any
inter-agency action-oriented focus on a particular situation.

4.1. ... and the case of the Issaks

In an article in the *New York Times* on 13 August 1989, Holly Burkhalter of Human Rights Watch in Washington D.C., challenged the US government to take action to address the situation of Issaks in northern Somalia by more effective coordination of non-governmental monitoring and reporting, governmental pressure, and public opinion. She recommended actions to pressure the Government of Somalia to make reforms, to ameliorate the situation of the Issaks, and thus create conditions conducive to the eventual return of the thousands of Issak refugees from Ethiopia and Djibouti.

As the US Government Accounting Office has reported, few Issaks are likely to return until they are confident that it is safe to do so. Two primary requirements of that safety are the removal from, or 'barracking' in, of the Somali military presence in northern Somalia, and the resolution of the status and rights of the Ogadeni refugees still in that area (GAO, 1989, p. 11). Human Rights Watch, in its 20 June 1989 testimony before the House Banking Subcommittee on International Development Institutions and Finance, proposed additional objectives which should be met for US assistance to Somalia to continue:

> *ceasing torture, murder and political imprisonment of Somali citizens; reforming laws and regulations which permit imprisonment without trial and other abuses; dismantling the security agencies that have arrested thousands of people and created a climate of fear and lawlessness; permitting international human rights monitoring groups to visit all areas of the country to conduct fact-finding assessments; and disciplining those within the military who are responsible for the wanton destruction of the north and the murder of thousands of Somali civilians during the past year (Burkhalter, 1989, pp. 10-11).*

In her *New York Times* article, Ms Burkhalter further recommends coordinated US actions targeted at various international fora, including the World Bank, the International Monetary Fund and the African Development Bank, and additional action within the Bush Administration to address this situation more effectively.

The recommendations of this paper (see section 3.3 above), suggest that such actions could include:

• Better coordination of US responses at various international fora (such as the United Nations Development Program, the UN

Human Rights Commission, the International Committee of the Red Cross, the UN High Commissioner for Refugees, etc.) to keep an international focus on Somali violations of human rights and on the steps needed to ameliorate the situation and thus permit the eventual return and reintegration of Issaks currently internally and externally displaced.

• Better integration of public statements, public and private actions, and the programmes of various US executive departments and agencies, according to an agreed-upon national strategy involving, for example, the US Department of State (for better coordination between human rights and foreign policy) and the US Agency for International Development (for redirecting or targeting economic assistance).

• Better coordination of actions between the public and private sectors involved with one or more of the human rights, refugee relief, international development and foreign policy aspects of the situation in Somalia.

5. CONCLUSION

True coordination of actions according to an agreed-upon strategy is necessary to any focus on root cases and aversion of new flows of refugees. While not necessarily requiring additional financial resources, focusing on a particular situation – and then coordinating and integrating policy-making and program decision-making according to an agreed-upon strategy – has its bureaucratic constraints. Agencies within the government can be expected to resist such coordination, while current experience suggests that the possibilities for close cooperation and coordination between the government and outside agencies in the future are not yet overly promising. There is a need to bring human rights and refugee agencies together, and then to introduce the results of this collaboration into official government policy-making. Years of working in virtual isolation according to narrowly-defined and narrowly-perceived organizational mandates will make this bridging effort difficult.

5.1. International and national inaction: The Issaks and the failure of early warning: A case study

To demonstrate both the problems and potential benefits which might result from such coordinated action, an exercise involving inter-agency research and discussion should be developed, for example using the situation of the Issaks as a case study. The issues to be addressed could include:

Prediction and prevention

Who was monitoring the deteriorating situation of the Issaks in Somalia? What did we know (US government and US NGOs, and governments and NGOs elsewhere), and when did we know it? What did we (individually or collectively) do about it? Were actions taken coordinated or integrated into a general strategy? Would better coordination and focus of these activities have speeded our response and improved the situation of the Issaks in Somalia?

Assistance to victims

What did we do in response to this crisis once it happened? Who (in the US government, in the US and international NGO community, and in the international arena) did what? Were these responses coordinated and focused? Would greater coordination or focus have speeded up our overall response or made it more effective? Was the specific situation of the Issaks in Somalia ever separately addressed in planning for refugee assistance, refugee resettlement policies and programmes, and/or the need for, or desirability of, any official US designation of the Issaks as a group 'of special humanitarian concern' to the refugee programme of the United States?

Continuous monitoring of the situation

Which agencies (and where) are monitoring which aspects of any improvements in, or deterioration of, the problem situation (which 'box(es)' of the matrix)? Which agencies are collating this information into action-oriented reports most easily utilized by policy and resource allocations decision-makers? How are future actions in favour of the Issaks in Somalia being planned, focused and coordinated?

Lessons learned, recommendations for the future
What did we or can we learn from the experience of our response
to the situation of the Issaks in Somalia about averting (preventing) new flows of internally or externally displaced persons of
national and international humanitarian concern, and then
responding to such flows, if and when they happen again?

6. POSTSCRIPT

Since January 1990, when this article was first published, the
situation in Somalia has obviously changed dramatically for the
worse. Previously local problems in Somalia have spread
nationwide as the central government of Siad Barre collapsed
and the country fragmented into competing fiefdoms. These
developments have proven to be outside the ability of the international community to either influence or control. At the same
time, experience involving additional human rights situations,
most especially that involving the Kurds in northern Iraq following the end of the war in the Persian Gulf, reinforce many of
the statements and observations made in this paper concerning
the need for clearer official and unofficial institutional mandates,
greater specificity as to lead organizations, and increased
coordination of national and international responses to humanitarian emergencies.

In addition, bridge-building between the 'human rights
community' and the 'refugee community' and between the various non-governmental entities and their governmental counterparts involved in these issues, remains elusive. Lessons which
could be learned still need identification and discussion. There is
still need for additional thought and conceptualization, and even
greater need for thoughtful action in response to new and continuing international humanitarian crises. However, books such
as this current volume, and seminars such as that held by the
International Peace Research Institute, Oslo, those conducted by
the Centre for Refugee Studies at York University, and the
recently-concluded one organized by the *International Journal of
Refugee Law* are positive steps in the right direction.

NOTES

1. This article was first published as 'Human Rights Monitoring and the Failure of Early warning: A Practitioner's View' in *International Journal of Refugee law*, vol 2, no. 1, January 1990, pp 56-82, to which the editors wish to express their acknowledgements for granting permission to reprint.

2. The views expressed are the author's personal views and are not necessarily shared by the Immigration and naturalization Service (INS), the Department of Justice or the United States Government.

3. Gersony, R., *Why Somalis Flee.*

4. See, for example, the U.S. State Department's chapter on Somalia in its *Country Reports on Human Rights Practices for 1987*, (February 1988). This report notes the importance of clan identity to the political base of Somalia's President Mohamed Siad Barre (who 'recognizes the continuing strength of the traditional, clan-based political coalitions and uses clan politics as a means of maintaining his rule'); and that 'clan politics and clan rivalries occasionally erupt into violence' (p. 268). However, it makes only passing reference to the fact that 'some members of the Issak clan of the North actively support the insurgency of the anti-government SNM' (p. 268) after reporting the existence of the Somali National Movement (SNM) as an 'antiregime organization ... periodically conducting military attacks against Somali government and army establishments, primarily in northern Somalia' (p. 263). The report did record the political detention of a number of northern Somalis following 'mass arrests in the North in the wake of the conflict between the army and the SNM' (p. 265).

5. See also *Gersony report*, above, pp. 3-29; Burkhalter testimony, noted above, 20 June 1989, page 3.

6. See also *Gersony report*, above, pp. 24-26.

7. Telex MSC/6898 dated 20 October 1989 from UNHCR Headquarters, Geneva, Switzerland.

8. This conclusion is based on the author's discussions by phone with the representatives of six relief and/or development agencies operating in Somalia between 1980 and 1988.

9. Human Rights Internet, letter to the author dated 16 October 1989.

10. The Group was mandated to undertake a 'comprehensive review' of the ways, 'within existing relevant international instruments, norms and principles', to improve international cooperation to *avert* new flows of refugees, 'having due regard to the principle of non-interference in the internal affairs of sovereign States'.

11. The report specifically referred to the prohibitions contained in Article 2, paragraphs 4 and 7 of the United Nations Charter (10 December 1948), in the Declaration on the Inadmissibility of Intervention in the Domestic Affairs of States and the Protection of their Independence and Sovereignty (21 December 1965), and in the Declaration of Principles of International Law concerning Friendly Relations and Cooperation among States in Accordance with the Charter of the United Nations (24 October 1970).

12. See, for example, the Preamble to the Declaration on Principles of International Law concerning Friendly Relations.

13. Correspondence between the author and the IRBDC, Canada (letter dated 28 September 1989) and with Human Rights Internet (letter dated 16 October 1989).

14. See, for example, the work of agencies such as Amnesty International, the various Human Rights Watches, the Lawyers Committee for Human Rights, the U.S. Committee for Refugees, etc.

15. The Group of Governmental Experts foresaw that mass flows of refugees could result from a number of causes, including purely economic and even natural causes. However, for the purposes of this paper, only human rights abuses and monitoring root causes of potential Convention refugee status, that is, individualized persecution, are discussed.

16. As defined by the 1951 Convention and described in greater detail in *Handbook on Procedures and Criteria for Determining Refugee Status*, Geneva, UNHCR, 1979.

17. Wiseberg, Laurie S., Executive Director, Human Rights Internet, letter to the author, 16 October 1989.

18. See UN doc. ST/SGB/225. The fuller description of the functions and organization of this Office, as incorporated into the *UN Organizational Manual* through UN doc. ST/SGB/Organization, 3 October 1988, is contained in the annex to this article; see below, pp. 000-000. See also Ramcharan (1989).

19. Lawyer's Committee for Human Rights, *Report of the 1988 Project*, (mimeograph version), September 1988, pp. 96-107. See also id., *Linking Security Assistance and Human Rights*, 1989.

20. Department of State, *1988 Human Rights Report*.

21. Ibid., Introduction, p. 1.

22. Lawyer's Committee for Human Rights, *Report of the 1988 Project*, above note, p. 126.

23. Ibid., pp. 125, 131.

24. Lance Clark of the Refugee Policy Group in Washington, D.C., has written an excellent paper - due for publication in the near future - on early warning scenarios and the analysis of factors and events precipitating actual displacements of refugees.

REFERENCES

Burkhalter, H., 1989. 'Human Rights in Somalia', Human Rights Watch testimony before the United States House of Representatives Banking Subcommittee on International Development Institutions and Finance, 20 June 1989.

Donnelly, J., & R. Howard, 1988. 'Assessing National Human Rights Performance: A Theoretical Framework', *Human Rights Quarterly*, vol. 10, no. 2, pp. 214-48.

HRW/LCHR, 1989. *Critique: Review of the Department of State's Country Reports on Human Rights Practices for 1988*, July 1989, p. 7.

Immigration and Refugee Board Documentation Centre (IRBDC), 1989. 'Position of the Issaks in Somalia before May 1988', report dated 28 September 1989, Ottawa, Canada.

Ramcharan, B.G., 1989. 'Early Warning at the United Nations: The First Experiment', *International Journal of Refugee Law*, vol. 379.

Stohl, M., et al., 1986. 'State Violation of Human Rights: Issues and Problems of Measurement', *Human Rights Quarterly*, vol. 8, no. 4, pp. 592-606.

Thoolen, H., 1989. 'The Development of Legal Databases in Refugee Work', *International Journal of Refugee Law*, vol. 1, pp. 89-100.

United Nations, 1986. *Report of the Group of Governmental Experts on International Cooperation to Avert New Flows of Refugees*, UN doc. A/41/324, 13 May 1986.

United States Government Accounting Office (GAO), 1989. *Somalia, Observations Regarding the Northern Conflict and Resulting Conditions*, Report GAO/NSIAD-89-159.

US Department of State, 1989. *Country Reports on Human Rights Practices for 1988*, February 1989, p. 1.

Table 1: HUMAN RIGHTS MATRIX

Rights	Most Serious Violations/Abuses		
Life	Arbitrary deprivation of life, political killings or disappearances, by GE	Arbitrary deprivation of life, political killings or disappearances, by NGE, with government unwilling to prevent/protect	Arbitrary deprivation of life, political killings or disappearances, by NGE, with government unable to prevent/protect
Liberty	Slavery or involuntary servitude, by NGE, with government unwilling to prevent/protect	Slavery or involuntary servitude, by NGE, with government unable to prevent/protect	Arbitrary arrest *and* prolonged detention, by GE
Security of Person	Torture, inhuman treatment, by GE.	Torture, inhuman treatment, by NGE, with government unwilling to prevent/protect	Torture, inhuman treatment, by NGE, with government unable to prevent/protect
Economic Rights	Denial of Right to work and/or lawful means of subsistence through employment, by GE	Denial of choice of employment by GE	Denial of equal pay for equal work, by NGE or GE
Educational and Cultural Rights	Denial of right to education, by GE or NGE	Discriminatory denial of right to free elementary and/or secondary education available to others, by GE or NGE	Discriminatory denial of equal access to higher, technical or professional education based on merit, by GE or NGE
Personal Rights	Interference with freedom of thought, conscience and religion and its manifestation through teaching, practice, worship and observance, by GE	Interference with freedom of thought, conscience and religion and its manifestation through teaching, practice, worship and observance, by NGE, with government unwilling to prevent/protect	Interference with freedom of thought, conscience and religion and its manifestation through teaching, practice, worship and observance, by NGE, with government unwilling to prevent/protect
Legal, Political, and Nationality Rights	Discriminatory denial of equal treatment before the law	Denial of access to effective legal remedies to redress violations of fundamental rights granted by a constitution or law	Discriminatory denial of right to freely participate in the government (governing process and/or services) of his/her country
Social, Family and Property	Arbitrary deprivation/ confiscation of property, by GE	Arbitrary deprivation/ confiscation of property, by NGE with government unwilling to prevent/protect	Arbitrary deprivation/ confiscation of property, by NGE with government un-willing to prevent/protect
Personal Integrity and Privacy	Arbitrary interference with personal privacy, integrity, and/or correspondence, by GE	Arbitrary interference with personal privacy, integrity, and/or correspondence, by NGE with government unwilling to prevent/protect	Arbitrary interference with personal privacy, integrity, and/or correspondence, by NGE with government unwilling to prevent/protect

GE - Governmental Entity
NGE - Non-Governmental Entity

Continues...

Table 1: HUMAN RIGHTS MATRIX (continued)

Rights				
Life	Death penalty through 'due process', discriminatorily applied, by NGE	Death penalty, by NGE, with government unwilling to prevent/protect	Death penalty, by NGE, with government unwilling to prevent/protect	Random violence, by NGE, with government unable to prevent/protect
Liberty	Arbitrary detention, by NGE, with government unwilling to prevent/-protect	Arbitrary detention by NGE, with government unable to prevent/protect	Arbitrary arrest, by GE	Internal exile, by GE
Security of Person	Cruel, degrading treatment, by GE	Cruel, degrading treatment, by NGE, with government unable to prevent/protect	Cruel, degrading treatment, by NGE, with government unable to prevent/protect	Surveillance and/or harassment, by GE
Economic Rights	Discrimination in advancement in employment despite merit and seniority, by GE or NGE	Discriminatory denial of safe/healthy work environment, by GE or NGE	Denial of protection against unemployment and/or of unemployment compensation and other employee benefits available to others, by GE	Discriminatory denial of right to join trade unions available to others, by GE or NGE
Educational and Cultural Rights	Denial of parental right to choose the kind of education to be given to their children, by GE or NGE	Denial of freedom of choice of course of study, by GE or NGE	Discriminatory denial of free choice of educational institutions if otherwise qualified, by GE of NGE	Discriminatory fees charged in excess of those charged others for education, by GE or NGE
Personal Rights	Arbitrary interference with freedom of opinion and its expression through media and/or peaceful assembly, by GE or NGE	Compulsion to join and belong to an association, by GE	Compulsion to join and belong to an association, by NGE, with government unable to prevent/protect	Compulsion to join and belong to an association, by NGE, with government unable to prevent/protect
Legal, Political, and Nationality Rights	Discriminatory denial of access to effective legal assistance available to others	Arbitrary denial of nationality	Denial of freedom of movement or residence within one's country	Denial of right to leave and return to one's country
Social, Family and Property	Denial of right to social services/security available to others similarly situated	Discriminatory denial of social protection/benefits equal to those of others similarly situated	Discriminatory restrictions on housing and/or relegation to substandard housing	Discriminatory higher charges for same/similar housing available to others
Personal Integrity and Privacy	Arbitrary interference with family/home, by GE	Arbitrary interference with family/-home, by NGE, with government unable to prevent/protect	Arbitrary interference with family/-home, by NGE, with government unable to prevent/protect	Slander/libel against honour or reputation, by GE

Continues...

Table 1: HUMAN RIGHTS MATRIX (continued)

Rights			Less Serious Violations/Abuses
Life	Random violence, by NGE, with government unable to prevent/protect	Credible threat against life, by GE	Credible threat against life, by NGE
Liberty	External (forced) exile, by GE, or denial of return/reentry into one's country	Arrest and detention, by government in excess of normal punishment for same offenses	Intimidation and/or threat(s) against liberty
Security of Person	Surveillance and/or harassment, by NGE, with government unable to prevent/protect	Surveillance and/or harassment, by NGE, with government unable to prevent/protect	Credible threat(s) of cruel, inhuman or degrading treatment
Economic Rights	Discriminatory denial of right to protection and material interest resulting from production of scientific, literary or artistic work, by GE	Discriminatory denial of reasonable limitation on working hours and paid holidays enjoyed by others, by GE or NGE	Discriminatory denial of rest and leisure time available to others, by GE or NGE
Educational and Cultural Rights	Discriminatory imposition of greater duties to community service than required from others	Discriminatory denial of right to freely participate in the cultural life of the community	Discriminatory denial of right to freely enjoy the arts and share in scientific advancement and its benefits
Personal Rights	Harassment and/or discrimination because of thought, conscience, religion and its expression, by GE	Harassment and/or discrimination because of thought, conscience, religion and its expression, by NGE, with government unable to prevent/protect	Harassment and/or discrimination because of thought, conscience, religion and its expression, by NGE, with government unable to prevent/protect
Legal, Political, and Nationality Rights	Denial of right to change one's nationality	Discriminatory denial of equal access to fair and public hearing/trial by an impartial tribunal	Discriminatory harsher punishments for crimes/violations similar to others
Social, Family and Property	Discriminatory denial of right to live anywhere one can otherwise afford	Interference in owning property alone or in association with others	Discriminatory interference in rights available to others to freely choose a spouse and found a family
Personal Integrity and Privacy	Slander/libel against honour or reputation, by NGE, with government unwilling to prevent/protect	Slander/libel against honour or reputation, by NGE, with government unable to prevent/protect	Credible threat against privacy, family, home, correspondence, honour or reputation

GE - Government Entity
NGE - Non-Government Entity

3

Dangerous States and Endangered Peoples: Implications of Life Integrity Violations Analysis

Helen Fein[1]

1. CONCEPTION AND SCALING OF LIFE INTEGRITY VIOLATIONS

1.1. Background: Discriminating perpetrators from other states

In order to assess whether one could discriminate states perpetrating (or attempting) genocide or mass political killings from other states before these crimes were corroborated, an exploratory study paired four states (in different regions) committing genocide or political killings between 1975-1984 with matched states which were non-perpetrators during that period (Fein 1988). States were matched by region, length of political experience since independence, similar colonial experience, similar degree of cultural heterogeneity, and dominant religion. These four pairs (of perpetrator and non-perpetrator) were compared for four or five year periods starting from the political or regime change which prefaced the perpetrator's resort to mass killing. Drawing on methods of content analysis, we devised the Life Integrity Violation Analysis Form (later described) which checked the presence or absence of certain practices noted in the *Amnesty International Report* for the given years. These pairs (perpetrators listed first) follow: Ethiopia/Nigeria (1974-78); Cambodia/ Sri Lanka (1975-78); Iran/Turkey (1979-83); and Argentina/ Venezuela (1976-80).

Perpetrators differed from the non-perpetrators by their use of a pattern of summary and extrajudicial execution (and abducted or 'disappeared' persons), lack of any due process of law (or indeed any process), and a pattern of deaths in police custody from the beginning of the period observed. Torture was reported for three of four perpetrators but was also widely used by one of the nonperpetrators (Turkey). Mass killing was reported by AI for only the last three years in Ethiopia and the last two in Cambodia. Spirer (1988) analyzed the likeness among perpetrators and non-perpetrators through use of similarity coefficients, showing that both perpetrators (mean .71, median .73) and non-perpetrators (mean .76, median .71) were much more alike than perpetrators and non-perpetrators (mean .40, median .42). This indicated that we can identify the set of states which have a pattern of violations with the potential for escalation to mass murder. Discussion then focused on the ideologies and goals of these states which in part determined who were the victims.

1.2. Lives at risk: An analysis of 50 states in 1987
This led to the pilot study reported herein, a more systematic analysis of violations of life integrity in fifty states and six occupied regions[2] in 1987 (Fein 1990a). The concept of life integrity, stemming from the right to life, is an innovation in social research measuring human rights violations. 'Life integrity rights' comprise six related claims: the right to life; to bodily inviolability; to security from arbitrary punishment, seizure, and detention; to own one's body and labour; to free movement without discrimination; to marry and to form a family. This study examines the level of violation of the first three rights on the basis of the *Amnesty International 1988 Report*.

The states included were selected because they had perpetrated genocides or ethnic massacres in the past, were engaged in civil strife in 1987, had large numbers of 'minorities at risk' (see Gurr & Scaritt 1989) or showed signs of escalation of abuses in 1987 and were located in areas of high conflict. These states are located in Africa, Asia, the Middle-East, Central and South America.

The Soviet Union could have been included by these criteria, but it was excluded because perestroika seemed to imply that the Soviet state would be less likely to violate life integrity now than it was formerly. The unexpected consequences - including pogroms and state failure to protect people - and possibility of further violations have now shown this was a mistake. Future studies should include the USSR and expand the number of vulnerable states studied. Had the USSR been included, the evidence of mistreatment of prisoners and misuse of psychiatry in 1987 implies that it would have been in the B (Bad) class of violators.

The method is based on content analysis of violations in 1987 reported in the *Amnesty International 1988 Report*. This report focuses on several major violations of theoretical interest: torture and state killings outside war - legal, summary, and extrajudicial executions However, not all the life-integrity claims whose violation needs assessment (see Table 1) are monitored by AI nor are all of AI's concerns indexed in this study; capital punishment (later discussed herein) is omitted. AI was chosen as the single best source to begin such study because of the range and quality of AI's research, the universality and clarity of its mandate and the limits of our own resources. Ideally, one would use several data sources, including other human rights non-governmental organizations and governmental assessments of human rights - the United States currently assess the human rights situation of most states in the world, while a group of smaller, like-minded industrial countries assess a substantial number.

The survey schedule used herein, the Life Integrity Violation Analysis form (LIVA), was designed and pretested by Helen Fein. LIVA is a structured, 32-page, 37-item form (with eight open-ended questions) which research assistants use to code the presence or absence of specific violations and practices and their prevalence (or estimates of same) based on the *AI Report*.

Both governmental and non-governmental violations were coded, including patterns of extrajudicical and summary execution, mass killings and massacres, disappeared or abducted persons, deaths in custody; planned starvation, deportations, and separations of families; torture, ill treatment of prisoners, and rape and sexual abuse by government agents; detention of political prisoners and prisoners of conscience; repressive sanctions outside control facilities; deaths in custody and police immunity from sanctions. All underlined terms were defined in a coder glossary, drawing on definitions in international law, Amnesty International definitions, and previous usage of terms in human rights recording (see Reiter et al., 1986; Schmid 1988, p. 75). Wherever possible, characteristics (and numbers) of victims were coded, and the prevalence of and sanctioning of practices were assessed.

Both Helen Fein and one of two research assistants (working independently after training) coded all cases; two thirds of states were coded by two or three coders. Training of coders led to high inter-coder reliability.[3]

1.3. The concept of life integrity

Understanding the prevalence of human rights and wrongs (or their violation) is often confounded by different presuppositions and divisions. Some may question the basis and universality of the concept of rights. Many debate priorities among human rights, assuming there are but two classes: political and civil rights, aspects of freedom or democracy; and social and economic rights, aspects of equity or just distribution.

We begin from a different approach, without judgement on the underlying philosophic justifications for rights. Rights are regarded sociologically as expressions of human need - which means all humans can enjoy them - and claims successfully wrested by peoples: rules with sanctions, norms governing expectations. These claims tend to expand as previously won rights are exercised.

However, both international law and common experience suggest that there are some claims one needs to secure before others: the right to life, to be free from violation of the body and the integrity of the person, family, and group. The right to life is basic in both domestic and international law - indeed 'all other human rights become meaningless if the basic right to life is not duly protected' (Von Aggelen, 1986, p. 743).

The right to life is not an absolute right in international law; neither capital punishment nor war is categorically outlawed by any international covenant (Sieghart, 1983, pp. 130-131). But respect for the right to life is obligatory in times of war and peace. Both homicide and genocide are now general crimes in domestic and international law.

Linked to the right to be are other rights implying the claim to be let alone: the right to be not violated, to be free from arbitrary fear, to be the owner of one's body and labour, to be mobile, to be part of a family. Foremost among them is the right to be free from invasion of one's body and mind: from torture, rape and sexual abuse, and humiliating punishments. Freedom from fear of arbitrary seizure is also basic to enjoying other rights. There is general agreement (see covenants in Figure 1 following) as to the value of being free rather than being owned, of being able to move without discrimination, and of living as part of a family and community from which one derives identity and meaning.

Violations of many of these rights (noted in Table 1) are criminalized in international law and the domestic law of many states. Four of the six are subjects of special conventions: listed in the order of their passage, the outlawed practices are slavery, genocide, racial discrimination and apartheid, and torture.

At times these practices have been labelled violations of physical or legal integrity or the integrity of the person; at other times they have been termed gross violations of human rights, basic human rights, or non-derogable rights. In 1977, US Secretary of State Vance discriminated between civil and political rights and 'the right to the fulfilment of...vital needs' from 'the right to be free from governmental violations of the integrity of the persons': his examples included torture; cruel, inhuman, or degrading treatment or punishment; and arbitrary arrest or imprisonment.

We label the violations of the rights specified in Table 1 as life integrity violations because they imply an integrated set of claims defending the biological and social integration of persons and groups: of body and mind among all humans (denied by genocide, murder, and torture); of self-ownership, mobility and social dignity (denied by slavery, segregation and apartheid); of self and family (denied by prohibiting marriage and family development); and of the reciprocal guarantees for protection of human groups (denied by genocide). How these rights are related to civil and political rights and to social and economic rights is a question which demands empirical inquiry; indexing life integrity rights separately will enable researchers to probe this.

Indexing life integrity violations requires us first to specify the observable practices which exemplify each class of violation and then to find or put together sources documenting them. Relying only on one source - the *AI 1988 Report* - we can only do this for (1) The right to life; (2) The right to personal inviolability; and (3) The right to be free of fear of arbitrary seizure, detention, and punishment. The results of this analysis are described below.

Table 1: Life Integrity Rights and Their Violations

Rights	Violations	International Law against violation / date in force**
1. The right to life	Genocide*, Mass killing, Summary/extrajudicial executions, "Disappearances"	UN Genocide Conv. 1951, UDHR 3, ICPR 6
2. The right to personal inviolability / not to be hurt	Torture, rape and sexual abuse, Inhuman and degrading treatment and punishment	UN Torture Conv. 1987, UDHR 5, ICPR 7
3. The right to be free of fear of arbitrary seizure, detention and punishment	No due process or any process, Arbitrary detention, Lack of fair trial	UDHR 3, ICPR 9
4. Freedom to own one's body and labour	Slavery, Forced labour, Debt slavery and equivalent institutions	Slavery Conv. 1927, Supplementary Conv. 1957, Convention concerning abolition of forced labour 1959
5. The right to free movement without discrimination	Group macro-segregation (apartheid), Micro-segregation, Group detention, Forced resettlement	Convention on the suppression & punishment of crime of apartheid 1976, Int. Conv. on the Elimination of all forms of racial discrimination, 1969 ICPR 9, 13
6. The right to create and cohabit with family	No marriage or family formation permitted, Kidnapping and adoption or involuntary transfer of children*	UDHR 3, ICPR 9

* Besides mass killing, genocide also may include a) murder through starvation and poisoning of air, water or food and b) the involuntary transfer of children when such practices are directed against a national, ethnic, religious, or racial group with intent to destroy the group.

** Reference is to articles of the following:
  UDHR - Universal Declaration of Human Rights, 1948;
  ICPR - International Covenant on Civil and Political Rights, 1976.

1.4. Findings

The study found that violation of the right to life and violations of the right to inviolability are uni-dimensional. This means that states which practice mass killing also practice calculated individual killings and torture; states which go no further than calculated individual killing also practice torture routinely, with few exceptions. Table A (end of chapter) shows that violators form an almost perfect Guttman scale: the coefficient of reproducibility is .976.

Our aim was to seek answers to some simple questions which might preface later inferences rather than to test hypotheses. To start with: What states were the most dangerous? Who were the victims of the state? Which peoples were endangered and why? How is the level of state violation related to the use of violence by challengers to the state? How is the level of state violation related to the type of government? (Students of the state can also relate these stages of violation to the stages and functions of state repression, terror and genocide.) Lastly, what are the anticipatable effects of such violations: e.g., how is the level of state violation related to the number of refugees generated by states? A brief precis of findings follows.

Five levels of violation were theoretically distinguishable: from the worst conceivable - E: Epidemic Genocide - in descending order through D: Danger or Disaster level, C: Calculated Killings, and B: Bad to A: Apparently none of the above. No states at level E - epidemic genocide - were found. Ten states were in the top-ranking D level of violators, the danger of/or disaster level, perpetrating indiscriminate mass killing and massacre (see Table A). In six of the ten cases this was directed against a national group or collectivity seen to be a basis for violent opposition to the regime in power. Below this rank, another thirteen states regularly produced calculated deaths (level C), selectively killing individuals who were most likely to be chosen because they were class (labour or peasant organization) activists, protestors, alternative political leaders or human rights workers monitoring the killings and disappearances of the earlier victims.

In another 26 cases, states were classed as bad (class B): torture is the most common type of deliberate violation of the body. In some of these, there were occasional killings or single massacres resulting from crowd confrontations, deaths induced by maltreatment or torture, or some evidence of systematic torture, beating or ill-treatment of prisoners, and rape by state agents. Class B states were subdivided into two sub-classes (not used in statistical analysis) to discriminate those states in which there were many deaths arising from apparently unpremeditated state actions (B1) - from police fire (usually in response to disorders) or torture and ill- treatment in prisons – from other (B2) states.

In six states (level A) none of these practices were found to exist during the period investigated; these include three cases with an extensive pattern of 'disappearances', torture, and extrajudicial execution in the last decade.

Although one cannot predict with certainty what the number of states in each class would have been if every state in the world had been included, there is reason to believe that most of the excluded states would have been either A or B states. The back cover of the AI Report 1988 states that torture is practised in at least a third of the world's nations, indicating we missed possibly a dozen states that employ torture.

Looking at the indicators of lack of due process, we found little difference among B, C, and D states. The threat of arbitrary seizure and punishment exists in levels D, C, and B states, although detainees would appear to have a better chance of survival in B states. Coders' judgements among these states usually differed in rankings demarcating the most basic criterion at the bottom of the scale: whether the detention of prisoners was acknowledged. Prisoners in states which do not acknowledge their detention are more likely to be killed than those in states where such imprisonment is acknowledged and recorded.

1.4. Who were the victims and the perpetrators?

Most often the victims of mass killings slain in level D and C states are indigenous people or members of an ethnic group or residents of a region which was used as the base of an armed rebel organization (Fein 1990a, p. 9.) Only the Baha'is in Iran were selected for their deviance from Islam rather than for any political opposition to the state. Some group victims have been and still may be subject to genocidal massacres (Kurds in Iraq, tribal people in Bangladesh, the Dinkas in Sudan) while in other cases the threat has abated: the Baha'is in Iran, the Bush Negroes of Surinam. The continuity of attacks against Iraqi Kurds and the pattern of involuntary resettlement of them buttress charges of Iraqi genocide.

States with violent challengers - whether armed insurgents or terrorists - were more likely to be higher violators (at levels C and D) than other states in the study (r= .551) - see Table B (at end of chapter). But correlation cannot tell us which is cause and which is effect or how state and insurgent violence interact; several explanations which cannot be tested from these data are proposed (Fein 1990a, pp. 25-26). Nonstate actors killed many more times the number killed by state actors in four cases: India, Mozambique, Nicaragua, and Zimbabwe. In three of these four cases, the non-state killing forces were known or believed to be armed by a superpower or a regional power.

Most states at level B were one-party states and military-ruled states and occupied areas. However, there was about the same number of multi-party states in levels D and C as one-party and military-ruled states. This would indicate that such practices can also occur in democratic and democratizing states.

1.5. What happens to endangered people who manage to escape?

There are many effects of life-integrity violation, beginning - but not ending - with the death, injury, traumatization, and humiliation of the victims. Their impact is not on the victims alone but on the global state system: they lead to refugee flight and mass homelessness.

If we look at all violators in this study together - the B, C, and D states - the impact is stark. These 45 states - 26% of the states in the world in 1988 - produced more than 96% of the world's refugees in 1988. From one to over 10 percent of the population have fled from 14 states. We must also note that in a few states the use of mass killing by government challengers (e.g., in Mozambique) also impels people to flee.

There is a positive but slight relationship between the level of violation in 1987 and the ratio of refugees generated in 1988 (r= .149). This is not surprising, because the number of refugees includes an accumulation from earlier flights; thus, the refugee population may be both a sum and residue from genocides and related atrocities that can have occurred more than a decade ago rather than the practices of a state today. The continued exile of refugees from China (Tibet), Cambodia, Burundi, and Ethiopia testifies to this. The massacres in 1988 and 1989 in three of these four (excepting Cambodia) testify to the realistic basis of refugee fears of returning to dangerous states.

The violators of life integrity traced herein are from 6 times to 12.5 times more likely to be in the top 20 refugeegenerating states than are other states: they comprise 15 of the top 20 refugee-generating states (Fein 1990a, p. 17). They produce not only mass homelessness - and often chronic hopelessness - but also severe economic and social strains on the receiving countries which are, in most cases, among the poorest on earth.

2. WARNING SIGNS AND BYSTANDERS: WHAT IS TO BE DONE?

If we look again at Table 1 and relate the classification of states at different levels of danger to contemporary events, we may note a few changes. But at least half of the states at level D (Danger/disaster) still present acute threats to the lives of some of their citizens - and in one case to citizens of a neighboring country and others.

The first case in point is Iraq. Iraqi aggression and violations in Kuwait have instigated a belated international response which, at the time of writing (December 1990) may lead to large-scale war. Much of the responsibility for rearming Iraq can be ascribed to international collaboration - including providing Iraq with the capacity for chemical and biological warfare - and the lack of earlier sanctions against Iraq for genocide and crimes against humanity. These included gassing part of its Kurdish population in 1987 and 1988. Since early 1988, Iraq has forcibly relocated 500,000 Kurds, destroying more than five hundred of their villages and towns (Saeedpour 1988; Korn 1990, Ch. 5).

The second is the Sudan, which exemplifies how genocidal massacres have led to famine and flight both in the Horn of Africa and in Southern Africa. Sudanese massacres and policies which prolong the civil war and government manipulation of food aid - trading grain for weapons - have again led to another impending famine in which millions may risk starvation (*New York Times*, October 5, 1990; Clay 1988).

Besides Iraq and the Sudan, there are continued high levels of killing in Sri Lanka, India, and Brazil by the state, and also by anti-state terrorists in the first two. Further, several states have now probably moved up to Class C or D in the risks they pose.

The lack of international response, for whatever reasons (usually those of Realpolitik), was not 'neutral'. It reinforced the power and audacity of the perpetrators who had no reason not to believe they could get away with new violations. When states did respond to this class of violators, they intervened - directly or indirectly - on the basis of national interest or sympathy with an embattled group within the target state. Violations of life integrity in Sri Lanka and massacres on all sides in Lebanon did lead to interventions by neighbouring states. But in both these cases, the intervenors' forces also committed mass or group killings and instigated reactive anti-state mass killings, leading to a cumulating disaster. In Afghanistan, US aid to the embattled antigovernment mujahadin lead to a negotiated settlement and withdrawal of Soviet forces. But the habit - among some mujahadin forces - of violating the life integrity of their opposition among Afghanis persisted, making an internal settlement impossible till now.

In perhaps two cases of the ten in class D in 1987, there have been substantial improvements. Haiti has held democratic elections in 1990 without further massacres. In Surinam, a new constitutional civilian government (overthrown by an Army coup in December 1990) appears to have eliminated military massacres against Bush Negroes since early 1988. The US Committee for Refugees and Amnesty International had publicized the earlier killings.

Given the persistence of patterns of violation leading to mass killing and war, we must ask: what could be done to stop such killings and to deter genocide and wars resulting from the aggression of the perpetrators of genocide?

Were there the political will on the part of leading states, regional organizations, or the international community to respond to violations of life integrity, we could use indicators of the level of these violations to invoke states' obligations to respond. For a monitoring scheme and an 'early-warning' system alike depend both on political will to pay the costs of sanctions, deterrence or intervention, and reliable reports on life integrity violations and patterns of discrimination.

State terror and genocide have been repeated in part because of the inviolability of perpetrators in the international system, *and* the lack of censure or sanctions from other states, regional and international organizations, from trading partners, patrons and allies. Thus, we must consider not only how to target or move dangerous states to change but also how to move the movers to act.

Perhaps political will could be expanded if states could be persuaded that intervening to stop life integrity violations is not just an act of altruism based on identification with the victims. Were one to add up the costs of ignoring life integrity violations, as in the above cases of Iraq and the Sudan, including the cost of defense, food aid, refugee support, environmental degradation and wasted development funds, the costs of a preventive response would probably reveal themselves as low.

In order to assess the readiness of states to commit genocide, we also the need to translate social theory into political intelligence. Besides violations of life integrity, other characteristics of states which are associated with genocide include:

* Ideology;

* Revolutionary totalitarian and authoritarian regimes;

* Challenges to the legitimacy of ethno-class domination;

* Transfer of power in states with competing and polarized ethnic groups;

* Development policies which lead to conflicts over land with indigenous peoples outside the polity.

In all these cases, a necessary - but not sufficient - precondition for victimization is exclusion of the victim from the perpetrator's universe of obligation: they are people (or non-people) who do not count, do not need to be protected, to whom the perpetrators owe no obligation or accountability (Fein 1990b, pp. 36-7).

To consider how to protect groups at risk, after their identification, and how to target states, we shall focus our strategy on the perpetrator, taking into account the victims insofar as their behaviour may precipitate their destruction, or may facilitate, or impede it. In the first case, political acts of sets of potential victims may evoke retributive or pre-emptive violence from state actors. Thus, potential victims may be counselled by intermediaries as to the most effective use of nonviolent sanctions both to provoke change and to save lives- -the lives of their constituency. In the second case, the organization of potential victims for resistance or change may deter state violence; in the worst case, victims may be organized for mutual aid and for flight.

To target the perpetrator, we need to consider all kinds of power: a) influence and normative appeal, b) economic resources (sanctions and assistance) and c) physical force - humanitarian and other interventions. Table 2 suggests that if we want to stop violations, the type of response should be proportional to the risk to the victims: the rapidity of our escalation from a) appeal to b) sanctions (and incentives) and to c) intervention should depend on the danger. At the minimum, levels of violation afford a crude index for estimating the appropriate, necessary, and proportional response.

This guide (Table 2) to bystander response must be tempered by several other considerations:

a) The readiness of the perpetrator to respond to nonviolent appeals;
b) The resources and potential power of the sanctioner (whether an IGO, a regional governmental organization, or an NGO);
c) The likelihood that the strategy chosen can help the victims versus the likelihood that it will lead to further killings and chaos;
d) The vulnerability and strengths of the victims.

Other indicators - e.g. characteristics, location, and organization of groups at risk - will enable us to estimate the size, strengths, and vulnerability of the potential victims and assess or create constituencies which might come to their aid.

The problems resulting from unilateral intervention, and from multilateral interventions such as that of ECOWAS in Liberia in 1990, suggest that there is a need to create forces trained in multilateral intervention and peace-keeping, to intervene in such situations.

Responding to life-integrity violations in democratic states often poses other problems involving the need to change norms as well as to use sanctions. In Brazil, indiscriminate killings of criminal suspects and calculated killings of leaders of peasant, trade union, and indigenous peoples' organizations continued in 1988 and 1989: Amnesty International reports 'extermination groups' as well as 'death squads' (*AI Report* 1990, pp. 47-50). Homeless and delinquent youth became especially vulnerable. By November 1990, Amnesty International reported, 'At least one child a day is killed by death squads' (*New York Times*,

November 13, 1990). This should lead us to ask: why do Brazilians tolerate such practices and how can their implicit authorization be reversed?

On the other hand, the government has moved to curtail settlers' invasion of Indian areas - invasions which have led to some killings and to a greater number of deaths from diseases and food shortage related to the influx. International sympathizers with the indigenous people played a role in mobilizing concern through the Rain Forest Coalition - a network of NGOs concerned with related (ecological) issues - thus raising the costs of tolerating violence against indigenous people in Brazil. This indicates one model for other NGOs to follow.

Table 2: *Suggested Response Levels to Life Integrity Violations*

	Responses to Perpetrator		
	I Normative:	II Economic sanctions:*	III Physical:
Level of Life Integrity Violation:	1. Appeal 2. Condemnation 3. Warning	1. Reduction 2. Cut-off 3. Embargo	1. Peace-keeping force 2. Multilateral humanitarian intervention 3. Other intervention
E. Epidemic** genocide...	-	Embargo	Intervention or war
D. Disaster or danger of disaster	Warning	Embargo Cut-off	All three
C. Calculated deaths	Warning	Cut-off	-
B. Bad	Condemnation Appeal	Reduction	-
A. Other violations	Appeal	-	-

* The table illustrates only negative economic sanctions (assuming the simultaneous cut-off of military aid); but assistance can serve as a positive and negative sanction.
A complementary approach (advocated at times by International Alert) is to tie the successful conclusion of negotiations and mediated solutions to aid packages, using development assistance as an incentive.

** This stage, best describing the genocides of Nazi Germany during 1941-45, was not found in the present study. Early response to anti-Jewish discrimination and violations of life integrity might well have checked Germany's use of epidemic genocide during the war.

Scenarios of response to endangered peoples demand hard thinking: who shall plan, who shall target the perpetrators, and who shall pay the costs? Perpetrators include not only governments but also anti-government paramilitary and terrorist groups and the classes and public which legitimate killing endangered peoples – who, as in the case of Brazilian delinquents, may be viewed as 'dangerous' people.

3. A RESEARCH AFTER-NOTE

We need continued research on *Lives at risk*, employing multiple sources to refine the scale, to measure aspects of life integrity not indexed, and to track changes in the level of violation over time, as indicators for basic research and policy research. Longitudinal study could enable us to understand better the trajectory of escalation and determine, for example, whether there are underlying differences between D and C states or whether they are basically the same but are just responding to different levels of threat to the ruling elite. Our aims are to 1) detect signs and portents of escalation of violence toward genocide and mass killing; 2) relate levels of violation to underlying and intervening causes; and 3) relate violations of life integrity to other kinds of rights violations. Further, were states and non-governmental organizations to become committed to preventive action, we could 4) trace the impact of government intervention and aid to other states on their level of violation; 5) consider the efficacy of different strategies of response at different levels of violation; and 6) trace the impact of NGO campaigns against various classes of violators.

An independent non-profit organization, such as the Institute for the Study of Genocide (the sponsor and publisher of *Lives at Risk*), may be better qualified to pursue this research than governmental or intergovernmental organizations who may be under pressure to support national policies, to protect client or member states, and to rationalize state or organizational interests. However, to apprehend people(s) at risk and to deter genocide and political killing demands an investment in time and resources. The question we should ask supporters of such aims is: does not our concern for the global integrity of life demand that we put resources into monitoring peoples at risk comparable to the resources we devote to monitoring the weather or the state of the environment?

NOTES

1. I wish to thank Hayward R. Alker, Jr. (Massachusetts Institute of Technology) and Nils Petter Gleditsch (International Peace Research Institute, Oslo) for their helpful critiques and suggestions on an earlier version of this article.

2. An occupied region or province is a region of disputed sovereignty which a neighbouring state has invaded, either integrating it in its polity or extending military rule over it. These include Tibet (China), East Timor (Indonesia), West Irian (Indonesia), Israeli-occupied territories, and Syrian-occupied Lebanon. The temporary intervention of India in Sri Lanka in which no claim of sovereignty was made was not included in the study originally but is cited in Tables A and B because grave violations of life integrity were noted in the *AI Report 1988*. States in which a native administration was put into office or sustained there by another state's intervention include Afghanistan and Cambodia.

3. There was a mean of 87% agreement between coders and a mode between 85 and 89%. All cases of disagreement were reviewed and resolved by Helen Fein.

Table A: Major Life Integrity Violations in 1987 in States/Regions in Study

Highest level of violation	Pattern of mass killing /massacre	Pattern of extrajudicial /summary executions	Pattern of torture /ill treatment of prisoners and/or rape
D. Danger/disaster			
Afghanistan	O	O	O
Brazil	O	O	O
Haiti	O	O	O
India	O	-	O
India/Sri Lanka	O	O	O
Iraq	O	O	O
Sri Lanka	O	O	O
Sudan	O	O	O
Surinam	O	-	-
Syria/Lebanon	O	O	O
C. Calculated deaths			
Bangladesh		O	O
Burma		O	O
Colombia		O	O
El Salvador		O	O
Guatemala		O	O
Iran		O	O
Libya		O	O
Peru		O	O
Philippines		O	-
Somalia		O	O
Syria		O	O
Uganda		O	O
Zaire		O	O
B. Bad (1)			
Angola			O
Chile			O
China/Tibet			O
Indonesia/Irian Jaya			O
Indonesia/East Timor			O
Indonesia			O
Israel/occ. territories			O
Madagascar			O
Nigeria			O
Saudi Arabia			O
Turkey			O

O Applies　　　　　　　　　　　　　　　　　　　Continues...

Table A: (continued)

Highest level of violation	Pattern of mass killing / massacre	Pattern of extrajudicial / summary executions	Pattern of torture /ill treatment of prisoners and/or rape
B. Bad (2)			
Burundi			O
Cambodia			O
China			O
Ethiopia			O
Fiji			O
Kenya			O
Morocco			O
Mozambique			O
Nicaragua			O
Pakistan			O
Paraguay			O
Rwanda			O
S. Africa			O
Vietnam			O
Zimbabwe			O

A. Apparently none of above
Malaysia
Argentina
Equatorial Guinea
Israel (excluded occupied territories)
New Caledonia
Uruguay

From *Lives at Risk: A study of Violations of Life-Integrity in 50 States in 1987* based on the Amnesty International 1988 Report (New York: Institute for the Study of Genocide, 1990).

See *Lives at Risk* for discussion of sub-groups within levels.

Table B: Violence of Challengers to State Power and Level of State Violation of Life Integrity in 1987

Level of state violation of life integrity	Types of challenges and level of violence presented				
	Internal war; armed opposition; attempted assassination of head of state		Terrorism	Communal violence or violent disorders	Non violent protest or mass demonstrations
	highest (5)	high (4)	medium (3)	low (2)	least (1)
D. Danger...					
Afghanistan	●				
Brazil			●	○	○
Haiti			●	○	○
India	●		○	○	
Iraq		●			
Sri Lanka	●		○	○	
Sudan	●			○	○
Surinam		●			
Syria/Lebanon	●				
C. Calculated...					
Bangladesh			●	○	○
Burma		●		○	○
Colombia		●	○		○
El Salvador		●			○
Guatemala		●			
Iran[1]					
Libya[1]					
Peru	●				
Philippines[2]	●		○	○	
Somalia		●			
Syria[1]					
Uganda		●	○		
Zaire		●			

○ applies
● indicates the most violent level of challenge in this state
[1] none noted
[2] coup or aborted coup by the military noted

Table B: (continued)

	Types of challenges and level of violence presented				
Level of state violation of life integrity	Internal war; armed opposition; attempted assassination of head of state		Terrorism	Communal violence or violent disorders	Non violent protest or mass demonstrations
	highest (5)	high (4)	medium (3)	low (2)	least (1)
B. Bad (1)					
Angola	●		○	○	
Chile					●
China/Tibet					●
Indonesia/Ir. Jaya		●			
Indonesia/E. Timor		●			
Indonesia[1]					
Israel/occ. terr.				●	
Madagascar				●	
Nigeria				●	○
Saudi Arabia				●	
Turkey		●	○		
B. Bad (2)					
Burundi[1 2]					
Cambodia		●			
China					●
Ethiopia	●				
Fiji*				●	
Kenya				●	○
Morocco					●
Mozambique	●				
Nicaragua	●				
Pakistan			●	○	○
Paraguay					●
Rwanda[1]					
South Africa		●	○		
Vietnam[1]					
Zimbabwe		●		○	
A. Apparently none					
Malaysia					
Argentina				●	
Eq. Guinea[1]					●
Israel					
New Caledonia				●	○
Uruguay[1]					●

Source: *Amnesty International 1988 Report*

60 *Dangerous States and Endangered Peoples*

Table C: Life Integrity Violations 1987 and Refugees Generated 1988

Refugees per 100,000 population	Level of state violation		
	D. Disaster	C. Calculated deaths	B. Bad
Over 7000	Afghanistan[2*]		Mozambique[3]
6000-6999			China/Tibet[5] Cambodia[6]
5000-5999		Somalia[8]	Angola[7]
4000-4999			Burundi[9] Rwanda[10]
3000-3999	Iraq[11]	El Salvador[12]	
2000-2999	Surinam[16]		Ethiopia[14]
1000-1999	Sudan[18]		Nicaragua[17]
10-999	Haiti Sri Lanka	Bangladesh Burma Guatemala Iran[20] Philippines Uganda Zaire	Chile Fiji Indonesia / E. Timor / Irian Jaya Pakistan South Africa Vietnam Zimbabwe
Under 10	India Brazil	Colombia Libya Peru Syria	China Indonesia Kenya Madagascar Morocco Nigeria Pakistan Paraguay Saudi Arabia Turkey

* numbers [n] indicate rank among the top 20 cases in the world, by ratio of refugees generated per 100 000 population 1980. Palestinian refugees were omitted because the divergent definition of their status from that of other refugees makes them non-compatible.

** Of the states in level A, Equatorial Guinea and new Caledonia were rated at the level of 10-999 refugees per 100,000 population, while Argentina, Israel, Malaysia, and Uruguay had under 10 refugees per 100,000 population.

Sources: US Committee for Refugees *World Refugee Survey: 1988 in Review* (Washington:1989) and unpublished statistics from correspondence with USCR.

REFERENCES

Amnesty International, 1990. *Amnesty International Report 1990*, London: AI.

Amnesty International, 1989. *Amnesty International Report 1989*, London: AI.

Amnesty International, 1988. *Amnesty International Report 1988*, London: AI.

Charny, Israel, 1982. *How Can We Commit the Unthinkable? Genocide: The Human Cancer*. Boulder, Co.: Westview Press.

Clay, Jason, 1988. 'Food as a Weapon: State-Produced Deaths by Starvation in Ethiopia and Sudan', *The ISG Newsletter* (Institute for the Study of Genocide, New York), vol. 1, no. 2, pp. 8-10.

Fein, Helen, 1990a. *Lives at Risk: A Study of Violations of Life Integrity in 50 States in 1987 based on the Amnesty International 1988 Report*, New York: Institute for the Study of Genocide.

Fein, Helen, 1990b. 'Genocide: A Sociological Perspective', *Current Sociology*, vol. 38, no. 1, pp. 1-126.

Fein, Helen, 1988. 'Discriminating States of Horror through Life Integrity Violation Analysis', paper presented at the 83rd Annual Meeting of the American Sociological Association in Atlanta, Ga., August 28, 1988.

Gurr, Ted Robert and James R. Scaritt, 1989. 'Minorities Rights at Risk: A Global Survey,' *Human Rights Quarterly*, vol. 11, no. 3, pp. 379-405.

Harff, Barbara and Ted R. Gurr, 1987. 'Victims of the State: Genocides, Politicides and Group Repression since 1945', *Internet on the Holocaust and Genocide*, vol. 13, pp. 1-7.

Korn, David A, 1990. *Human Rights in Iraq*, New Haven: Yale Univ. Press.

Kuper, Leo, 1985. *The Prevention of Genocide*, New Haven: Yale Univ. Press.

Littell, Franklin, 1988. 'Essay: Early Warning', *Holocaust and Genocide Studies*, vol. 3, no. 4, pp. 483-90.

New York Times, October 1 - November 30, 1990.

Reiter, Randy et al., 1986. 'Guidelines for Field Reporting of Basic Human Rights Violations', *Human Rights Quarterly*, vol. 8, no. 4, pp. 628-53.

Saeedpour, Vera Beaudin, 1988. 'Iraq Attacks to Destroy the Kurds', *The ISG Newsletter*, vol. 1, no. 2, pp. 2-11.

Schmid, Alex P., 1988. *Research on Gross Human Rights Violations: A Programme*, Leiden: COMT.

Sieghart, Paul, 1983. *The International Law of Human Rights*, Oxford: Clarendon Press.

Spirer, Herbert E., 1988. 'Quantitative Analysis of Life Integrity Violations', unpublished paper, Stamford, CT: University of Connecticut, 1988.

United States Committee for Refugees, 1988. *World Refugee Survey: 1987 in Review*, Washington, DC: USCR.

United States Committee for Refugees, 1989. *World Refugee Survey: 1988 in Review*, Washington, DC: USCR.

Von Aggelen, C., 1986. 'Review: The Right to Live in International Law', *American Journal of International Law*, vol. 80, p. 743.

4

Peaceful Settlement of post-1945 Conflicts: A Comparative Study[1]

Hugh Miall

1. INTRODUCTION

It is clearly desirable that major internal and international conflicts should be settled early, and particularly before they become violent. Peace researchers have devoted a great deal of study to armed conflicts, but peacefully resolved conflicts have received less attention. If we want to encourage early intervention to resolve conflicts, it is relevant to test propositions from contemporary theories of conflict resolution against the historical experience of conflicts that have been settled without becoming violent.

This chapter reports findings from a continuing study of conflicts that have been peacefully resolved between 1945 and 1985. In order to draw conclusions about factors which influenced whether conflicts were peacefully resolved in this period, it was necessary to compare settlements in both armed and peaceful conflicts.

Most published work on conflict resolution concentrates on violent conflicts, but there is a set of studies which examine both peaceful and violent conflicts. Northedge and Donelan (1971) examined 50 international disputes between 1945 and 1970, of which over half were resolved peacefully or became quiescent without a resort to force. Holsti (1966) analyzed 77 major international conflicts between 1919 and 1965. In 49 of them (64 per cent) there was some form of third party intervention, and these conflicts showed least evidence of destructive violence. Haas et al (1972) assessed the effectiveness of the UN and regional conflict managing organizations in 146 international conflicts between 1945 and 1970. Among his findings were that in the period 1945-70 the UN had helped to settle about a third of the cases referred to it, but that the organization had shown relatively little interest in conflicts in which there was no fighting. Butterworth (1976; 1978) expanded this data set to include cases without conflict management, to ask the question: do conflict managers make a difference?

Recently Sherman (1987) has compiled a fuller data set than his predecessors to examine the UN's effectiveness. Brecher and Wilkenfeld (1988) looked at factors influencing peaceful and violent outcomes of international crises.

2. FACTORS CONDUCIVE TO PEACEFUL SETTLEMENT

A number of factors may be canvassed as conducive to peaceful settlement of conflicts. This paper examines three.

2.1. The nature and intensity of the conflict

The first proposition is that some conflicts are inherently simpler to resolve peacefully because the degree of conflict of interest is less, or the threat to the goals and values of the parties is minimal. A conflict in which parties threaten one another's existence is more likely to become violent than one which does not affect a party's central goals. It is suggested that conflicts over interests may be easier to resolve than conflicts over justice or power (Ury 1988), so that one strategy for seeking peaceful resolution should be to reformulate a conflict apparently over power or justice into one over interests.

2.2. Agreed procedures and third party intervention

The second proposition is that conflicts are more likely to be peacefully resolved if parties choose agreed procedures to deal with them (irrespective of the substance of the disagreement). Even signalling an intention to accept some form of mutually agreed procedure can help to create the momentum for a settlement. Accepting third-party intervention is such a signal, and it is widely held that early third-party intervention, for example mediation, makes peaceful resolution of conflict more likely.

2.3. 'Integrative' outcomes

The third proposition is that outcomes should integrate the interests of the parties. Common to many theories of conflict resolution (e.g. Burton 1987, Fisher & Ury 1983) is the idea that what is perceived as a zero-sum conflict should be transformed into a positive-sum situation in which the parties have common interests in a settlement.

A simple version of this theory is the idea that peacefully resolved conflicts should have 'win-win' outcomes. A rather more sophisticated version is that while parties' overt positions may clash, their underlying interests may be reconcilable (Pruitt and Rubin 1986). Parties should be helped to explore the conflict in order to identify the potentially integrative outcomes.

Figure 1 shows the classic diagram of a zero-sum conflict where states E and I contest control of the territory S. The two sloping lines show the utility or preference curves of the two states. Any gain by one party means a loss for the other.

Figure 1: Zero-sum Conflict over one Good

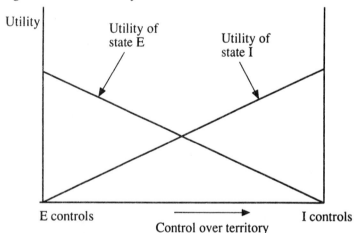

Figure 2 suggests that the conflict can be resolved if it is disaggregated into the parties' underlying interests. Here the utility curves are two planes, aligned at right angles to one another, so that a point exists which is a maximum for both parties. In this example the conflict over territory can be disaggregated into state E's need for sovereignty and state I's need for security. Since these can be independent of one another, a mutually satisfactory outcome is possible.

Figur 2: *Non-Zero-Sum Conflict over one Good*

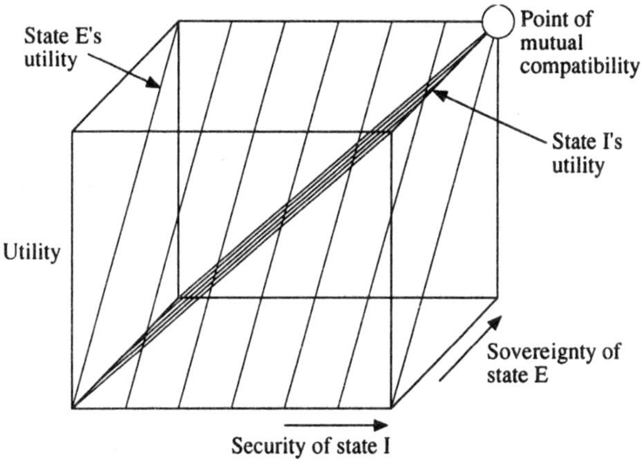

3. METHODOLOGY

3.1. Research design

The initial plan was to classify conflicts into four categories, by whether they were peaceful or violent, and by whether they were resolved or unresolved (see Figure 3).

Theories about factors conducive to peacefully resolved conflicts could then be tested by comparing differences between the resolved and unresolved conflicts, and between the violent and peaceful conflicts. Cases in all four categories need to be examined in order to confirm or disconfirm propositions about how conflicts are peacefully resolved (Richardson 1952).

However, a large number of conflicts are neither full wars nor free of military coercion, and besides 'resolved' and 'unresolved' conflicts there are those that were partly, but not wholly resolved by the cut-off date of the study, 1985, and those that lapsed without being resolved. To accommodate these, a three-by-three classification was adopted, as in table 1.

Figure 3: Plan for Classification of Conflicts

	Resolved	Unresolved
Peaceful	a	b
Violent	c	d

3.2. The selection

It was decided to include domestic, international and mixed conflicts. A strict distinction between internal and international conflict is difficult to maintain, since much conflict starts within states and then spills over their borders, while international conflict often exacerbates domestic conflicts.

A main methodological difficulty of the study was to define a population of conflicts. Scholars have had difficulty establishing clear and agreed criteria for defining wars. It is even harder to find a boundary for a population of peaceful conflicts. To help fix ideas, Figure 4 shows a schema of the stages that an armed conflict may go through, and of the forms of conflict management that may operate at different stages. The Figure suggests that it is the stage of overt non-coercive conflict that should be the focus of study. It is only when a conflict has become overt that processes of resolution or dispute settlement can go into operation.

Conflicts were included based on the following criteria:

• The participants must perceive that they are in conflict.

• The conflict must have a focus. There must be a clash over interests, values, relationships or goals.

• The conflict must be between nations or must involve significant elements of the population within a nation. That is, they must be international or major civil conflicts.

• The outcome must be important to the parties. Domestic conflicts are included only if the outcome is important to the society as a whole, and if their resolution requires something other than the normal functioning of an existing political institution. Industrial conflicts, coups d'etats and institutionalized political conflict between political parties were excluded.

Figure 4 *Phases in conflict and forms of conflict management*

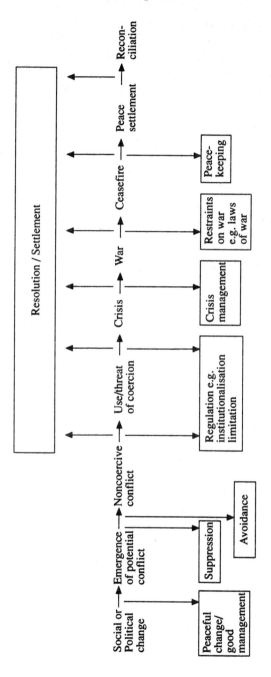

3.3. Distinguishing one conflict from another

Any method of classifying and counting conflicts requires distinctions to be made between conflicts. The difficulty is that often one conflict leads to another, and separate conflicts become linked and entangled. Sydney Bailey (1988) speaks of the 'hybrid nature of many conflicts'. The Arab-Israeli conflict, for example, 'began as a conflict between Jewish underground groups and the British administration. As soon as the UN Partition Resolution was passed on 29 November 1947, it became a conflict between underground Arab organizations and the Jewish communities. When the State of Israel was declared on 15 May 1948, the Arab states intervened and it became an inter-state conflict.'

Butterworth (1976) deals with this problem by splitting conflicts into separate cases whenever a change of party or issue occurs. However, this seemed inappropriate in a study focusing on how conflict is resolved. For this purpose it is preferable to treat conflicts as wholes. So if a conflict has several different phases, but the same basic issues are involved and the same parties participated, it is treated as a single case. For example, successive wars between Egypt and Israel are treated as a single Egypt-Israel conflict. On the other hand, the conflict between Syria and Israel is treated as a separate dispute.

3.3. The list of conflicts

The decision to adopt a broad definition of a political conflict, covering a longer phase than simply an armed conflict, meant that a new list of conflicts had to be compiled. Although there are existing lists of armed conflicts (Singer 1988), crises (Brecher 1988), cases that referred to the UN (Allsebrook 1986) and general international conflicts (Butterworth 1975), no good lists yet exist of peacefully resolved conflicts. A list of about 350 non-militarized and armed conflicts was drawn up, using reference sources and existing lists. The lists consulted include those of Allsebrook (1986), Beer (1981), Bebler (1987), Brecher (1988), Butter-worth (1976), Day (1987), Holsti (1966), Kende (1986), Luard (1986), Northedge and Donelan (1971), Singer (1982), Sivard (1987) and Zacher (1979). Sherman's (1986) comprehensive list was not available to the author at the time of the study.

3.4. The conflicts selected

From this list of 350 conflicts, 81 in Europe, the Middle East and Africa were selected for analysis. Due to the difficulties of establishing a complete population, no attempt was made to draw a random sample. Instead, conflicts were selected which give a coverage of conflicts from the three continents of conflicts which were peaceful and violent, and conflicts which were resolved and unresolved. Once the conflicts are broken down into these categories, a comparison of factors which discriminate between them can be made. Because the sample is non-random, caution must be used in generalizing statistical conclusions from it.

A computer database was constructed with standardized information about the conflicts and their outcomes. This information will be published in a separate monograph.

3.5. Violence and coercion

A simple distinction between 'peaceful' and 'violent' conflicts is difficult to sustain in practice. Three variables were included to represent peacefulness/violence. These are: the degree of coercion used, the extent of hostilities, and the number of fatalities.

Following Butterworth (1976), coercion was indicated as one of five categories: no coercion, no military coercion, threat of force, display of force, use of minor force, use of major force. Here non-military coercion includes measures like economic sanctions intended to achieve a political objective. Display of force includes the mobilization or deployment of armed force for demonstrative purposes, but not its use to secure an objective. The category of 'minor force' indicates the use of very limited military force, with no attempt to make a major attack on an adversary's military forces. 'Major force' indicates the use of substantial military forces to secure objectives by military means.

3.6. Classification of conflicts

The following definitions were adopted in the three-by-three classification (Tables 1 and 2):

• *Peaceful*
Conflicts in which no hostilities took place and there was no use of coercion.

Table 1: Classification of Conflicts By Level of Violence and Type of Resolution

Resolved	Lapsed, quiescent or interim	Unresolved
Peaceful		
• Algeria - Tunisia • Cameroon's (British) independence • Cyrenaica • Gadaduma Wells • Ifni • Liberia's boundaries • Mauritania - Morocco • Wadi Halfa • Åland Islands • Albania - Greece (Northern Epirus) • Austria (status of) • Belgian - Netherlands border • Minquiers Islands • Norway - UK fishing • Saar • Bahrain -Iran:Bahrain's independence • Kuwait - Saudi Arabia	• German reunification • Romania - Soviet Union • South Tyrol	• Gibraltar
Minor violence		
• Gabon - Congo • Ghana - Ivory Coast, Niger, Upper Volta, Togo • Ghana - Upper Volta • Malagasy independence • Malawi independence • Mauretania - Mali • Niger - Dahomey • Sudan independence • Tunisia independence • Denmark - UK fisheries • Iceland - UK fisheries • Poland • Trieste • Saudi Arabia - Oman, Abu Dhabi • Syria - Lebanon	• Malawi - Tanzania • East German uprising • Iceland - UK: cod war • Syria - Turkey (Hatay)	• Albania - Yugoslavia (Kosovo) • Albania - Soviet Union • East - West confrontation in Europe • Greece - Turkey • Hungary - Romania (N. Transylvania) • Bahrain - Quatar • Kurds - Turkey

Continues...

Table 1: (continued)

Resolved	Lapsed, quiescent or interim	Unresolved

Major violence

Resolved	Lapsed, quiescent or interim	Unresolved
• Algeria - Morocco	• Tutsi - Hutu	• Angola
• Algeria independence	• Berlin	• Ethiopia - Somalia:
• Cameroon independence	• Czechoslovakia	the Ogaden
• Morocco independence	1968	• Ethiopia - Eritrea
• Mozambique indepen-	• Hungary	• Mozambique civil
dence	• Egypt - Israel	war
• Nigerian civil war	• Jordan -	• Namibia
• Tunisia - France (Sakiet	Palestinians	• South Africa
& Bizerte)	• Oman - Iman's	• Sudan civil war
• Zaire independence (the	rebels	• Uganda
Congo)		• Western Sahara
• Zimbabwe independence		• Cyprus
and majority rule		• Northern Ireland
• Yemen (South - North)		• Iraq - Iran
• Yemen civil war		• Iraq - Kuwait
• Yemen: conflict over		• Israel - Palestinians
Aden and independence		• Oman - Dhofar rebels
of S.Yemen		

• *Minor violence*
Conflicts that involved some coercion or some hostilities but not the use of major force.

• *Major violence*
Conflicts involving major hostilities or the use of major force by at least one side.

• *Resolved*
Resolved conflicts as of 1985, where the major parties accepted the conflict was over.

• *Lapsed, quiescent or interim*
Conflicts which had reached interim settlements as of 1985 (some major issues settled, others left outstanding), and conflicts which lapsed or became quiescent without being resolved.

Unresolved
Unresolved conflicts as of 1985.

4. FINDINGS

This section summarises the findings of the analysis of all 81 conflicts. Subsequent sections focus on two types of conflict: territorial conflicts, and conflicts involving ethnic or minority issues.

4.1. All conflicts: Whether a conflict is peaceful and whether it is resolved

Table 1 lists all 81 conflicts by whether they were resolved, partially resolved or unresolved, and whether they were peaceful, violent to a minor degree or violent to a major degree. Table 2 shows the number of conflicts in each category.

The chi-squared test measures whether there is an association between two attributes. In this case, the null hypothesis would be that there is no relationship between whether conflicts are peaceful and whether they were resolved. The table shows that on the contrary there was among these 81 conflicts a significant association between conflicts being peaceful and conflicts being resolved (chi-squared = 12.6).

Table 2: All Conflicts: Level of Violence by Type of Resolution

	Resolved	Partially Resolved	Un-resolved	Total
Peaceful	17 (21%)	3 (4%)	1 (1%)	21 (26%)
Minor Violence	15 (19%)	4 (5%)	7 (9%)	26 (32%)
Major Violence	12 (15%)	7 (9%)	15 (19%)	34 (42%)
Total	44 (54%)	14 (17%)	23 (28%)	81 (100%)

Type of conflict and peaceful conflict resolution
Are some types of conflict more likely to be peacefully resolved than others? The conflicts were classified into eight types (Tables 3-10) by whether they involved the following issues: control of government, ethnic issues, ideology, independence, jurisdiction, minorities, resources, territory (the categories are not mutually exclusive). The breakdown in each type by level of violence and type of resolution was then compared with that of all conflicts.

This comparison shows that territorial conflicts are significantly more peaceful than average, having more peaceful cases and fewer cases with major violence than would be expected. Territorial

Table 3: *Control of Government*

	R	PR	UR
P	0	0	0
mV	0	0	0
MV	4	4	6

14

Table 4: *Ethnic*

	R	PR	UR
P	3	1	0
mV	4	1	4
MV	3	2	10

28

Table 5: *Ideology*

	R	PR	UR
P	0	1	0
mV	1	1	4
MV	3	2	7

19

Table 6: *Independence*

	R	PR	UR
P	4	0	0
mV	4	0	0
MV	6	1	6

21

Table 7: *Jurisdiction*

	R	PR	UR
P	3	2	1
mV	4	1	1
MV	1	4	4

21

Table 8: *Minorities*

	R	PR	UR
P	0	2	0
mV	0	1	4
MV	1	2	4

14

Table 9: *Secession*

	R	PR	UR
P	0	0	0
mV	1	0	1
MV	3	1	4

10

Table 10: *Territory*

	R	PR	UR
P	5	3	1
mV	6	2	4
MV	3	1	8

33

Key: R = Resolved PR = Partially Resolved UR = Unresolved
P = Peaceful mV = Minor Violence MV = Major Violence

conflicts do not differ significantly from all conflicts in their distribution between resolved, partly resolved and unresolved. Resource conflicts are only slightly different from average in terms of peacefulness, but slightly more than average were resolved.

Conflicts involving a struggle for control of government and ideological issues were more violent than average. Indeed, all the cases involving contested control of government involved major violence. All the conflicts involving an attempted secession were also violent, with more cases of major violence than the average. Among minority conflicts, there were few resolved conflicts. Fewer ethnic conflicts were peaceful and resolved than average.

To summarize, territorial and to a lesser extent resource conflicts appeared more likely to be peacefully resolved. Ideological conflicts, struggles for control of government, ethnic and secession appeared more likely to be associated with violence.

Table 11: Level of violence by Whether International or Civil

	Number of International Conflicts	Number of Civil or Civil/International Conflicts	Total	
Peaceful	17 (43%)	4 (10%)	21	(26%)
Minor Violence	17 (43%)	9 (22%)	26	(32%)
Major Violence	6 (15%)	28 (68%)	34	(42%)
Total	40 (100%)	41 (100%)	81	(100%)

Peaceful outcomes and international disputes
The conflicts were classified into those that were purely international conflicts, and those that were either civil or mixed civil/international. The association between this attribute and the type of resolution and level of violence is shown in Table 11. There was a strong association between international disputes and peaceful outcomes: 85% of the international conflicts were conducted without major violence, compared with only 32% of the civil conflicts. There was no significant association between whether the conflicts were international and whether they were resolved, partially resolved or unresolved.

Duration of conflict and violence
The median duration of the resolved conflicts was examined in the three categories of peacefulness/violence. Results are shown in Table 12. Conflicts involving major violence had a higher median than peacefully resolved conflicts, but conflicts involving minor violence had the lowest median duration. Even in the peacefully resolved conflicts the median duration was seven years.

Early third-party intervention and peaceful resolution of conflict
There is a growing interest in the idea that the international community should make an effort to catch emergent conflicts at an early stage. If third party intervention helps to settle disputes, then it is desirable that the intervention come sooner rather than later, and in particular before hostilities have broken out. Was it the case that there was early third-party intervention in the peacefully resolved disputes considered here?

Table 12: Median Duration of Resolved Conflicts by Level of Violence

	Median Duration (years)
Peaceful	7
Minor Violence	3
Major Violence	13

The database collected by Butterworth (1976) includes information about the types of intervention carried out by third parties to conflicts, and the timing of their interventions. From this we can isolate the conflicts in which interventions aimed at resolving a conflict were made (namely, conciliation, mediation, good offices, arbitration and investigation), as distinct from interventions such as coercion or exhortation. The conflict resolving interventions were then divided into those made before hostilities had broken out, and those made after. All other cases were counted as no intervention: For 12 conflicts, the available information was insufficient.

Table 13 shows the resulting classification by level of violence and timing of intervention. The first, second and third columns suggest an association between peaceful resolution and early intervention. Excluding cases where information is missing, 44% of all peacefully resolved conflicts had some form of third party intervention, by definition at a peaceful stage of the conflict. In contrast only 12% of the violent conflicts had early third party intervention. Less than a third of the cases with third party intervention at the phase of peaceful conflict became wars, while half of the cases without early intervention ended in war. No significant association was found between timing of intervention and whether conflicts were resolved, partially resolved or unresolved. This finding is further investigated in a study to be published later.

Level of violence and power disparity
Did differences in the relative power of the parties affect how their conflicts were resolved? It was not possible to investigate this subject in detail, but Butterworth (1976) gives an index of power disparity based on the Cox-Jacobson scale, which classifies nations into smallest powers, small powers, middle powers, large powers, and superpowers. The scale cannot be used for non-state actors. Table 14 shows differences in power compared with level of violence. There is no significant association.

Level of violence and previous antagonism
Butterworth also provides data about the previous relationships of the parties in dispute. Table 15 classifies conflicts into those in which the previous relationship was antagonistic, and those in which it was not. There was a significant relationship among these 81 conflicts between previous antagonism and the likelihood of a dispute being violent (chisquared = 7.0).

4.2. Conflicts involving territorial issues
Table 16 classifies the conflicts involving territorial issues by the level of violence involved and by whether they were resolved.
　　The outcomes of these conflicts were divided into four categories: those in which one side obtained the disputed territory, those in which one side obtained the territory but the other was compensated, those in which the territory was partitioned, and those in which the territory was shared. In one conflict (Bahrain's independence) neither of the original contestants (Britain and Iran) obtained the territory.
　　Table 17 shows the breakdown of these outcomes by the level of violence in the conflict. We see that in all the conflicts, including those which were peaceful resolved, a clear award of territory to one side was the most frequent outcome. An outcome other than this occurred in only a third of the peaceful cases.

Table 13: *Number of Conflicts with Third Party Intervention before or after the Outbreak of Hostilities, by Level of Violence*

	Intervention during Peaceful Phase of Conflict	Intervention after Hostilities	No Intervention	Information Missing
Peaceful	8	N/A	10	3
Minor Violence	2	5	12	7
Major Violence	4	20	8	2
Total	14	25	30	12

Table 14: *Level of Violence by Power Disparity*

	Roughly Equal	Somewhat Unequal	Very Unequal
Peaceful	8	5	6
Minor Violence	8	2	9
Major Violence	10	11	11
Total	26	18	26

Table 15: *Level of Violence by Previous Relationship*

	Previous Relationship non-Antagonistic	Previous Relationship Antagonistic
Peaceful	8	10
Minor Violence	10	9
Major Violence	6	26
Total	24	47

One of the four cases resolved after major violence involved an outcome other than an outright award to one side; this was the Egypt-Israel settlement. The most common alternative outcome was award of territory to one side, with some form of compensation to the other; this might take the form of shared rights in minerals or oil in the disputed territory (Algeria-Tunisia) or an agreement to share the use of a disputed river (Liberian boundaries). There is no support here for the theory that peacefully resolved conflicts should be 'win-win'. Clarity of outcome appears to be more important.

The methods parties used to reach a settlement are summarised in Table 18. This shows the percentage of conflicts in which various procedures for reaching settlements were used, broken down by the level of violence in the conflict. No single factor was found which would predict for peaceful resolution; in other words, no one factor was found that was present in all the peacefully resolved cases and absent in the violently resolved cases.

The involvement of third parties turned out to be the single most important factor of those examined in resolving conflicts. Third parties had an important role in 16 out of the 30 territorial conflicts examined. They were important in half of the conflicts resolved without major violence, and in three-fourths of the conflicts resolved after major violence. Change of government was a significant factor in 7 out of the 30 conflicts, including two of the 4 conflicts involving major violence and 5 of the 18 conflicts resolved without violence. Finding an agreed procedure was important in a third of the peaceful conflicts, and moving to an agreement in stages was important in a third of them (not the same third). Elections and plebiscites were significant in three of the peacefully resolved conflicts, and the granting of autonomy or cultural rights was important in 6 of the 26 conflicts resolved without major violence.

Although no single factor accounts for the difference between the peacefully and violently resolved conflicts, the picture is different if factors are taken in combination. Table 18 shows the percentage of conflicts which were resolved through either the compensation of one side, or the acceptance of an agreed procedure, or the granting of autonomy, or the use of a plebiscite. All of these represent co-operative or integrative solutions to some degree. It was found that at least one of this combination was present in 14 out of the 18 (78%) peaceful conflicts, in 4 of the 8 (50%) conflicts involving minor violence, and in one of the 4 (25%) conflicts involving major violence.

Table 16: *Conflicts Involving Territorial Issues*

Peaceful	Minor Violence	Major Violence
Resolved		
• Algeria – Tunisia	• Gabon – Congo	• Algeria – Morocco
• Cyrenaica	• Ghana – Upper Volta	• Algerian independence
• Gadaduma	• Wells Mauritania – Mali	• Yemen (Aden)
• Ifni		
• Liberia's borders		
• Mauritania – Morocco		
• Wadi Halfa		
• Åland Islands		
• Albania-Greece (N.Epirus)		
• Austria		
• Belgian – Neths. border		
• German borders		
• Minquiers Is.		
• Saar		
• Bahrain – Iran		
• Kuwait – Saudi Arabia		
Partially Resolved		
• Romania – Soviet Union	• Malawi – Tanzania	• Egypt – Israel
• South Tyrol	• Syria-Turkey (Hatay)	
Unresolved	• Albania – Soviet Union	• Ethiopia – Somalia
	• Greece – Turkey	• Namibia
• Gibraltar	• Hungary – Romania	• Western Sahara
	• Bahrain – Quatar	• Cyprus
		• Iraq – Iran
		• Iraq – Kuwait
		• Israel – Palestinians
		• South Africa

Table 17: *Resolved and Partially Resolved Territorial Disputes by level of Violence and Type of Outcome*

	Territory to One Side	Territory to One Side Compensation to other	Partition	Condominium
Peaceful	12	5	1	0
Minor Violence	4	2	1	1
Major Violence	3	1	0	0
Total	19	8	2	1

4.3. Conflicts involving ethnic and minority issues

Table 19 shows the conflicts involving ethnic and minority issues by whether they were peaceful and whether they were resolved.

The Åland Islands, South Tyrol, Trieste and Northern Epirus are cases where such conflict was resolved without hostilities. In the Åland Islands case, the conflict was resolved by granting the Swedish-speaking islanders autonomy and self-government, though the islands remained Finnish. The islanders use the Swedish language for education and government, and are proud of their islands' status as autonomous, neutral and demilitarised.

In the case of South Tyrol, the 1969 agreement gave the German-speaking minority self-determination in educational and cultural matters, linguistic rights, and some autonomy of economic management. The Trieste dispute was resolved through a territorial partition, with cultural guarantees for the minorities created on either side. The Northern Epirus dispute between Greece and Albania appears to have been resolved through Albanian acceptance of Greek cultural and political rights. The Greek minority is taught Greek in schools and is well represented in the Albanian political system. Indeed, it was a Greek Albanian who negotiated the end of the notional 'state of war' between Greece and Albania in 1985. In the cases of South Tyrol, Hatay and Northern Epirus, members of the ethnic groups involved were also given the option to leave if they wished.

How were the violent ethnic conflicts eventually resolved? We have noted three cases of resolved conflicts following major violence: the Nigerian Civil War, Zimbabwe and Zaire. In the case of Zaire, the effort of the Katangans to secede was crushed, and a strong unitary government was established, which then became a military dictatorship. This kind of resolution may work if the defeated group is either completely destroyed or reconciled to its defeat. If it is only dispersed or driven underground, resentment may resurface at a later time. Indeed, if the fighting in Shaba by Katangan exiles is interpreted as a continuation of the conflict, then this conflict has not been resolved.

In the Nigerian and Zimbabwe cases, although there was a clear victor, the victor pursued a policy of reconciliation. The Zimbabwe conflict was ended before any party had been utterly defeated. Certainly the white minority government did not give up without being exposed to a great deal of pressure. The combination of international sanctions, greater isolation following Portugal's withdrawal from her colonies, the South African calculation that it was preferable to have a moderate black government than a

Table 18: Percentage of Resolved and Partially Resolved Territorial Conflicts in which Particular Settlement Strategies Played a Significant Role

Percentage of Resolved Conflicts in which a Significant Role was Played by:	Peaceful	Minor Violence	Major Violence
Third Parties	50	50	75
Agreed Procedure	33	17	25
Agreement Reached in Stages	33	17	25
Granting of Autonomy or Cultural Rights	22	33	0
Elections/Plebiscites	17	0	0
Change of Government	28	0	50
Compensation *or* Agreed Procedure *or* Autonomy *or* Elections	78	50	25

Table 19: Conflicts Involving Ethnic and Minority Issues

Peaceful	Minor Violence	Major Violence
Resolved		
• Åland Islands • Albania – Greece • Saar	• Gabon – Congo • Mauritania – Mali • Sudanese independence • Trieste	• Nigerian Civil War • Zaire (Congo) • Zimbabwe
Partially Resolved		
• South Tyrol • Romania – Soviet Union	• Syria – Turkey (Hatay)	• Tutsi – Hutu • Jordan – Palestinians
Unresolved		
	• Albania – Yugoslavia (Kosovo) • Greece – Turkey • Hungary – Romania • Kurds – Turkey	• Angola • Ethiopia – Somalia • Ethiopia – Eritrea • Namibia • Sudan • Northern Ireland • Cyprus • Iraq – Iran • Israel – Palestinians • South Africa • Uganda

protracted civil war and pressure from Mr. Kissinger eventually forced the white government to accept the principle of majority rule. Having conceded this, the further steps, from the Muzorewa government to free elections on a one-person one-vote basis, presented an alternative to a fight to the finish in the guerrilla war. The settlement was marred by ethnic fighting between the Shona majority and the Ndebele minority. Nevertheless Mugabe followed a policy of conciliation, working with both the whites and Nkomo to form the new state.

In the case of Nigeria, despite the utter defeat of Ojukwu's Biafra, General Gowon did not slaughter the Ibos, as had been feared, preferring instead a policy of reconciliation. When power returned to civilian hands in 1969, the framers of the new federal constitution set up a system which represented the ethnic groups with reasonable fairness. More states were created and more executive powers were given to the states. This tended to enhance the representation of all the ethnic groups at the local level, while containing and reducing the struggle for power at the centre (Horowitz, 1985). The new constitution treated the Ibos on a par with other ethnic groups.

The findings which emerge from a comparison of these conflicts are these:

1. Of all the ethnic conflicts studied, the only ones which were resolved peacefully were those in Europe.

2. Of the ethnic conflicts which were resolved without major violence, all also involved a territorial dispute, with the exception of Sudanese independence, which however involved a conflict over jurisdiction to territory. In contrast, none of the conflicts resolved after major violence involved issues of territory or jurisdiction. Of the violent ethnic conflicts which remain unresolved, half also involve territorial disputes.

This, rather surprisingly, suggests that ethnic conflicts which also involve territorial claims are more likely to be resolved. In most of these cases a dispute over territory was settled in the interests of one of the contending states, with offsetting guarantees for the ethnic group belonging to the other.

The finding directs attention to the nature of governments' involvement with ethnic conflict. If territorial issues are involved, conflicts become a matter between governments, and they may be more easily defused at this level.

3. In the peacefully resolved conflicts, governments were not fully aligned and identified with the interests of the ethnic groups. Indeed, ethnic passions seem to have cooled when the focus of the dispute shifted toward intergovernmental negotiations, in the cases of South Tyrol, Trieste, Northern Epirus, Mauritania-Mali and Sudanese independence.

In contrast, in the conflicts which led to major violence, there was often either an identification between the government and one ethnic group, or a struggle between ethnic groups for the control of government. For example, in the Nigerian Civil War, it was the capture of government by a coalition of parties from the North and West which led the Ibos to feel excluded and to mount a coup in 1966; the Ibo-dominated government they formed then led to resentments in the North and massacres of Ibos. The Sudan is a classic case of a government identified with one ethnic group imposing its values on another. The decision to make the 'Sharia' compulsory also in non-Muslim areas has been one of the Southerners' most bitter grievances. Similarly the effort of the Ethiopian government to impose an Ethiopian national identity and the use of the Amharic language in Eritrea has led to violent resistance, as has Iraq's efforts to impose Arabic culture on the Kurds. South Africa and Israel are well-known cases where the government is wholly identified with one of the groups involved in an ethnic conflict.

There seems to be a chance that ethnic conflicts can be contained in cases where governments stand aloof from ethnic conflicts, or at least regard ethnic issues as less critical than the ethnic groups themselves. Governments then may become effectively third parties, or at least agencies which have normal channels of communication, and are subject to the diplomatic energies of the international community. On the other hand, where governments themselves become identified with an ethnic group, they clearly became parties themselves, and may make an existing dispute more violent.

4. All the ethnic conflicts which became a struggle for control of the government led to major violence, usually civil war.

5. In the cases of peacefully resolved ethnic conflicts, the parties on each side were ultimately prepared to acknowledge and take account of each other's interests. In the cases of South Tyrol, Northern Epirus, the Åland Islands and Trieste, the

ethnic minorities were prepared to accept the sovereignty of the nations in which they found themselves. In turn these nations were prepared to acknowledge the ethnic minority's special needs for identity, granting them cultural guarantees and a measure of political autonomy.

In contrast, when ethnic groups attempted to impose a settlement, either by making a secession attempt, or by using control of the government to dominate an ethnically divided society, violence was the result. Thus neither attempting secession nor seeking to establish a dominant national identity by excluding ethnic groups is likely to result in peaceful resolution of conflict.

All the ethnic conflicts in which secession was attempted led to violence. Six secession attempts are included (Biafra, Katanga, Eritrea, the Ogaden, Southern Sudan, the Kurds). All involved major violence. Indeed, these conflicts accounted for a total of over 3.2 million civilian and military casualties. To date, none of these secession attempts have succeeded.

In the cases where violent conflicts were finally resolved, societies needed to find a settlement which acknowledged the reality of the interests of the divided groups. The Nigerian case is interesting precisely because, although one of the parties (Biafra) was destroyed, the subsequent federal constitution acknowledged and balanced the interests of the groups that the parties in conflict had comprised.

5. CONCLUSIONS

The study suggests some clear differences between internal and international conflicts. Among the conflicts in the study, conflicts over interests (such as territory or resources) were easier to resolve peacefully than conflicts over values and relationships (such as ethnic conflicts) and than internal struggles for power. The international dispute settlement system is in fact reasonably well equipped to handle disputes of the first type. Diplomats are rather good at negotiating over tangible assets like territory and resources.

There is more difficulty when fundamental differences of values are concerned, perhaps because values are nonnegotiable. In inter-state conflicts, the UN and the regional organizations operate a functioning dispute settlement regime. But this system was not designed to cope with internal conflicts and is inadequately equipped to do so.

With regard to 'integrative' resolutions, the results of the study on territorial disputes does not lend support to the theory that 'win-win' outcomes are necessary for peaceful resolutions; clarity of outcome was more important. But 'integrative' solutions were important to the peacefully resolved ethnic and minority conflicts. The factor crucial to peaceful settlements was that the parties were prepared to acknowledge one another's concerns.

The study indicates that agreed procedures are important, although there is no certainty that they will produce peaceful outcomes. In particular the study gives some historical support to the contention that early third party intervention can assist peaceful resolution. It suggests there is a need to develop dispute settlement regimes appropriate to conflicts at various levels.

NOTE

1. This study was carried out with financial support from the United States Institute of Peace, whose help is gratefully acknowledged. The opinions, findings and conclusions or recommendations are those of the author and do not necessarily reflect the views of the USIP.

REFERENCES

Allsebrook M., 1986. *Prototypes of Peacemaking: The First Forty Years of the United Nations*, UK: Longman.

Bailey, S.D., 1988. *Personal Communication.*

Bebler, A., 1987. 'Conflicts Between Socialist States', *Journal of Peace Research*, vol. 24, no. 1.

Beer F.A., 1981. *Peace Against War*, Oxford: W.H.Freeman & Co.

Brecher M., Wilkenfeld J. & S. Moser, 1988. *Crises in the Twentieth Century*, 2 vols, Oxford and New York: Pergamon.

Burton J., 1987. *Resolving Deep-rooted Conflict: A Handbook*, University Press of America.

Butterworth R.L., 1976. *Managing Interstate Conflict.* 1945-74. Data with Synopses. Pittsburgh.

Butterworth R.L., 1978. 'Do Conflict Managers Matter?', International Studies Quarterly, vol. 22, June, pp.195-214.

Day A.J., ed., 1987. *Border and Territorial Disputes*, London: Longman.

Donelan M.D. & M.J. Grieve, 1973. *International Disputes: Case Studies*, London: Europa.

Fisher R. & W. Ury, 1983. *Getting to Yes*, London: Penguin.

Haas E.B., J.S. Nye & Butterworth, 1972. *Conflict Management by International Organizations*, Morristown NJ.

Holsti K.J., 1966. 'Resolving International Conflict: A Taxonomy of Behaviour and Some Figures on Procedure', *Journal of Conflict Resolution*, vol. 10, no. 3.

Horowitz, D.L., 1985. *Ethnic Groups in conflict*, Berkeley and London: University of California Press.

Kende I., 1986. 'Local Wars since 1945' in Laszlo E. and Yoo J.Y., eds, *World Encyclopaedia of Peace*, New York: Pergamon, pp. 545-9.

Luard E., 1986. 'War in International Society', London: I.B.Tauris.

Northedge F.S. & M.D. Donelan, 1971. 'International Disputes: The Political Aspects'.

Richardson L.F., 1952. 'Is it Possible to Prove any General Statements About Historical Fact?', *British Journal of Sociology*, vol. 3, pp. 77-84.

Sherman F.L., 1987. 'The United Nations and the Road to Nowhere', Ph.D. dissertation, Dept of Political Science, University of Pennsylvania.

Sivard R.L., 1987. *World Military and Social Expenditures*, Washington: World Priorities Inc.

Small M. & J.D. Singer, 1982. *Resort to Arms: International and Civil Wars 1816-1980*, California: Sage.

Ury W., J. Brett & S. Goldberg, 1988. *Getting Disputes Resolved*, San Francisco and London: Jossey-Bass.

Zacher M., 1979. *International Conflict and Collective Security 1946-77*, Praeger.

5

Famine Early Warning and Local Knowledge: The Possibilities for Pro-active Responses to Stress

Peter J. C. Walker

1. INTRODUCTION

Traditionally, at least from the perspective of the developed North, famines are seen as catastrophic events which render the victims helpless and dependent upon outside aid for survival. In many people's minds a straight linkage is made between food production in the famine affected country and food consumption. Thus most famine early warning systems use a simple food balance model to predict if there will be a food shortage and hence a famine. Crop surveys, agro-meterological modelling and remote sensing of biomass production are used to gauge crop production or precursors of it. These are then balanced against country average figures for food consumption, storage, seed-needs exportation, etc., to arrive at a prediction of whether the country in question will have surplus or deficit food.

Since the work of Sen (1981) on food entitlement, there has been good reason to question the all embracing validity of this model. As Sen showed, famines often occur in food surplus countries. He demonstrated that first, famine is a question of losing one's entitlement to food (i.e not being able to buy it, borrow it, claim it or produce it). Secondly, he showed that famine is a process not an event. It may take years to shift from a stable sustainable local economy to one where lives are threatened through the lack of food. The process, once started, is not inevitable. Communities may move towards a less food-secure situation and then recover for a few years. Faced with this sort of recurring stress, famine prone households have developed ways of coping. Often these coping mechanisms can be seen as sequential; a logical set of measures taken to safeguard the future of the household. Given such a sequence it should be possible to identify the early stages of famine, before mass starvation sets in. Further, if the local logic behind the coping mechanisms is clearly understood it should also be possible to develop famine relief strategies which build upon the local coping mechanisms and work in partnership with the affected peoples rather than as an imposed outside system.

2.   HOW DO PEOPLE TRADITIONALLY RESPOND TO FAMINE?

A number of studies, to be discussed below, have shown that victims will respond to an attack on the sustainability of their livelihoods, not to the threat to their personal food supplies. Most communities suffering famine have experienced it a number of times in their history. They have accumulated a traditional wisdom of the consequences of prolonged drought or civil war and are therefore well aware of the possible consequences of the inception of such a process. Famine victims do not respond to stress from a position of ignorance, but from a position of knowledge – knowledge both of the stress processes their community suffers, and the long term consequences of their individual actions.

This traditional knowledge is neither fossilised nor stagnant. It is a means of survival. Traditional wisdom, like any system of knowledge, is constantly evolving. Recently the term traditional knowledge has been replaced in the literature by 'local knowledge', since the knowledge in question is not evolving in isolation; the local community often incorporates ideas from outside.

Just as local knowledge and coping strategies evolve, so do the factors causing famine, and the political and economic context within which it occurs. So today, famine victims have recourse to sources of casual employment denied their grandfathers. Equally, today's famine victim has to cope with stresses unknown to his or her forefathers. Civil wars fought with submachine guns and aircraft are a stress on a peasant society, unknown fifty years ago. Obviously coping strategies do not always work. The imposed stress may be too much for the community to absorb, or may have evolved so rapidly that there has not been time to develop sustainable responses to it. Despite their failures, they most certainly have their successes, in terms of delaying, mitigating, sometimes averting disaster and often ensuring survival despite the disaster.

The logical and sequential nature of coping strategies provides, for the outsider, an insight into the manner in which famine develops and an indication of possible appropriate forms of warning and relief. However, caution should be exercised when creating generalisations from the literature. Its breadth and depth are in fact pitifully limited. There is no mass of data upon which to build theories, only a few isolated case studies. Most of these examine coping strategies in Africa during the famines of the 1980s.

3. TRADITIONAL RESPONSES IN AFRICA

Corbett (1988), in a review of the African literature, makes the point that household food shortages are frequently anticipated well in advance and thus strategies are carefully planned to minimise the impact of stress. in Sudan, De Waal found that after harvest failure 'people know that they have to make their resources cover a full twelve to fifteen months and husband them accordingly.' Watts (1983) makes the same assertion for famine victims in Nigeria, and Rahmato (1987) shows a similar logic behind the actions of peasants in Wollo province, Ethiopia. In a study of famine responses in Showa province, McCann (1987) maintains that 'the response to drought and subsequent famine is not chaotic, but is a process determined by pre-existing social and economic institutions.' Similarly Walker (1990) has shown how households in Southern Ethiopia tackled famine as a process, laying particular emphasis on the use of kinship relationships to protect themselves.

Reaction to stress is not an ad-hoc, purely reactive process. The potential victim takes preemptive action to stave off or mitigate the effects of future problems, within a coherent framework of ideas. A few examples of these preemptive actions are given below.

3.1. Ethiopia

Walker reports on reactions to and perceptions of famine in the Rift Valley 200 km south of Addis Ababa, the capital of Ethiopia. During the famine of 1984-85 households went through a number of strategies to cope with the resultant stress.

First, normal hungry season strategies were used. Grain consumption was deliberately cut back before the family grain store had emptied. In most years people's grain stores are empty by the middle of the rainy season (August). During the famine many stores were empty by May. Men travelled to the capital (Addis Abeba) to look for seasonal labour and returned at the end of the rainy season to begin ploughing. Women and some men travelled to 'distant' markets where grain was cheaper than in their area. They bought grain, brought it back and sold some of it at a higher price, consuming the rest. Two wild plants, known locally as *Zeru* and *Lume*, were gathered by women and used to supplement diets. Finally, women tried to grow larger than normal quantities of a 'one month maturing' cabbage called *Denkele*. (This is a traditional hungry season crop.)

When these strategies failed, irreversible, more drastic strategies were used. People sold their cattle, then oxen, then household goods, then the houses themselves (bit by bit). An ox could be sold for 40-150 birr (US$ 20-75) and a cow for 70 birr. Animals were either sold in the local market to outside traders or taken to 'far off areas' to sell direct. Either way, the wealth represented by the animals, left the area. Maize could be bought for 120 birr/quintal. In normal times maize would cost 40-60 birr/quintal and an ox would fetch 300 birr, a cow 250-300 birr. Thus for the purchase of large quantities of food, famine prices were inflated by a factor of 400-600%.

For those not rich enough to have oxen or cattle to sell, household goods were traded. During 1984 one stool was bartered for one tin (1 kg) of maize, a goat skin for 2 tins. Normal prices would be 5 birr for a stool, 10 birr for a goat skin and 25 cents for 1 kg maize. Thus famine prices for buying small quantities of food were inflated by a factor of 2,000%. Many of the women, who are the ones predominantly involved in petty trading, pointed out that they could not have traded for larger quantities anyway as the only means of portage they had were their backs. Ownership of donkeys in the area was the prerogative of the better off households.

The poorest people with less valuable assets were clearly most vulnerable and hardest hit. The price of food for them was three to five times higher than for the better off households. Many resorted to eating a wild plant called *Mucho*. This plant was known to cause stomach cramps, but was resorted to all the same.

If the above strategies did not suffice, people migrated out of the area in search of relatives who could give them food. Some households split up with the man and wife going to their respective families. Many people talked of going to the *Enset* growing areas in the hills as Enset can survive the drought. Enset is an indigenous perennial crop, looking rather like a banana tree. It takes five to six years to mature and will not grow in the lowlands described here. They emphasised, however, that one could only get food from relatives, no stranger would be fed. Further, it was felt that this 'social asset' was something that could only be called upon once. If a famine occurred next year, so soon after the last, relatives who themselves were not well off might legitimately refuse to give food.

As a final strategy people moved right out of the area to the towns to beg and search for work. It was at this stage in people's coping strategies that relief food became available in the area.

3.2. Sudan

In a study of survival strategies in West Sudan, De Waal asserts that the overall objective of households is to maintain the subsistence basis of their livelihoods. He identifies three sequential stages of destitution in which this subsistence base is progressively eroded. The first involves the use of unusual sources of income which do not eat into the subsistence base of the household. In the second stage, activities are undertaken which do cut into the subsistence base, and in the third stage, it is assumed that the subsistence base has collapsed and that households are reliant upon charity. Corbett, quoting De Waal & El Amin (1986), lists the responses made during each of these three stages:

First Stage of Destitution.

- Gathering of wild foods.
- Selling animals which are surplus to requirements.

- Borrowing money or food from relatives.
- Other forms of inter-household assistance.
- Work as day labourers.
- Sale of non-essential possessions.
- Migration with herd to distant pastures.

Second Stage of Destitution.

- Sale of animals which are required for subsistence.
- Borrowing food or money from merchants.
- Sale of required possessions.
- Paid work which interferes with the running of the household farm.
- Clientage.
- Out-migration to seek work or charity in towns.

Third Stage of Destitution.

- Starvation.
- Dependence on charity.

As De Waal points out, many of the first stage strategies are ones employed in times of 'normal' stress, or those which are routinely used by very poor families. When households first seek to protect their subsistence base during famine times, they do so using *normal* strategies. In its early stages, famine is no different from the seasonal poverty routinely experienced by African and Asian peasantry. Thus the practising of coping strategies in a community does not necessarily mean that this community anticipates 'mass starvation' in the future.

3.3. Traditional responses in the Indian sub-continent

Peasant strategies for dealing with famine in the Indian sub-continent have not attracted as much attention in recent years as those in Africa, perhaps because of the more developed State methodologies for coping with famine on the sub-continent. Jodha (1975), in a study of how coping strategies in Rajasthan can be used to trigger famine relief, makes the point that farmers in famine prone areas manage their economy in such a way as to offset the impact of drought years by the use of assets gained during food years. 'The seasonal migration or sale of assets (accumulated during good years) during a drought year are part of the adjustment mechanism evolved by farmers.' Thus the occurrence of these strategies should be viewed as 'normal', i.e, as actions evolved to cope with the year to year variation in household harvests and income. However, when faced with the prospect of famine, farmers resort to increasingly irreversible coping strategies. Jodha distinguishes five classes.

1) Reconstruction of current farming activities to maximise effective availability of products.
2) Minimising of current commitments.
3) Disposal of home-produce and purchased goods held in stock for future use, such as marriage dowries.
4) Sale or mortgage of assets.
5) Out-migration.

As with African peasant strategies, the Indian strategies should be seen as sequential. Strategies at the beginning of the series are largely reversible and do not eat into the subsistence base of the household.

In a study of the 1978/79 drought in Bangladesh, Brammer (1987) has shown how farmers reacted to the loss of their normal crops by planting irrigated wheat, or considerably expanding the area under 'famine-millets'. In other words, they adjusted their farming activities to maximise effective availability of products (Stage one of Jodha's model).

Torry (1986), in a detailed study of the psychology and morality behind Hindu peasant adjustments to famine, emphasises the central role that inter-personal exchanges play in the normal survival pattern of Indian peasants. 'Only a fraction of village households have the land to feed themselves during good years. The structure of food sharing is such that a significant proportion of households in many villages normally survives with the tiniest margin of food security.' Famine, he maintains, 'obstructs the circulation of food gifts and credit amongst households.' As cheap credit from relatives disappears, impoverished households have to look to money lenders for cash. This is a very costly adjustment. Those who have land may mortgage or sell part of it. Such forced sales bring short term gains but if the household is unable to reclaim its land, its members will emerge from the famine in a more vulnerable state than when they entered it.

4. DISCUSSION

4.1. The objectives behind coping strategies

It is clear from the foregoing examples that famine victims, predominantly peasants and landless labourers, do not view the famine process from a standpoint of helplessness and panic. Previous experience of seasonal problems, and of famine itself, have allowed communities to develop a series of adjustments to increasing stress. The purpose of these adjustments is to protect the household's long term viability. The avoidance of destitution rather than starvation, is the goal. Often indeed, as Jodha's work in Rajasthan shows, becoming malnourished may actually be a calculated part of the coping strategy.

4.2. Famine strategies as an extension of normal strategies

Adjustments are not picked off the shelf, like a contingency plan, when famine threatens. Rather they evolve out of the normal mechanisms for coping with annual stress. Thus, those strategies quoted as being the first response to famine, such as the increased use of wild foods, the cutting back on food consumption or the increased use of intra-family support, are the same strategies used by the household through the lean time often experienced prior to harvest, or through temporary hardship caused by unusual weather conditions.

Famine survival strategies are, for the victim, a logical extension of every day survival strategies. The same rationale of protecting one's long term options for the future is employed. This contrasts sharply with the outside agencies' approach to famine mitigation, where free hand-outs and the external control of relief are justified on the grounds that the purpose of emergency aid is to address the existence of mass starvation.

4.3. The importance of kinship structures

In all coping strategies, kinship structures play an important part. Often, as seen in the work of Cutler, their role is not fully appreciated because such structures tend to be private affairs which are largely inaccessible to the first line of defence. In times of stress, elderly parents may move in with their children. Relatives living outside the famine hit area may be sought out to provide loans or to take on the responsibility of caring for children. In times of extreme stress it is expected that the richer and more powerful members of a community will show a degree of patronage. These patrons may well be the same people who, in normal times, charge high rates of interest for loans or control the grain trade in a village. An examination of credit needs in rural Bangladesh showed that peasants resisted accepting credit from outside their village, even when the terms offered were far better than those of local money lenders. Their rationale, they explained, was that by borrowing from the village moneylender they were building up a stock of good will, so that when famine struck they would be able to call on the moral obligations of the locally powerful. If they borrowed outside the village, no such assistance was assured.

4.4. The sequence of coping strategies

Assembling together all the examples of coping strategies from Africa and India, a common pattern emerges in the sequence of measures people adopt to tackle famine. The support structures, both kinship and non-kinship related, seem to fall into four classes.

1. Those strategies which people would employ to overcome normally experienced seasonal stresses:

   • Altering cropping and pasturing practices.
   • Rationing food.
   • Increased use of kinship transfers and loans.
   • Diversification of income sources.
   • Temporary migration in search of work during slack periods in the farming calendar.
   • The sale of non-essential possessions.
   • Sale of excess animals.

None of these strategies affect the underlying basis of the potential victim's economy. Thus, for the subsistence farmer, his land, tools, seed and labour potential remain intact. For the pastoralist, his breeding herd is intact. For the landless labourer, his ability to work at peak employment periods is preserved. All these strategies are reversible. They do not force the practitioners down a path which limits their options for the future.

2. If stress is prolonged then strategies are employed which trade off short term gain for long term problems:

    • Essential livestock are sold.
    • Agricultural tools are sold.
    • Money is borrowed from outside kinship relations.
    • Land is mortgaged.
    • Land is sold.
    • Children are taken into bondage.

The essential difference between stage one and stage two strategies is that those in the second stage directly undermine the basis of the victims normal means of survival. The sale of essential livestock or land means that the victim sees his household's position as being so desperate that its members should sacrifice future security for present survival. If one wished to mark the true beginnings of famine, as opposed to seasonal food shortage, this might well be the appropriate place.

3. If all these fail the victim can only resort to outside charity:

    • Distress migration.
    • Reliance upon food aid.

4. If coping mechanisms fail then the final stage may be reached:

    • Starvation.
    • Death.

As the famine victim moves along this sequence, the household's options for future survival are progressively curtailed. Distress migration, particularly if it is across an international boundary may have so curtailed victims' options that they have no way of re-entering their old mode of survival.

4.5. The localised nature of coping strategies
The above sequence of strategies is of course a generalisation. Not every famine prone community will have access to all these strategies or be able to use them all. Landless labourers have no land to sell. Traditionally, in much of Africa land is not privately

owned and as such cannot be sold. Wild foods may not grow in an area where a famine is developing. Secondly, not every household in a 'famine' area starts off from the same level of vulnerability. The larger farmer, the more prosperous pastoralist and the well connected merchant may never have to move past stage one, whereas those who only just survive will find themselves very quickly at the bottom of the coping sequence.

4.6. Intra-household effects

A further point which is only just touched upon in the literature is that famine has a disproportionate affect on the various members of a household. Whilst it is accepted on medical grounds that the old, the young and pregnant and lactating mothers are the most 'at risk' during a famine, a number of studies suggest that the coping strategies households adopt may alter this. Rahmato makes the point that whilst it is normally accepted that in Ethiopia men have control over the production of food, this should not be equated with control over the consumption of food. He hints that in times of great stress the woman as controller of food preparation and dispensation becomes relatively more powerful compared with the man who has lost his ability to produce or acquire food. Anecdotal evidence from Darfur supports this. De Waal has shown that mortality amongst boys between the age of five and nine was significantly higher than for girls during the Darfur famine. He attributes this to girls, who would traditionally help their mothers in the kitchens, having access to food at the food preparation stage. Young boys on the other hand, have to await the food arriving on the table before they can eat. Thus, just as coping strategies will have a differential effect across households within the community, they may also have a differential effect within households.

5. LESSONS FOR FAMINE EARLY WARNING

The first and most obvious lesson is that the above analysis points very clearly to that phenomenon which a warning system should be trying to predict. Famine warning should not be about predicting mass starvation. It must be geared to warning about the erosion of the subsistence base of the victim's society. The real crisis emerges when famine victims shift from using reversible, non asset stripping strategies, to non-reversible ones which cut into their long term options. It is at this point that the warning needs to be sounded.

Secondly, the socio-economic responses to stress which we call the famine process, are extremely complex, typically localised and often producing contradictory signals. To understand the motivations of and constraints upon individual households, warning systems which utilise those data must themselves be localised in nature.

Thirdly, rather than responding to secondary signals generated by the actions of potential victims, there is scope for warning systems to tie into the knowledge and rationale which the victims are using to direct their actions. Why wait until a householder has sold his land before accepting it as a warning signal? Why not react to the householder's assertion that he is going to have to sell his land? The implication of this, of course, is that there is scope for questioning who controls a locally based warning system – should it be some outside agency, or the victims themselves? Since the purpose of a warning system is to elicit aid for the stressed community, this itself carries implications for the form that aid should take.

At present, the standard practice of relief agencies is to intervene at the junction of stages three and four. To delay the input of emergency aid to this point is to totally misunderstand the nature of the victims' real needs. Some agencies are beginning to realise this. In 1987/88, in Ethiopia, emphasis was put on moving emergency aid into the countryside to pre-empt the mass movement of people, i.e. at the junction of stages two and three. This may still be too late. By the time people start to think about moving they have already lost many of their assets, and closed the door on many future options. From the point of view of preserving livelihoods, not just lives, there is a growing case for emergency intervention between stages one and two. This after all, seems to be the point at which the victim feels the famine beginning.

Further, warning systems tied into this 'destitution' definition of famine will produce forecasts rather than warnings. The famine process does not inevitably end in mass-starvation, only to be averted by outside relief. The cessation of a civil war, a good season's rainfall, or changes in government policy may avert the final stage, and in any case, mass starvation is not the threat perceived by the victims. They are concerned about irreversible destitution.

This approach also opens up the opportunity to use relief methods which are intimately linked to the capabilities of the recipient society. Relief which builds upon coping strategies, rather than cutting across them, will do far more to reinforce the long term sustainability of the economic system than present day food hand-outs. It also suggests that the term 'famine early warning system' may be a misnomer. What is actually being suggested is a local pro-active information system.

6. BUILDING A LOCAL PRO-ACTIVE INFORMATION SYSTEM

Given this background and approach a local pro-active information system would need to serve the following six purposes:

- Warn of the impending beginning of the famine process.

- Be capable of monitoring the development of that process.

- Be able to recommend sustainable strategies for reversing the famine process.

- Be able to steer and monitor the application of these strategies.

- Be able to evaluate their effectiveness after they have been applied.

- In the event of the failure of these strategies, it must be able to switch to monitoring those parameters which will predict the likelihood of mass starvation.

6.1. The nature of the information needed

Information is needed which describes the determinants and definition of poverty within the chosen community. Since our thesis is that famine is internally defined and derived from an extension of those forces which normally control the wealth, or poverty, in a community, any warning or information system must start off from an understanding of the local basis of these definitions.

Secondly, the system needs to be informed about the nature of the threat as perceived by the potential victims. As an extension of this, we need to know just what it is the victims seek to safeguard in the event of a famine threat. Are they trying to safeguard their nutritional status, or their long-term economic viability? If the latter, how do they define it?

Thirdly, the system must build upon past experiences, and so must seek information on how previous famine crises have been coped with – both in the absence and presence of outside aid.

Finally, the system needs explicit information on when the 'point of no return' is reached. When are people knowingly adopting coping strategies, and who is adopting them?

6.2. Who should gather this information?

The person being asked to gather the above information must be in a position to understand the inner workings of the community being examined and in a position to recognise and confront the fundamental causes of the diversity in vulnerability found within the community.

This creates something of a paradox. To gain an intimate understanding of the community implies a very close association with it. To map the shifts in vulnerability requires a high degree of trust between the reporter and the community. However, to recognise and challenge the causes of vulnerability calls for the informant to distance themselves from the more powerful in the community and direct their energies towards the most vulnerable, those who will be hardest hit by famine.

This paradox can be overcome. It is accepted that the information gatherers must be members of the community being examined. There are obvious practical reasons for this. To gather information, they must speak the local language, and understand local customs. To operate an information system with continuity over a number of years, they must be resident in the community. Recognising the above paradox highlights the need for informants to have support.

First, it must be clearly understood that the informants are the most important part of the information system. It is their information and primary analysis upon which the rest of the system is based: they are worth investing in, both in terms of finance and training: training in simple things like how to construct a statistically valid sampling regime, and training in the much more complex issues of how to recognise the most vulnerable members of the community. Training is needed not only to impart skills, but to overcome prejudices. Informants must be willing to have dialogue with women, migrants, landless labourers and nomads as well as village leaders, land owners and merchants.

Informants need support. The informant must be made to feel, quite rightly, that he or she is an important part of the system, not just a minion at the base, for ever giving and never receiving. Those higher up the system must be willing to have dialogue with the informants over their interpretation of information. Equally, there needs to be in place a system of monitoring which watches for slackness in the rigour with which information is gathered and analyzed.

6.3. How should the information be gathered?

The gathering and understanding of information is not a linear process. It must be evolutionary and participatory. Upon setting up an information system, we should be sure how the prime causes of famine will be manifested in that community, or who the chief sufferers will be. This information, which is partly defined by the community, can only be extracted in a discursive manner.

Each round of discussions improves our understanding of the famine process and enables questioning and information gathering to be better targeted. This form of information gathering also helps counteract the feeling of exploitation which many vulnerable communities have when subjected to extensive questioning. If the potential victims are helping to evolve the information on famine threats, their onset, and ways of coping with them, they will be far more willing to work in partnership with the aid agency. Further, the value of ensuing data will be greatly enhanced.

6.4. Analysis and synthesis of the warning message

Primary analysis of the information must take place at its source. The interpretation of such things as changes in migration patterns, changes in land ownership structure, and the nature and price of goods for sale in the market can only take place within the framework of local knowledge. An informant's report should be of the form 'here is our information, this is what we think it means and this is how we derive this analysis.'

This then needs to be supplemented by analysis at a higher level. A regional and national picture needs to be created which can expose the non-local causes of famine and highlight those classes of society and geographical areas most at risk.

A local informant may highlight the sudden increase in food prices in their area, attributing it to merchant profiteering. An analysis at national level, however, may show that it has got far more to do with the sudden curtailment of structural food aid to the country or to changes in a government's 'cheap food' policy. Local informants may tell of increasingly frequent crop failures and the growing fuel-wood crisis in their area. Access to satellite data and the nation's meteorological service may show that this is not a local phenomenon but part of a pan-national problem of desertification and increasingly unreliable rainfall.

6.5. What message should the system disseminate?

The system should not create a single message, but rather a network of messages, moving out and targeted to, an ever widening audience. The message must state clearly what the threat is, and what action the receiver of the message is being urged to take.

The listener must receive a two part message. 'Here is the problem, and here is what you can realistically do about it.' When this message is targeted internally – that is from the informants to their headquarters – there must be an onus upon the headquarters to act. There is little point in investing in warning system if one then ignores the warnings! The actions being suggested must be firmly based upon the known local capacities and coping mechanisms. Any outside action should extend, not supplant local initiatives.

7. CONCLUSIONS

Attempts have been made in a number of African states to implement warning and information systems along the above proposed lines. The Sudanese Red Crescent has experimented with such a system in West Sudan and the British Save the Children Fund has carried out similar work in Mali. Both experiments have found that the usefulness of this approach lies not so much in predicting when massive food aid will be needed, but in building up a strong partnership between the local community and the relief agency which allows appropriate and sustainable action to be taken to safeguard livelihoods long before the final crisis point of starvation is reached. This is a very positive development as it reinforces the claim long made by academics, that the strict divisions between development and relief aid are inappropriate.

On a less positive note we should bear in mind that the above approaches have little chances of success where famine results from conflict situations. During the eighties the conjunction of famine and war seems to have been the norm in Africa. Traditional ethnic disputes have been fuelled by governments and rebel forces and fed by modern armaments. The destruction of food production and the attempts to control the distribution of humanitarian food aid are now becoming more common. Let us hope that this trend can be reversed in the nineties as it is axiomatic that no sustainable development can take place where civil or inter-state war is raging.

REFERENCES

Bangladesh Rural Advancement Committee, 1984. *Peasant Perceptions*, Dhaka, Bangladesh, BRAC.

Brammer, H., 1987. 'Drought in Bangladesh: Lessons for Planners and Administrators', *Disasters Journal*, vol. 11, pp.21-9.

Corbett, J., 1988. 'Famine and Household Coping Strategies', *World Development*, vol. 16, no. 10, pp. 1099-1112.

Cutler, P., 1984. 'Famine Forecasting; Prices and Peasant Behaviour in Northern Ethiopia', *Disasters Journal*, vol. 8, pp.48-56.

Cutler, P., 1986. 'The Response to Drought of Beja Famine Refugees in Sudan', *Disasters Journal*, vol. 10, pp. 181-8.

De Waal, A., 197?. *Famine that Kills*, London: Save the Children Fund.

De Waal, A. & M. El Amin, 1986. *Survival in Northern Darfur 1985-1986*, Nayala, Sudan: Save the Children Fund.

Jodha, N.S., 1975. 'Famine and Famine Policies: Some Empirical Evidence', *Economic and Political Weekly*, 11 October 1975, pp. 1609-18.

McCann, J., 1987. 'The Social Impact of Drought in Ethiopia: Oxen, Households and Some Implications for Rehabilitation', in Glantz, M., ed., *Drought and Hunger in Africa*, Cambridge, UK: Cambridge University Press.

McCorkle, C.M., 1990. 'Towards a Knowledge of Local Knowledge and its Importance for Agricultural RD&E', *Agriculture and Human Values*, vol. 6, no 3, pp. 4-12.

Oxfam Health Unit, 1984. *Practical Guide to Selective Feeding Programmes*, Oxford, UK: Oxfam.

Rahmato, D., 1987. *Famine and Survival Strategies. A Case Study from North-east Ethiopia*, Addis Abeba, Ethiopia: Institute of Development Research.

Sen, A., 1981. *Poverty and Famines: An Essay on Entitlement and Deprivation*, Oxford, UK, Clarendon Press.

Torry, W.I., 1986. 'Morality and Harm: Hindu Peasant Adjustments to Famine', *Social Science Information*, vol. 25, pp. 125-60.

Walker, P.J.C., 1990. 'Coping with Famine in Southern Ethiopia', *International Journal of Mass Emergencies and Disasters*, vol. 8, pp. 103-16.

Watts, M., 1983. *Silent Violence, Food Famine and Peasantry in Northern Nigeria*, Los Angeles: University of California Press.

6

The United Nations and the Resolution of Ethnic Conflict[1]

Stephen Ryan

Peace is a dynamic and indivisible concept and it is impossible to separate the internal, international or universal components

(Theo Van Boven).

1. INTRODUCTION

In the early 1960s Hannah Arendt predicted that revolutionary violence would replace interstate war as the predominant form of contemporary political violence (Arendt, 1963). A generation later, it now appears that she was correct to foresee the relative decline in importance of traditional wars fought between sovereign states. However, with the benefit of hindsight, it also seems that she was less perceptive in her view of what type of violence would become most prevalent in world society. For if any form of violence can be said to be dominant today it seems to be ethnic violence, which has proliferated remarkably since Arendt made her claim. Here an 'ethnic group' is defined as a group of people who define themselves as distinct from other groups because of cultural differences. Culture has been defined as:

> *...the set of concepts in terms of which a given population thinks and acts. A concept is a shared way of grouping experiences and of acting and reacting, and usually has a name. A culture is a system, and not just a collection of concepts: the notions which constitute it are interrelated and interdependent in various complex ways, and it is plausible to suppose that they could not exist at all in isolation (Gellner, 1988, p. 274).*

A culture, therefore, gives meaning and direction to the individuals who belong to it; and is the core of ethnic identity. When an ethnic group adopts a political programme that calls for the creation of a separate state to coincide with these cultural boundaries, it becomes a national group. For, according to Gellner (1983), the key to nationalism is the idea of one nation, one state. The proliferation of ethnic conflict has occurred in at least three types of situation. In the democratic West an 'ethnic revival' has led to increased assertiveness among minority ethnic groups (Basques, Bretons, Scots, French-Canadians). In the Third World, decolonization has left many states with multi-ethnic populations and disputed borders, resulting in bitter violence in Congo, Nigeria, Bangladesh, Sudan, Ethiopia, Lebanon and a host of other countries. In Eastern Europe and the USSR, political liberalization has raised fears that serious ethnic conflict will increase in this part of the world also.

So wherever we look in the world, there appears to be unresolved ethnic conflict underway. It seems clear, therefore, that the term nation-state is a misnomer in the vast majority of cases. For the legal boundaries of the state rarely coincide with the cultural boundaries of nations. In a famous study Connor (1972) found that of 132 states examined, only 12 were 'essentially homogeneous from an ethnic viewpoint'. In another study, Nielsson claimed that the 'conventional concept of the nation-state fits only one-quarter of the members of the global state system' (1985, p. 33) because only 45 out of 164 states could be described as single nation-group states (i.e. where between 95 and 100% of the population are from a single national group). Azar (1990, p. 2) has noted that there are at present over 70 protracted conflicts in the world that are identity-related.

It seems inevitable, therefore, that the present world society, where there is no neat convergence between state frontiers and cultural boundaries, should experience ethnic conflict. It is not inevitable, however, that such conflict should become violent, protracted and destructive. Yet this is often what happens, and it is the extent to which the UN can respond constructively to such conflicts that is the focus of this paper. How, in other words, can the UN contribute to ethnic conflict resolution?

States themselves are often not able to respond constructively to such conflicts. This will especially be the case where the state is itself a party to the conflict because the government is under the control of a dominant ethnic group, who then use their power in a way that is detrimental to other ethnic groups in the same state. In such circumstances, the very legitimacy of the state will be called into question by one or more of the parties, and it is then likely that the mechanisms existing within that state for conflict resolution (courts, security forces) will also be regarded as illegitimate. Sometimes governments and their agents will add to this sense of illegitimacy by adopting heavy-handed tactics in response to ethnic unrest. This will usually involve the use of special legislation or the declaration of martial law. For example, between 1985-87 states of emergency or martial law were declared in a number of states experiencing ethnic conflict, including Fiji, Bangladesh, Turkey, Pakistan, Sudan, Sri Lanka and Zimbabwe (UN Doc. E/CN.4/Sub.2/ 1987/19). Such legislation may well be regarded by the affected groups as evidence of continuing oppression and will do nothing to remove the underlying causes of the conflict.

It is difficult to take issue, therefore, with writers like Galtung (1981), who have pointed out that in many ethnic conflicts the state is not a neutral arbitrator (a third party), but is part of the conflict (a second party). We have only to look at the activities of the security forces of some states in responding to ethnic unrest to witness this type of partial involvement. Amnesty International (1984; 1989), for example, has condemned both Sri Lanka and Turkey for the way in which they have treated their Tamil and Kurdish minorities.

Furthermore, other states are often unable or unwilling to play a constructive role (Ryan, 1988). They may be disinterested in a particular ethnic conflict; they may intervene to exploit it for their own ends (e.g. the exploitation by the USA and Iran of Iraq's problems with its Kurdish minority, or the exploitation by the USSR and Afghanistan of ethnic problems in Pakistan); or intervention by one state will trigger a competitive intervention by another (Greece and Turkey in Cyprus, Israel and Syria in Lebanon, Cuba and South Africa in Angola etc.).

The UN, however, as the guardian of international peace and security has no particular national interest to pursue and is therefore less likely to exploit ethnic conflict for its own ends. This is a point made by Beitz, who argues that the problem of partiality in intervention may be resolved by 'intervention under the auspices of an international organization (like the UN) which might not (I do not say will not) be subject to the partiality that characterises the decisions of particular governments' (1979, p. 85).

However, if there are some who, for this reason, can envisage an active role for the UN in ethnic conflict resolution, there are others who have their doubts that the organization can play a significant positive role. One reason for this is that the UN, despite its name, is an organization of states, and is primarily concerned with relations between these sovereign entities. Since many states feel threatened by ethnic sentiments held by groups of their population, they have, it is claimed, a vested interest in keeping ethnic issues off the UN agenda. Van den Burghe, for example, has claimed that 'the United Nations is first and foremost an organisation of states, not of nations, and since most states are, in fact threatened by the claims of nations, it is little wonder that the UN is pro-state and antination' (in Kuper 1981, p. 161). This is an argument echoed by Shiels, who claims that 'ethnic separatist movements are not likely to be aided by the United Nations or regional groups, which tend to have pro-nation-state biases' (1984, p. 10).

A further reason for doubting that the UN can play an effective role is that since many, but by no means all, ethnic conflicts are fought out within the borders of a single sovereign state, they can be characterized as being within the domestic jurisdiction of the state concerned. This effectively inhibits UN involvement because of Article 2(7) of the UN Charter. So during the Nigerian Civil War, the UN Secretary General decided that 'It was...impossible for me to act during one of the most tragic events of the decade of my tenure: the civil war in Nigeria in 1967... There was never any doubt in my mind that the conflict was strictly an internal matter and, therefore, outside the jurisdiction of the United Nations' (U Thant, 1977).

Indeed, one could provide a long list of ethnic conflicts from which the UN has been excluded. During the Bangladesh war of secession in 1971, for example, although the UN played a limited humanitarian role (Ramcharan, 1983, Ch. 4), its political involvement has been described by Buckheit as 'limited and ineffective' (1978, p. 209).

What is really interesting about the role of the UN, however, given these limitations, is not how infrequently the organization has become involved in ethnic conflict, but how much time the organization has in fact devoted to such issues. For many of the key events in the UN's history have been linked to ethnic conflict, even if the UN has been concerned not with the ethnic conflicts per se, but with their international implications. From the very first UN meetings (Soviet support for Azerbaijani independence in Iran, Palestine, Kashmir) right up to the present day, the organization has not been able to avoid altogether an interest in such conflicts. Nor has it been possible to keep the UN out of all ethnic conflicts, or to keep ethnic issues off the organization's agenda.

This overlapping interest is not difficult to explain. It suffices to refer to Article 1 of the UN Charter, which states that two of the purposes of the organization are to maintain international peace and security, and to promote and encourage respect for human rights and fundamental freedoms for all. The recent past has clearly shown that ethnic conflicts threaten both ideals. Threats to international peace and security are an ever-present aspect of some of the most violent and protracted ethnic conflicts. This is because such conflicts threaten to spill over onto the international arena. Stanley Hoffmann once stated that the world is full of Austria-Hungaries. This raises the spectre of the so-called 'Sarajevo analogy' which points out the possibility that internal conflicts can drag in interested outside powers, which then escalates the conflict (e.g. Cyprus and Lebanon). But there is also a 'Munich analogy', which arises when an ethnic group is spread over more than one state and there then arises an irredentist movement committed to reuniting this group. There have been several examples of militant irredentist states: the Greek pursuit of the Megali Idea against Turkey in the 19th and 20th centuries; Hitler's pursuit of the Volksgemeinschaft in Europe; and Somalia's attempt to redeem its co-nationals in the Ogaden region of Africa. A final threat to international peace and security arising out of unresolved ethnic conflict is the problem of international terrorism, often rooted in the attitudes of dissatisfied ethnic groups (IRA, PLO, ASALA etc).

As for the promotion and encouragement of human rights, we should also remember that the victims of ethnic conflict are not killed or maimed only in open inter-communal clashes. They can be murdered through the activities of death squads. They can be imprisoned for political activity. They can be forcibly removed from their traditional homelands, or they can be prohibited from expressing their own cultures. A successful response to ethnic conflict does not depend solely on the creation of a stable and well ordered-state, but also on the establishment of a just society where the rights of all citizens are respected. The UN should, therefore, have an important role to play in ethnic conflicts – not just through conflict resolution measures, but also through its promotion of human rights activities, which are increasingly regarded as the legitimate concern of the international community.

2. THE PROCESSES OF ETHNIC CONFLICT RESOLUTION

There are many ways in which the UN can become involved in protracted and violent ethnic conflict. Miller (1967) has identified UN involvement in 'local disorder' under the headings of mediation, peace-keeping, observer missions and resolutions. Schachter (1974) has offered a more comprehensive list composed of: public debate and the expression of international concern; quiet diplomacy, good offices and conciliation; inquiry and reporting; assistance to ascertain the will of the people; observation and surveillance; peace-keeping and policing; economic assistance and technical cooperation; determination of the government entitled to representation at the UN; sanctions and enforcement measures; and the elaboration of norms and criteria of conduct. For the purposes of this paper we will reduce these headings to four.

Mitchell (1981) has set out the various aspects of violent conflict that have to be addressed in order to promote conflict resolution. They are violent behaviour, negative and destructive attitudes and the perceived conflict of interest. If these aspects to be addressed are combined with Galtung's (1976) famous tripartite classification of peace strategies (peace-keeping, peacemaking and peace-building) we can set a standard by which UN action in the area of ethnic conflict resolution can be judged. For it can be argued that effective conflict resolution demands positive action in at least all three of these areas: peace-keeping, which involves the physical separation of groups engaged in violent behaviour; peace-making, which is the process by which the parties to the conflict can negotiate a settlement of the incompatible interests which divide them; and peace-building, which attempts to alter destructive attitudes through encouraging contact between the ordinary people on all sides of the conflict. Whilst these categories can be applied to several types of conflict, we are here concerned only with violent ethnic conflict.

However, an examination of the role of the UN in ethnic conflict resolution will be incomplete if it deals solely with these three strategies of peace-keeping, peace-making and peace-building. For all of these approaches are essentially reactive. They are responses to outbreaks of violence. Given that prevention is generally better than cure, we should also look at how the UN might adopt a more proactive role. Here, the development of an early warning system is an encouraging sign (see, e.g. Rupesinghe, 1988), but there is no time to examine this here. Instead we shall look at the role the UN can play in avoiding violent conflict through the protection of ethnic minorities. If an effective regime of minority group protection could be created, the incidence of violent ethnic conflict could be reduced.

The UN, when faced with violent ethnic conflict situations that threaten international peace and security or which violate human rights standards, has been involved in all four of these activities (peace-keeping, peace-making, peace-building and the protection of ethnic minorities) with varying degrees of enthusiasm and commitment. The rest of this paper will attempt to assess the actions of the organization under each heading. The hope is that an analysis (even one this brief) can provide a basis by which to judge the worth of the UN in the area of ethnic conflict resolution. We can then avoid the temptation either to embrace it too enthusiastically or reject it too quickly. For the organization's record, although disappointing overall, is not entirely negative.

2.1. Peace-keeping and the United Nations

The most visible and dramatic form of UN involvement in ethnic conflict is the installation of peacekeeping forces in states troubled by violent and protracted inter-communal conflict. At present there are two such operations underway. The United

Nations Force in Cyprus (UNFICYP), created by Security Council Resolution 186 in March, 1964; and the United Nations Interim Force in Lebanon (UNIFIL), created in March 1978 by Security Council Resolution 425. There is also a small observer mission in Kashmir (UNMOGIP), which has been in operation along the India-Pakistan border since 1948, and has never involved more than 70 observers (Alam, 1982). We should also note that the largest and most controversial peacekeeping force ever created by the UN - in the Congo (ONUC) - was also deployed in an area of bitter ethnic conflict.

Although the mandate of each force will change, in all cases their main function is to reduce violent behaviour by interposing military units between the warring groups. This is not to suggest that these forces do not undertake other valuable tasks. They can facilitate the withdrawal of the parties from direct confrontation (Skjelsbæk, 1989). UN troops have to negotiate with local commanders of rival groups, and therefore, at the micro-level also perform an important peace-making role. They also engage in work that could be characterized as peace-building. In Cyprus, for example, UNFICYP escorts farmers into the buffer zone to allow them to cultivate their land; it facilitates meetings between representatives of both communities; and the civilian police contingent (UNCIVPOL) escorts people on visits across the inter-communal divide and investigates complaints of criminal activity with an inter-communal content.

However, as Thakur (1988) reminds us, the primary purpose of peace-keeping remains to bring about and preserve a cessation of hostilities. Peace-keeping, then, is a military activity; but unlike the actions of the British army in Northern Ireland, for example, these military forces do not attempt to enforce a particular solution. Rather they attempt to keep the sides apart without prejudging a final political settlement. This can happen, of course, only if the parties to the conflict have already accepted a ceasefire. The fact that there is no attempt by the UN to implement a particular solution; that UN forces are meant to fire only in self-defence; and that such forces are not meant to interfere in the internal affairs of the host state helps to maintain UN impartiality and preserves whatever practical and moral pressure it can bring to bear. This is vital if a peacekeeping force is to become part of the solution rather than part of the problem.

There is no doubt that UN peacekeeping forces do valuable work. In Cyprus just over 2,000 UNFICYP troops control a buffer zone between the Greek and Turkish Cypriot parts of the island. Here they have installed observation posts which, together with mobile patrols, try to spot quickly any breaches of the ceasefire agreement. If this breach is a shooting incident, rapid action can stop a minor incident from escalating. If it involves the construction of new fortifications, the UN can normally persuade the guilty party to return to the status quo position.

UNIFIL operates under more difficult circumstances. It is deployed in an area between the Litani River and the Israeli border. Under its mandate it is meant to confirm the withdrawal of Israeli forces; prevent a recurrence of fighting; restore international peace and security; and assist the government of Lebanon in ensuring a return of its effective authority. However, as the UN itself admitted in October 1985, the 'conditions still do not exist in which UNIFIL can fully perform its functions or completely fulfil its mandate'. Indeed, between 1978 and 1988 60 UNIFIL personnel were killed in shooting incidents or by mines. UNIFIL troops have been kidnapped by various local militias, and UN posts have been persistently attacked by the various factions. Nevertheless it has had some success in controlling the movement of armed persons in the UN zone. In January 1989 the force was composed of 5,889 troops from 9 states, along with 64 members of the UN Truce Supervisory Organisation who are under the authority of the UNIFIL commander (UN Doc. S/20416).

Whilst it is easy to find critics of UN peacekeeping forces it should also be remembered that no suitable alternative has yet been found for the work that they do in managing ethnic conflict. There have been some attempts, but all have been less successful than UN forces. The OAU force in Chad was a 'total failure' (Sesay, 1989, p. 2); was 'ineffectual' (Martin, 1990, p. 43); and did not live up to 'the ideal or the interests of the OAU' (Zartman, 1986, p. 28). The Indian Peacekeeping Force (IPKF) in Sri Lanka has also had to be withdrawn because of opposition both from some Tamil groups and from nationalist Sinhalese groups such as the JVP. Initial hopes that the force could contribute to the peace process on the island have not been fulfilled. It was soon drawn into violent clashes with Tamil guerrilla groups, and its manpower was increased from 6,000 to 50,000.

According to estimates, in its first year of its existence the IPKF killed 2,000 civilians, damaged 50,000 buildings and created 200,000 refugees; and prior to its withdrawal there were ominous reports of deliberate human rights violations by the IPKF (see evidence of Martin Ennals to UN Sub-Commission for the Prevention of Discrimination and the Protection of Minorities, UN Doc. E/CN.4/Sub.2/1988/SR.14 par.17). The Multinational Force (MNF) in Beirut also collapsed, this time following car bomb attacks on the US and French barracks in October 1983 which killed over 300 men.

Thakur (1987a; 1987b) has offered an interesting comparison between the MNF and UNIFIL, which has a wider significance for international peace-keeping. He claims that the UN force has had some success, whereas the MNF was a failure; and this is because UNIFIL based its operation on authority, whereas the MNF relied on power. As a result, UNIFIL was regarded by the various Lebanese factions as a legitimate presence whereas the MNF, because of its coercive actions, was regarded as illegitimate and so became a besieged entity incapable of playing a positive role in Lebanon. Because of overt US support for the Gemayel government, its training of the Lebanese army, and its use of naval forces to bombard hostile groups such as the Druze, Thakur claims that the MNF lost even the passive acquiescence of large sections of the Lebanese population. His conclusion:

> The decisions of the United Nations command authority because they are the outcome of an international political process of the assertion and reconciliation of national interests. The authority conferred by the claim to be acting in the interests of mankind can be legitimised only by the international community as a whole. The United Nations is so sanctified; the MNF was not... As Washington grew more firmly committed to the Gemayel government, so opposing factions identified the marines increasingly as part of the enemy forces. Once this happened, the presence of the marines was no longer impartial third party peace-keeping, but an obstacle to Lebanese reconciliation and peace. Such a transformation is inconceivable with UN forces. At worst they can become ineffectual peace-keepers, but never hurdles to peace (Thakur, 1987b, p. 474).

Thakur claims support for this conclusion from Brian Urquhart, and quotes with approval the observation of the former Under-Secretary General. Urquhart states that if a peace-keeping operation is forced into relying on military might to achieve its ends it 'will already have lost its status as a peace-keeping

operation and, in all probability, any reasonable hopes of reme-
dying the situation as well. It will cease to be above the conflict
and will have become part of it' (Thakur 1987a, p. 175). A
similar point is made by James, who writes that 'peace-keeping
forces are in the business of providing assistance rather than
banging heads' (1989, p. 372).

However, even though the available evidence shows that no
better alternative to UN peace-keeping exists, this does not
mean that the organization has no serious problems to address
in this area. Indeed several issues need to be mentioned. Most of
them exist for all peacekeeping forces, but there is one that is
especially applicable to interventions in internal conflict situations. The specific problem is the lack of effective government
authority that can exist in ethnically divided states. Unlike
interstate conflicts, where the UN is dealing with recognized
governments who can make agreements and have the resources
to carry them out, in ethnic conflict the central government will
have lost its legitimacy among sections of the population and is
not in a position to enforce any agreements it makes on behalf of
dissatisfied groups. The UN can then become bogged down in a
messy situation from which it is unable to extricate itself. This
also raises tricky problems for the UN about which groups it
should deal with (in practice UN forces have been able to make
de facto agreements with the parties on the ground). The UN
may have to decide whether to support the actions of the central
government in restoring its own authority – which can seriously
affect its perceived impartiality. Or, in order to be effective, it
might deal with all the warring groups, including those regarded
as 'illegitimate' by the government – which might bring down
the wrath of the host state on the organization. The problems
that arose in the Congo are instructive here. When this operation began Hammerskjold (who lost his life whilst mediating in
this conflict) stressed that the activities of ONUC were to be
independent of any efforts by the central government to restore
its authority in rebel provinces such as Katanga. Yet as the
conflict wore on the force was not able to maintain this distinction and was increasingly dragged into the internal politics of
the state (Luard, 1989, p. 230 ff.).

Four general problems with international peacekeeping
forces have been identified many times; we can deal with them
only briefly here. *First*, UN peace-keepers are not involved in

enforcement operations. To be effective they rely on the consent and co-operation of the parties themselves. If one or more of these parties decides to escalate the violence, there is little that the UN can do to stop this happening. UNFICYP could not stop the Turkish invasion of Cyprus in 1974, nor could UNIFIL stop the Israeli invasion of Lebanon in 1982. Such incidents remind us that the UN forces are better at stopping unintended escalations of violence than those deliberately planned and implemented by interested parties. *Second*, a reliable and efficient system of finance is needed. At the end of 1988 UNFICYP was over $164 million in deficit (UN Doc. S/20310) and UNIFIL was $304 million in deficit (UN Doc. S/20416). This can undermine the will of the contributing states to support UN operations.

This is not a new problem. Writing over 20 years ago, Young noted that 'the premature termination of ONUC and the sluggishness in launching United Nations Force in Cyprus (UNFICYP) are at least partially attributable to these financial problems. The Secretary-General has complained repeatedly, moreover, about the limitations caused by the increasing difficulty of financing peacekeeping operations' (1967, p. 341). He is still complaining today. *Third*, the UN offers no proper training for peacekeeping operations. *Fourth*, UN peace-keeping is sometimes criticized because by reducing overt violence it removes the incentive for the parties to negotiate and so contributes to the 'pacific perpetuation' of disputes. (There is a compliment hidden in this criticism, which is that the UN can be effective in reducing overt violence.) However, this argument is suspect, for it assumes that the continuation of violence will bring both sides to 'their senses'. This is highly questionable, for it seems to this observer that the continuation of violence is more likely to feed destructive processes that encourage violence than it is to encourage meaningful negotiations; and on the whole the pacific perpetuation of disputes is to be preferred to their violent perpetuation. Peacekeeping operations cannot resolve conflicts: they can only manage them so as to give the people who can resolve them a window of opportunity to negotiate a resolution to their differences in an atmosphere not poisoned by death and destruction. There is no guarantee this opportunity will be grasped. If it is not, one should not blame the peace-keepers, for they do promote a minimum degree of stability in dangerous situations.

2.2. Peace-making and the United Nations

This leads us to the next category of UN involvement in ethnic conflict. This is peace-making, which is the attempt to facilitate a resolution of the perceived incompatibility of interests that divide the parties. This can take several forms: a mediator might be appointed (as in Cyprus from 1964-65); the UN Secretary-General might use his unrivalled network of contacts to work behind the scenes with the warring parties; the Security Council or the General Assembly might pass resolutions which address specific conflicts and which might help set an agenda for their resolution (e.g. Resolution 242, with its land-for-peace approach to the JewishPalestinian conflict); or the concentration of diplomats in New York might provide an opportunity for informal meetings which can open the way for a resolution (such a meeting between representatives of the Greek and Turkish governments in 1958 led to the LondonZurich settlement of the Cyprus issue).

Haas (1986) has recently tried to quantify the relative success of the UN in the collective management of conflict by analyzing 319 disputes between July 1945 and September 1984 which included two or more states. It is important to bear in mind that Haas is dealing here not specifically with ethnic conflict. Nevertheless, 31% of the conflicts studied were 'civil wars'. Haas's findings are revealing. He claims that the UN's effectiveness in managing conflict is declining, and since the early 1960s there has been no overall consistency in stopping hostilities. The organization's record in settling disputes was 'nearly always dismal', but it has been more effective in isolating conflict and in abating (i.e. scaling down) hostilities. Overall, he concludes, the UN impact on the conflicts considered was 'marginal but not absent'.

It is, of course, dangerous to use these figures to make any statements about ethnic conflict in particular. But it is likely that the record of the UN in this area will be even worse than the rather poor record Haas has suggested. This is a purely intuitive argument, and it is difficult to find figures to support or disprove it. The main reason for suggesting it here is that the UN is often an inappropriate arena for ethnic conflict resolution because it is an organization which is composed of states and which finds it difficult to accommodate representatives of ethnic groups who do not form their own state. So one can sympathize with the argument of Bailey:

*The UN is not very well equipped to deal with non-state actors.
The Charter was drafted on the assumption that disputes arise
between states...there is no provision in the Charter by which
the Security Council or General Assembly may relate to
non-state agencies such as liberation movements, communal
minorities, or political parties (1982, p. 469).*

In his recent study of the history of the UN from 1955-65, Luard
has concluded that the UN had only a mixed record of success
overall in restoring peace, and that 'in general demands for a
cease-fire were occasionally successful in cases of external war,
but were largely ignored when they were directed at the parties
in domestic conflicts' (1989, p. 532). He goes on to criticize the
UN for placing more emphasis on the temporary cessation rather
than the long-term resolution of differences, and mentions the
increasing disinterest after 1958 in seeking a solution of the
Kashmir problem; the abandonment of the search for a political
settlement in Congo; and the failure in Cyprus to appoint a
mediator to replace Galo Plaza, who was forced to stand down
after pressure from Turkey. Azar has also been critical of UN
mediation efforts. He writes that formal thirdparty mediation
(which includes the UN) is rarely effective because more importance is put on concluding agreements than on searching for
options and non-binding outcomes. So although the UN is a
'perfectly logical body' for peace-making, it 'finds it difficult to
act outside the 'limelight', and also suffers from constraints
stemming from its permissible role in internal and regional
politics. The UN tends to appoint mediators who relay proposals
and counter-proposals between opposing sides, thus maintaining
the bargaining framework' (1990, p. 31). To this extent, the UN
remains committed to traditional methods of dispute settlement,
and appears to have been immune to new developments in the
field of conflict resolution theory.

There may be ways to improve the capability of the UN in
the area of peace-making in ethnic conflict. More attention could
be given to the work being done in the field of Alternative
Dispute Resolution (ADR). More training could be given in the
skills of conflict resolution, and more use could be made of outside specialists. It has even been suggested that a UN Mediation
Centre could be established, which would be involved in research
and training activities (Mapes 1985, p. 141). Ury (1987) has
called for the creation of an informal network of mediation
specialists that would act as a sounding board; interchange
practical knowledge; spotlight danger areas; identify sources of

information; provide a referral service; supply support staff; and offer pre-negotiation involvement. He does not mention the UN at all, and his emphasis on an informal network would seem to rule out the organization as an active participant in such a network. Indeed, the advantages of informality and unofficial status should not be ignored. Van Der Merwe reminds us that unofficial mediators, defined as 'people not employed by or responsible to national governments or intergovernmental organizations' (1989, p. 183) can be more effective than official mediators, especially where a government does not want to confer legitimacy on an ethnic group it wants to have talks with. Nevertheless, Ury's idea of greater sharing of knowledge and skills by mediation specialists is an interesting one, and there is no reason why the UN could not act on such proposals in a slightly different form.

In some ways, however, the apparent poor success rate of the UN in peace-making is not cause for too much concern because there are many alternatives to UN involvement. Regional organizations, individual governments and private organizations and individuals can all be effective peace-makers. In Sudan, for example, the 1972 Addis Abeba agreement which brought about a temporary abatement of ethnic conflict, was made possible, in part, by an initiative by the World Council of Churches (Assefa, 1987; Mitchell, 1989). Former US President Carter has done valuable work in both Sudan and the Horn of Africa. An unidentified individual was responsible for a meeting in Duisberg in February 1989 between the four main constitutional parties in Northern Ireland (the Protestant UUP and DUP, the Catholic SDLP and the Alliance Party).

2.3. Peace-building and the United Nations

Whereas a great deal has been written about UN peace-keeping and peace-making, very little work has been undertaken on the role of the organization in peace-building. This involves working with the 'ordinary people' from the parties to ethnic conflicts so as to reduce mutual antagonisms, correct stereotypes and other destructive attitudes, and build up trust. The idea is that peace can be promoted from the bottom up as well as from the top down. So whereas peace-keeping is about building barriers between those who want to fight, peace-building aims to build bridges between those who want to engage in constructive interaction to reduce violent conflict. Peace-building work usually involves the encouragement of contact between members of the opposed ethnic groups, usually focused on one of the following areas: superordinate goals, economic development, confidence building, and education for mutual understanding.

These are all areas where one could envisage a major role for the specialized agencies of the UN (UNESCO in the field of education, the UNDP, FAO and others in development, the UNEP and WHO in meeting superordinate goals in the areas of the environment and health). Yet the record of such bodies is disappointing, because it is too politically sensitive to attempt to work with governments *and* groups who may be opposed by governments at the same time. UN specialized agencies are meant to be non-political and cannot be seen to be interfering in the internal affairs of states.

Nevertheless, we may find some interesting examples of UN activity in inter-ethnic peace-building. One prominent case is the Nicosia Master Plan project, led by the UNDP, which is concerned with the redevelopment of the capital city of Cyprus, presently divided, like the island itself, into Greek Cypriot and Turkish Cypriot controlled zones. The plan

> ...*was to aim at transcending immediate political differences through technical collaboration designed to find solutions to common socio-economic, physical and environmental problems affecting the city. The underlying belief was that out of the routine co-operation between the technical specialists of the two communities...would emerge new bonds of understanding (UNDP Publicity leaflet, January 1987).*

Since 1980 teams of specialists from both communities have met routinely in the UN-controlled buffer zone to discuss various aspects of the plan, which was to chart the future of the city to the year 2000. In so doing the city was to be regarded as a single entity and particular attention was given to linking socio-economic growth with traffic management, conservation and recreation. Special emphasis was given to the old walled city.

The first phase of the plan, which drew up plans for the city to the year 2000, was completed in 1984. Phase two, lasting from 1984-86, examined in detail how these plans could be implemented. Now phase three involves attempts to get the plans implemented. It seems that the UNDP will fund a project to halt damage to the Selimiye-St. Sophia monument, and a joint West German/ UNHCR project will undertake work on the old walled city. West German money has also been allocated to convert a rundown building on the Greek side into a community centre and to restore a 16th century Ottoman inn on the Turkish side (Jensen, 1988, p. 18). UNESCO has also been interested in an initiative in Sri Lanka involving the study of conditions conducive to the implementation of development projects likely to ensure mutual understanding and cultural consensus through consultation between all the social partners, and through consideration by the decision-makers of the interests and aspirations of those population groups that are most vulnerable to the adverse effects of social change (UNESCO Budget proposal for 1988: UN Doc. 24/C/5, project number 68104).

This is an interesting idea, which has been echoed by a call from Hettne to redefine the development project to include the principle of 'ethno-development', which is concerned in the words of Stavenhagen, with the 'principles of development that bring out the potential of different ethnic groups rather than bringing them into feuds' (quoted in Hettne, 1990, p. 193). Such activities by the UN are all too infrequent; one might hope that in the future more attention could be given to such peacebuilding projects. Azar (1990) has similarly called for 'development diplomacy', which involves less emphasis on economic productivity and more emphasis on correcting overcentralization and uneven growth in multi-ethnic societies. This is because 'balanced and redistributive development strategies are more conducive to conflict resolution than those which are imbalanced and merely growth orientated' (Azar, 1990, p. 133). One encouraging sign of greater UN interest in such ideas is the recent conference on peace-building and development in Lebanon, held in April 1990, which was sponsored by the International Peace Research Association and UNESCO. One conclusions from this conference was that 'all United Nations agencies should be operating at full capacity in Lebanon now in order to help Lebanese in their peace and development efforts' (Final Report of the Conference on Peacebuilding and Development in Lebanon, 1990, p. 57).

Finally, the UN can contribute in a more indirect way to peace-building in ethnic conflict by ensuring that the victims of violence can obtain a minimum standard of physical and mental wellbeing. The UNHCR, for example, has done good work in assisting refugees in the Horn of Africa, Cyprus and Nicaragua (Misquito Indians), providing them with basic care and working for their peaceful return to their homes. UNRWA has done equally good work in the Middle East.

2.4. Conflict avoidance and the UN - protection of ethnic minorities

The proposal that both international peace and security and human rights could be strengthened by creating an international regime to protect minorities is not a new idea. The League of Nations established a system of minority treaties, supervised by a Minorities Section, which operated with varying degrees of success in the interwar period. The interesting features of this system were: that the guarantor of the treaty was an international organization, not individual states; it provided, through the Minorities Section, permanent supervision of how the states subjected to the system treated their minorities; and a judicial element was introduced into the process of protection by the role envisaged for the Permanent Court of International Justice. The effectiveness of this system has been analyzed elsewhere (Azcarate, 1967; Claude, 1969; Fawcett, 1979; Mair, 1928; Robinson, 1943; Thornberry, 1980). I mention it here because when attention was focused on what form the replacement organization to the League should take, there were, inevitably, discussions on whether a system of minority protection should be recreated.

In fact, rather than readopt such a regime, the UN decided on a course of action by which, in Claude's words, it 'definitely de-emphasised' (1951, p. 310) this issue. There were several reasons for this. First, the interwar years had revealed how a state (Hitler's Germany) could use the minority issue for its own territorial aggrandizement. So there were fears that reviving a system to protect minorities would, in the words of an Iranian delegate to the UN, 'lead to abuses, encourage political provocation and collusion with foreign states and result in violations of Article 2 of the Charter' (UN Doc. E/CN.4/Sub 2/SR.47, p. 10). Second, it was feared that the granting of minority rights would only freeze a situation of minority/majority antagonism and inhibit the development of a transcendental loyalty to the state. Third, and related to this, the US position on the minority issue had now changed. At Versailles, Woodrow Wilson had been one of the international champions of minority rights. By 1945 the USA now favoured an approach which reflected its supposed 'melting pot' heritage. This involved the promotion of the idea that the best way to deal with cultural difference was to encourage assimilation on the basis of equal treatment before the law. At the interstate level this expressed itself as support for an international bill of human rights rather than support for the principle of minority protection. This policy was reflected in the attitude of Eleanor Roosevelt, the first US representative on the Human Rights Commission and also its first chairperson. Arguing from the US experience, and claiming that the USA had no minorities problem, she consistently opposed the idea of special rights for ethnic groups. In this she received strong support from most Latin American states, who feared that special status provisions for minorities would increase instability within states. As Haksar (1974, p. 86) has pointed out, here we find a curious reversal. For instead of protecting minorities from state power, the UN seemed more concerned with protecting states from their own minorities. Not all states were happy with this negative policy on the issue of minority rights. Indeed there were attempts by the USSR, Lebanon, Yugoslavia and Denmark to include an article in the Universal Declaration on Human Rights on cultural minorities, but they came to nothing (Ryan, 1990).

A fourth reason for opposing a system of minority protection was the argument that since the situations in the various multi-ethnic states varied so much, it was not possible to provide a clear-cut, across-the-board system to deal with this issue. Rather, each case should be dealt with on an ad hoc basis. Finally, the mixed record of the League system may have reduced enthusiasm for the recreation of a similar system by the UN. As Claude put it:

> *Many champions of the rights of minorities had been so little impressed by the actual and potential benefits of the League system that they had come to believe that the game was hardly worth the candle. Some minorities were no longer inclined to base their hopes for liberal treatment on a system which, from their point of view, had promised too little and delivered even less (1969, p. 58).*

Therefore, during the early years of the UN, when the decision was made not to pursue the issue of minority protection, the hope was that a system of individual human rights protection, emphasizing non-discrimination, would be enough to deal with the potential problems inherent in multi-ethnic states. It is interesting, though, that the UN itself has not pursued faithfully this idea of individualism. For in its appointments to UN bodies it has adopted the system of regional quotas.

Supporters of an international regime of minority protection have always argued that a system of individual protection would not be enough and that the problems of cultural minorities would not disappear because the UN did not face up to them. (Writers in the immediate postwar period who favoured the idea of minority protection include Layburn, 1947; Vishniak, 1945). Modeen, for example, has written that 'Prohibition against discrimination is nevertheless not good enough...A national minority is a collective and its interests in education and other establishments of its own serving groups of minority members are the interests of a group and not of an individual. Minority protection should therefore be directed towards the collective population' (1969, p. 144). However an examination of the UN Charter and the 1948 Universal Declaration of Human Rights will show clearly that an approach based on individual rights and nondiscrimination has eased out ideas of minority protection within the organization. Nevertheless, the UN has not been able to avoid the issue of group rights entirely, and a brief examination of three areas of UN activity will reveal this.

Genocide
The issue of genocide was first taken up by the UN in November 1946, when a draft resolution was submitted to the General Assembly. This resulted in General Assembly Resolution 96(1) of 11 December 1946, which described genocide as a crime and called on the Economic and Social Council (ECOSOC) to produce studies to allow member states to enact the necessary legislation to prevent and punish such actions. After a lengthy period of consultation and deliberation, the Convention on the Prevention and Punishment of the Crime of Genocide was passed unanimously by the General Assembly on 9 November, 1948 (Resolution 260 A [111]).

This Convention reiterated the decisions of the Nuremburg Tribunal that genocide (defined as actions taken with the intent to destroy, in whole or in part, a national, ethnical, racial or religious group), was a crime. Actions which would constitute such a crime are: killing members of a group; causing serious bodily or mental harm; deliberately inflicting conditions of life calculated to result in the physical destruction of the group; and actions to prevent births within the group or the physical transfer of children out of the group. The Convention is meant to protect groups, not individuals; and as a Lebanese delegate noted at the time: 'for the first time in an international or constitutional document, mention was made...of the protection of the human group as such and not only of the individual' (Official

Record of the General Assembly, 3rd Session, Part 1, 66th Meeting of 6th Committee, 1948).

There are, however, criticisms about the way the Convention was drafted and the manner it has been implemented. An original draft article which would have made it a crime to destroy the language, religion or culture of a national, religious or racial group was taken out by the Sixth Committee of the General Assembly. Under Article VI it was proposed that an international tribunal might be established that would have jurisdiction with respect to states that had accepted its authority. This has not come into being. Article VIII allows contracting parties to call upon the competent organs of the UN to take action under the Charter to prevent or suppress genocidal acts; yet the article has been rarely used (if at all), despite several cases of genocidal activity since 1948, including Hutus in Burundi, Bah'ais in Iran, Ache Indians in Paraguay, ethnic Chinese in Indonesia (see e.g. Horowitz, 1980; Kuper, 1981; 1985).

It would therefore be fair to say that the work of the UN in the area of genocide has been less than impressive. Kuper has been especially critical of the organization, arguing that member states put political interests above human rights and that the 'UN cannot be relied upon to initiate and carry out preventive action against genocide' (Kuper, 1985, p. 19). He goes on to state that 'the impact on the outside observer...is of overwhelming hypocrisy' (p. 89) and claims that debates are characterised by 'cliche-ridden statements, an unctuous style of debate and a repetitive ritual of elaborate congratulations. In fact the UN condones genocide by delay, evasion and subterfuge' (p. 183). However, even Kuper has had to concede that if there is to be effective action against genocide it will probably have to involve the UN.

The sub-commission on the prevention of discrimination and the protection of minorities
The Sub-Commission on the Prevention of Discrimination and the Protection of Minorities (hereafter called the Sub-Commission), was established by ECOSOC in 1946. Today it is composed of 26 members (7 Africans, 5 Asians, 5 Latin Americans, 3 East Europeans, 6 West Europeans and North Americans), who are nominated by governments but are supposed to serve as independent experts. Since its creation the body has

rarely been able to press successfully for positive measures to protect minority groups. Perhaps its main success was the inclusion of Article 27 in the 1966 International Covenant of Civil and Political Rights (GA Resolution 2200 A (XX)), which was drafted by the Sub-Commission. It states that in those states in which ethnic, religious or linguistic minorities exist, persons belonging to such minorities shall not be denied the right in community with other members of their group, to enjoy their own culture, to profess and practice their own religion, or to use their own language.

Claude (1951) has pointed out that there were two general directions which the Sub-Commission could have taken. It could have remained a body of experts servicing the Human Rights Commission (HRC) - what Claude calls the scholarly approach. Or it could have adopted a more activist role, pressing to improve the legal and factual position of cultural minorities. One of the main reasons for the poor record of the Sub-Commission is that whenever it tried to play the latter role, the HRC, which has the power to determine the fate of Sub-Commission resolutions, made its disapproval very clear.

Humphrey (1984, p. 20), for example, a former director of the UN Human Rights Division, has stated that the HRC 'has never shown the slightest interest in what may be called the positive protection of minorities...every effort which the Sub-Commission made to protect minorities in a positive way was frustrated by the Human Rights Commission and higher bodies'. Sorensen, a former Sub-Commission Chairman, has written that its work was regarded with suspicion and distrust because it did not meet with the approval of the Commission on Human Rights. The reason was primarily that a number of countries were fundamentally opposed to the idea of protecting minority groups and claimed that their assimilation with the rest of the population was a necessity (1956, p. 324).

Twenty years later another student of the work of the UN in this area was equally critical. Lowe argued that the Sub-Commission was 'probably designed as a shelf upon which to place any minority questions that inconveniently came to the United Nation's attention' (1976, p. 40). As a result, the Sub-Commission had done little to improve the lot of minorities throughout the world (p. 125).

In fact, between the early 1950s and the mid-1960s the Sub-Commission preferred to concentrate on the prevention of discrimination, rather than the protection of minorities. The past generation has seen renewed interest in the latter issue, and the Sub-Commission has organized conferences (in Ljubljana in 1965 and Ohrid in 1974) on the promotion and protection of the human rights of minority groups. Some interesting reports have also been produced, most notably the 1977 Capotorti Report on the Study of Persons Belonging to Ethnic, Religious and Linguistic Minorities (UN Doc. E/CN.4/Sub.2/384). Furthermore, debates before the Sub-Commission during its annual meeting allow non-governmental organizations to publicize human rights violations, which can be the catalyst for international action. The Sub-Commission also has a working group charged with responsibility for examining allegations of human rights abuses received by the UN and bringing to the attention of the organization any pattern of gross violation of human rights that such an examination reveals.

In the 1980s the Sub-Commission began to request a more active role for itself (Hannum, 1981a; 1981b; Gardeniers, 1982; Garber, 1985). But so far the HRC has not responded favourably to such requests. During the 1988 session of the Sub-Commission, for example, Van Boven complained that the 'pace at which standard setting in respect of the protection of minorities was not proceeding was not satisfactory and...alternative models and mechanisms must be developed' (UN Doc. E/CN.4/Sub.2/1988/ SR.32). A draft resolution was also considered which invited Claire Palley to prepare a working paper on the ways and means by which the Sub-Commission might facilitate the peaceful and constructive resolution of situations involving racial, national, religious and linguistic minorities.

The Secretary-General was also to be requested to provide all the assistance necessary for the completion of this task (UN Doc. E/CN.4/Sub.2/1988/L.62). However, at its 45th session in early 1989 the HRC requested the Sub-Commission to 'restrict its requests to the Secretary- General...to requests relating to those studies which have received the prior explicit approval from the Commission' (Resolution 1989/36 par. 7). The Sub-Commission was also requested to give priority to those topics 'on which standards are being prepared, in accordance with the decisions taken by the Commission' (par. 3). The Sub-Commission, then, is clearly not yet to be allowed to play the activist role some of its members desire.

National self-determination
Articles 1(2) and 55 of the UN Charter refer to the principle (not the right) of the self-determination of peoples. They do not mention national or ethnic groups, though one could reasonably argue that such groups do constitute a 'people'. During the era of decolonization the principle of selfdetermination increasingly came to be regarded as a right. For example, the famous 1960 General Assembly resolution 1514 (XV), on the Granting of Independence to Colonial Peoples, states in Article 2 that 'all peoples have the right to self-determination' – though later in the same document, Article 6 states that 'any attempt aimed at the partial or total disruption of the national unity and territorial integrity of a country is incompatible with the principles of the Charter'. The two 1966 Human Rights Conventions also refer to the right of self-determination, though again, this should not be seen as right to be applied to cultural units, for it remains restricted to territorial units and within an anticolonial context. Therefore, the UN has revealed little sympathy for secession attempts throughout the international system.

There is one notable exception to this lack of sympathy for frustrated ethnic groups, arising out of the historic and legal peculiarities of the Israeli-Palestinian conflict, where the UN has a long term involvement due to its drafting of the partition plan for Palestine in 1948. Following the independence of Namibia, reference to the right of self- determination is now found most frequently in resolutions on this issue. There have been a plethora of General Assembly resolutions on this issue since 1974 which proclaim the right of the Palestinian people to self-determination. The UN has even established a Committee on the Inalienable Rights of the Palestinian people. Furthermore, as well as resolutions directed at specific situations, every year the General Assembly overwhelmingly supports a resolution on the 'importance of the universal realisation of the right of peoples to selfdetermination and the speedy granting of independence to colonial countries and peoples for the effective guarantee and observance of human rights'.

Even though the UN has tried to qualify heavily the right of self-determination, it is noticeable how even the acceptance of it in a limited way has had a much wider demonstration effect. Mazrui (1969), for example, has claimed that the ethnic revival in the West occurred shortly after the attention given to the issue of self-determination during the anti-colonial struggles in the Third World. It is also interesting to note how many groups engaged in ethnic conflict claim for themselves a right to self-determination, even where this would not be approved of by the UN (e.g. Sinn Fein in Northern Ireland and the Turkish Cypriot leadership in Cyprus).

This examination of the role of the UN is by no means complete. In order to be more comprehensive it would have to examine activities by the organization in several other areas. In 1960, for example, UNESCO passed a Convention Against Discrimination in Education, which in Article 5 (1c) stated that it 'was essential to recognise the right of members of national minorities to carry on their own educational activities, including the maintenance of schools and, depending on the education policy of each state, the use or the teaching of their own language.' The United Nations University has begun a project on ethnic minorities; and it would also be interesting to examine the work of the Committee on the Elimination of Racial Discrimination and the Human Rights Committee, established by the International Covenant on Civil and Political Rights. All of this, unfortunately, is beyond the scope of this study.

3. CONCLUSION

On the whole, the past record of the UN in responding to violent and protracted ethnic conflict is mixed. Where activities have been 'undertaken, they seem to have evolved in an ad hoc manner, and it is noteworthy that the UN Charter makes no mention of peace-keeping or peace-building activities, and does not mention ethnic groups. Yet the UN is responsible for ensuring international peace and security, and has undertaken a responsibility for ensuring the protection and promotion of human rights. It cannot therefore turn its back on ethnic conflicts altogether.

If future UN involvement remains true to its past record, we would expect the organization to have some success in managing ethnic conflict through peacekeeping operations, as long as such operations retain the support of the parties to the conflict. Certainly, no better alternative to UN peace-keeping has yet been devised by the international community. But although it may be able to help keep the warring sides apart, it is likely to be less successful in bringing them together again either to negotiate an end to their differences (peace-making) or to involve ordinary people in reconstruction and reconciliation projects (peace-building). Nor is it likely that the organization will make any progress in developing the idea of group rights, which could prevent ethnic conflicts from deteriorating into serious violence.

The consequences of these failures will be mixed. The inability to address the question of peace-building, and the apparent lack of effectiveness in peace-making are regrettable, but not fatal to conflict resolution initiatives since there are many alternatives to the UN in these areas (states, NGOs and private individuals). The failure to address the issue of minority protection is, however, more serious, since this seems to be an idea which the UN is best suited to promote. The organization is uniquely placed to create new international norms and standards. But this requires an act of political will that is lacking at present.

In all the activities examined here, the UN has undoubtedly been rendered less effective because it is an organization of states. It is sometimes said that the UN can be no more than a mirror of the world in which it operates. This is not strictly true: It would be more accurate to say that the UN reflects the state-centric view of its member governments. An important part of this view is that a clear distinction can be drawn between the internal and external affairs of states, and that the UN has no right to concern itself with the former, unless invited to do so by the state concerned. Yet as long as states continue to adopt such an attitude to outside involvement in how they treat and mistreat their peoples, it is unlikely that much progress will be made in attempts to create an effective international regime to protect the rights of peoples belonging to ethnic minorities.

This, though, might have a paradoxical effect. For if no such regime exists, it will be highly likely that more ethnic conflicts will become violent and protracted and escalate to become a threat to international peace and security. Such conflicts will then become part of the UN agenda anyway.

So whatever road the UN takes, it will not be able to avoid the problems associated with ethnic conflict. Therefore, the UN needs to look again at its attitude to all of these strategies. A more efficient system of finance for peace-keeping could be implemented. More interest in contemporary ADR theory could improve the organization's peace-making efforts. More work along the lines of the Nicosia Master Plan Project could add a valuable peacebuilding function to UN involvement in ethnic conflict. Attention could also be directed at how peace-keeping, peace-making and peace-building initiatives can interact with each other. As for the protection of ethnic minorities, the Genocide Convention could be strengthened and the status of the Sub-Commission on the Prevention of Discrimination and the Protection of Minorities could be improved.

My own belief is that a successful strategy to deal with ethnic conflict will have to involve a mixture of all four of the strategies of peace-keeping, peace-making, peace-building and minority protection. For political initiatives may not be successful if groups are not adequately protected in law, and legal protection will not be enough if violent ethnic conflict cannot be managed or resolved. At present, however, the UN is a long way from being able to provide either political or legal action to the level required to meet the terrible problems posed by protracted and violent ethnic conflict.

It may be argued that this is too harsh an assessment of the organization in the light of recent developments in international politics. Certainly the UN has shown in the last year or two that it is not as insignificant as some of its harshest critics have suggested. A 'new generation' of peace-keeping and observation forces have been dispatched to troubled areas of the world such as the Iran-Iraq border (UNIIMOG), Afghanistan (UNGOMAP), Angola (UNAVEM), Namibia (UNTAG) and Central America (ONUCA). These reflect the fact that the organization has been actively involved in several successful peacemaking initiatives in Afghanistan, the Gulf war, Central America, Namibia and Cambodia. The breakthroughs that have emerged from this involvement are based primarily on the quiet diplomacy and good offices of the Secretary-General and his immediate aides (Dedring, 1990). Furthermore, UN involvement in such cases shows an increasing willingness on the part of the UN to involve itself in matters that can be defined as domestic, and this has 'expanded the space' of operations for the organization (Dedring, 1990, p. 27). This expansion might make it easier in the future for the UN to intervene constructively in ethnic conflicts. Furthermore, we have already noted a growing interest by the UN specialised agencies such as the UNDP (Cyprus) and UNESCO (Lebanon) in peace-building. This too gives us grounds for some optimism about a future role for UN.

There is need for caution however. The remarkable advances at the UN in recent years have not yet spilled over into the area of ethnic conflict resolution, though they may have opened the door for such action in the future. No UN peacekeeping forces have been deployed to areas experiencing severe ethnic conflict since the deployment of UNIFIL in 1978. Instead we have witnessed the emergence of other forms of international peacekeeping in Sri Lanka, Chad and Beirut. This trend has continued recently with the dispatch of a West African peacekeeping force to Liberia.

In the area of peace-making, problems remain for the UN. We can give one example of this. Whilst it is true that the UN played an important role in arranging a ceasefire between Iran and Iraq in 1988, this merely released troops, who were redeployed by Baghdad against its Kurdish minority. The UN has not been able to do anything about this renewed oppression of an ethnic minority. Nor is there much evidence yet of a willingness by the UN outside of the Sub-Commission for the Prevention of Discrimination and the Protection of Minorities to pay significant attention to the issue of minority group protection. Therefore, despite the recent changes with regards to the role of the UN in the resolution of international and internal conflicts, we should reserve judgement on its ability to improve its record in the more specific area of ethnic conflict resolution.

NOTE

1. The research undertaken to write this article was made possible by the award of an ESRC Grant No. R000231101. My thanks to Jurgen Dedring for his comments on the first draft of this article.

REFERENCES

Alam, G. M. S., 1982. 'Peacekeeping Without Conflict Resolution: The Kashmir Dispute', *Fletcher Forum*, vol. 6, no. 1.

Amnesty International, 1984. *Sri Lanka: Current Human Rights Concerns and Evidence of Extra-Judicial Killings by the Security Forces*, London: Amnesty International.

Amnesty International, 1989. *Turkey: Brutal and Systematic Abuse of Human Rights*, London: Amnesty International.

Arendt, H., 1963. *On Revolution*, London: Faber (reprinted 1973 by Penguin, Harmondsworth).

Assefa, H., 1987. *Mediation of Civil war: Approaches and Strategies - The Sudan Conflict*, Boulder, CO: Westview.

Azar, E. E., 1990. *The Management of Protracted Social Conflict*, Dartmouth: Aldershot.

Bailey, S., 1982. 'The UN and the Termination of Armed Conflict: 1946-64', *International Affairs*, London, vol. 58, no. 3.

Beitz, C., 1979. *Political Theory and International Relations*, Princeton, NJ: Princeton University Press.

Buckheit, L. C., 1978. *Secession: The Legitimacy of SelfDetermination*, New Haven, CN: Yale University Press.

Claude, I. L. Jr., 1951. 'The Nature and Status of the Sub-commission on the Prevention of Discrimination and the Protection of Minorities', *International Organisation*, vol. 5, no. 2.

Claude, I. L. Jr., 1969. *National Minorities: An International Problem*, Westport, CT.: Greenwood.

Connor, W., 1972. 'Nation-building or Nation Destroying?', *World Politics*, vol. 24, no. 3.

De Azcarate, P., 1967. *Protection of National Minorities*, New York: Carnegie Endowment for International Peace.

Fawcett, J., 1979. *The International Protection of Minorities*, Minority Rights Group Report No. 41, London.

Galtung, J., 1976. 'Three Approaches to Peace: Peacekeeping, Peacemaking and Peacebuilding', in J. Galtung, *Essays in Peace Research*, Vol. 2, Copenhagen: Ejlers.

Galtung, J., 1980. *The True Worlds: A Transnational Perspective*, New York: Free Press.

Garber, L. & C. M. O'Connor, 1985. 'The 1984 United Nations Sub-Committee on the Prevention of Discrimination and the Protection of Minorities', *American Journal of International Law*, vol. 79, no. 1.

Gardeniers, T., H. Hannum & J. Kruger, 1982. 'The United Sub-Commission on the Prevention of Discrimination and the Protection of Minorities', *Human Rights Quarterly*, vol. 4, no. 3.

Gellner, E., 1988. *Plough, Sword and Book*, London: Collins Harvill.

Haas, E. B., 1986. *Why We Still Need the United Nations: The Collective Management of International Conflict, 1945-84*, Institute of International Studies Policy Paper on International Affairs No. 26, University of California.

Haksar, U., 1974. *Minority Protection and International Bill of Human Rights*, Bombay: Allied Publishers.

Hannum, H., 1981a. 'Human Rights and the United Nations: Progress at the 1980 Session of the Sub-Commission on the Prevention of Discrimination and the Protection of Minorities', *Human Rights Quarterly*, vol. 3, no. 3.

Hannum, H., 1981b. 'The Thirty-third Session of the United Nations Sub-Commission on the Prevention of Discrimination and the Protection of Minorities', *American Journal of International Law*, vol. 75, no. 1.

Hettne, B., 1990. *Development Theories and the Three Worlds*, Longman: Harlow.

Horowitz, I. L., 1980. *Taking Lives*, New Brunswick: Transaction Books.

Humphrey, J. P., 1984. *Human Rights and The United Nations: The Great Adventure*, Dobbs Ferry, NY: Transactional Publications.

International Peace Research Association, 1990. *Peacebuilding and Development in Lebanon*, Paris: Unesco.

James, A., 1989. 'Peacekeeping and Keeping the Peace', *Review of International Studies*, vol. 15, no. 4.

Janowsky, O.I., 1945. *Nationalities and National Minorities*, New York: Macmillan.

Jensen, L., 1988. 'Planning Together for Nicosia's Future', *World Development*, March.

Kuper, L., 1981. *Genocide*, Harmondsworth: Penguin.

Kuper, L., 1985. *The Prevention of Genocide*, New Haven: Yale University Press.

Layburn, J. G., 1947. *World Minority Problems*, New York: Public Affairs Committee.

Lowe, M. F., 1976. *International Organisation and the Protection of Minorities*, Geneva Institute for International Studies, Unpublished Thesis.

Luard, E., 1989. *A History of the United Nations*, vol. 2, London: Macmillan.

Mair, L.P. 1928. *The Protection of Minorities: The Working and Scope of the Minorities Treaties Under the League of Nations*, London: Christopher.

Mapes, M. C. Jr., 1985. 'Why Establish a National Peace Academy?', in C. D. Smith, ed., *The One Hundred Percent Challenge*, Bethesda, MD: Seven Locks Press.

Martin, G., 1990. 'Security and Conflict in Chad', *Bulletin of Peace Proposals*, vol. 21, no. 1.

Mazrui, A. A., 1969. *Post Imperial Fragmentation. The Legacy of Ethnic and Racial Conflict*, Denver, CO.: University of Denver.

Miller, L. B., 1967. *World Order and Local Disorders: The United Nations and Internal Conflicts*, Princeton, NJ: Princeton University Press.

Mitchell, C. R., 1981. *The Structure of International Conflict*, London: Macmillan.

Mitchell, C. R., 1989. *Conflict Resolution and Civil War: Reflections on the Sudanese Settlement of 1972*, Fairfax, VA: George Mason University, Centre for Conflict Analysis and Resolution.

Modeen, T., 1969. *The International Protection of National Minorities in Europe*, Åbo: Åbo Akademi.

Nielsson, G. P., 1984. 'States and Nation-Groups: A Global Taxonomy', in E.A. Tiryakian & R. Ragowski, eds, *New Nationalisms of the Developed West*, Boston: Allen and Unwin.

Ramcharan, B. G., 1983. *Humanitarian Good Offices in International Law*, Dordrecht, M. Nijhoff.

Robinson, J. et al., 1943. *Were the Minority Treaties a Failure?*, New York: Institute of Jewish Affairs.

Rupesinghe, K., 1988. 'Notes Towards a Research Programme: Ethnic Violence, Human Rights and Early Warning', *UNESCO Yearbook of Peace and Conflict Research 1986*, Paris: Unesco, ch. 23.

Ryan, S., 1988. 'Explaining Ethnic Conflict: The Neglected International Dimension', *Review of International Studies*, vol. 14, no. 3.

Ryan, S., 1990. 'Ethnic Conflict and the United Nations', *Ethnic and Racial Studies*, vol. 13, no. 1.

Schachter, O., 1974. 'The United Nations and Internal Conflict', in J.N. Moore, ed., *Law and Civil War in the Modern World*, Baltimore, MD: Johns Hopkins Press.

Sesay, A., 1989. 'The OAU Peacekeeping Force in Chad: What are the Lessons for the Future?', unpublished paper.

Shiels, F. L., ed., 1984. *Ethnic Separatism and World Politics*, Lanham: University Press of America.

Skjelsbæk, K., 1989. 'United Nations Peacekeeping and the Facilitation of Withdrawals', *Bulletin of Peace Proposals*, vol. 20, no. 3.

Sorensen, M., 1956. 'The Quest for Equality', *International Conciliation*, no. 507.

Thakur, R., 1987a. *International Peacekeeping in the Lebanon*, Boulder, CO: Westview.

Thakur, R., 1987b. 'International Peacekeeping, UN authority and US power', *Alternatives*, vol. 12, no. 4.

Thakur, R., 1988. 'International Peacekeeping', in R. Thakur, ed., *International Conflict Resolution*, Boulder, CO: Westview.

Thornberry, P., 1980. 'Minority Rights, Human Rights and International Law', *Ethnic and Racial Studies*, vol. 3, no. 3.

U Thant, 1977. *View From the United Nations*, Newton Abbot, David and Charles.

Ury, W., 1987. 'Strengthening International Mediation', *Negotiation Journal*, vol. 3, no. 3.

Van der Merwe, H., 1988. 'South African Initiatives: Contrasting Options in the Mediation Process', in C. R. Mitchell and K. Webb, eds, *New Approaches to International Mediation*, New York: Greenwood Press.

Vishniak, M., 1945. 'The International Protection of Minorities and the International Bill of Rights', *International Postwar Problems*, vol. 2, no. 3.

Young, O., 1967. *The Intermediaries*, Princeton, NJ: Princeton University Press.

Zartman, I. W., 1986. 'Conflict in Chad', in A. R. Day & M.W. Doyle, eds, *Escalation and Intervention*, Boulder, CO: Westview.

7

Political and Cultural Background of Conflicts and Global Governance

Kinhide Mushakoji

1. INTRODUCTION: THE GLOBAL CRISIS, SECURITY AND GOVERNANCE

This chapter is meant to provide a point of entry into the discussion on the political, and cultural background of conflicts and the conditions which guarantee global security and governance in the contemporary international system. It is an attempt to read the 'signs of the times,' especially in view of the recent events in the Soviet Union and in Eastern Europe.[1]

It seems today that the Cold War is over, and it is said that a new world order is forthcoming. Even if such a view is overly optimistic, it is true that the mist which has enveloped the international scene since the 1950s is clearing, permitting international issues of different kinds to be seen in their true form, no longer just as epiphenomena of the Cold War. In fact, many of these issues can now be seen to have had their origins in North-South contradictions turned into East-West conflicts. The dawning of the new era thus marks the end of the post-World-War-II hegemonic order, but it does not necessarily mean that the creation of a new world order is imminent. In fact, this transition is creating a chaotic and conflictual world situation, including a war of a new type, the Gulf War. The present disorder, however, is not necessarily negative, since the current chaos may play a creative role, serving as a gestation period for a more equitable new world order.

It is still premature to predict what awaits us at the turn of the century. In order to propose a possible reading of the 'signs of time', we start with a working hypothesis, to the effect that the world is in a deep crisis, and we must break the age-old assumptions about the world, the hegemonic order, the state, and other institutions whose legitimacy has never been put into question until today.

In fact, the global economic-political system is clearly in deep crisis. There is, on one hand, the new thinking of the Soviet Union which implies an official renunciation of its hegemonic role. The destabilization of the bi-hegemonic order of the Cold War may lead to a stable Pax Americana. This does not seem, however, likely, since the United States is not prepared to play a hegemonic role alone as it did in the 1950s and 1960s. Some even say that this hegemony has entered a declining phase. In support of this, we may say that the hegemonic order is in crisis with both hegemonic actors – the major hegemon and the challenging one – being unable to hold onto their leading positions. Behind these two trends, there is a deeper and a more general crisis of the state. All these trends converge into a general crisis of global governance which takes diverse shapes in the different parts of the world.

On the surface, this crisis appears to affect only the international political economy. In reality, it is a more fundamental political-cultural crisis; a crisis of Western civilization in which the basic values and beliefs underlying modern Western societies are put into question. The present chapter proposes a preliminary conceptual framework useful in grasping the true dimensions of this complex global crisis.

The complexity of this crisis can be identified in three contexts: hegemonic, technocratic, and politico-cultural. Moreover, these crises have in turn generated a situation which presents a fundamental challenge to the survival of life as we know it. This crisis has two main aspects – ecological and military – and can be seen in terms of a crisis in our definitions of, and thinking about, security.

It is crucial to stress the importance of the ecological crisis. Many hundred million years after the emergence of life on Earth, the human race has acquired the power to destroy all living beings, either through nuclear holocaust or through global biocide. Security in the face of the global crisis is thus made synonymous with the survival of all living beings, and ceases to be purely military. The ecological crisis, which may well lead to global biocide, is a consequence of modern techno-economic growth, a process led by politico-economic development under the successive hegemonic dynasties of Western powers of which the United States is the last defender, and the Soviet Union the last challenger.

It is within this global process of transformation that conflicts, security and governance must to be analyzed. The old stereotypes created by the nuclear security school of thought still prevail in terms of conflict and conflict management. Moreover, the tendency to consider the big powers as the only actors that can responsibly guarantee global security is not limited to military conflicts. Ecology constitutes another important aspect of global security which gives a special role to the industrial powers; according to them, it is they and they alone who can guarantee the survival of humankind thanks to their scientific and technological capacity.

Ecological viability is portrayed as a pseudo-common good but is thus, in reality, a club good of the industrial powers, who believe that to serve their own techno-economic interests serves *ipso facto* the best interests of humankind. The real concern is not the survival of the human race but the sustainability of the industrial development led by the industrial nations of the Trilateral regions: North America, Europe and Japan. They present the security of their economic interests as a global security issue, and claim to act in this respect on behalf of the whole of humankind. True enough, ecological security is in itself a common good to be shared by all living beings. The industrial nations, however, define this issue presupposing that it implies the sustainability of industrial development which guarantees the sustainability of their prosperity and leadership. The eventual need for, and possibility of, choosing some alternative paths for development which are ecologically and socially more healthy is excluded from their definition of ecological security.

It is, obviously, quite natural that the 'club' of industrial nations define their security in such terms as to best serve their interests. It is, however, unreasonable to justify the representation of this restricted definition of ecological security as a common good of humankind. Yet, on the basis of this claim, the industrially developed nations of the centre of the world system assume a leadership role in managing global environmental concerns, telling the developing nations what they should do or not do in view of guaranteeing the sustainability of industrial development. Thus ecological security is treated in a pseudo-globalistic context in which the club goods of the North are presented as the public goods of the global community including the south. At the same time, in the UN system, for example, environmental issues tend to be treated as a topic managed by the 'summit' of industrial nations, where numerous decisions are made before the questions are opened for debate among the smaller states.

Whereas nuclear security issues put the non-nuclear states under the exogenous security guarantee of the superpowers – a tendency strongly opposed by the former in such occasions as the evaluation of the Non-Proliferation Treaty, ecological security puts the peripheral states under exogenous security management by the so-called G7 summit process. It is commonly said that ecological issues serve to reinforce the interdependence of all the states. This is true in that the industrialized nations are dependent for their survival upon the ecological health and environmental sustainability of the developing world. It is also true, however, that ecological issues intensify the dependence of the nations of the South on the big industrial powers of the North in the name of global survival.

For most of the countries of the world, security (nuclear and ecological) is now predominantly exogenous, a situation which has prompted a wide range of reactions from states and non-state actors who refuse to be subjugated to external control because they feel insecure about accepting foreign 'protection' under whatever pretext.

The above discussion leads to a single conclusion. It is wrong to take for granted the assumption that the interests of the super-powers and of the other industrial nations can prevail regardless of all circumstances, and that no alternative approaches to nuclear and ecological security are possible. This assumption may have been realistic in the 1960s, when the hegemonic order led by the United States was stable. Nowadays, too many contesting actors and unmanageable factors exist. Governance, in this context, is one of the most important key concepts which can help us to ask the right question. It can be defined as the political, economic, and cultural processes of cooperation and competition involved in determining the legitimacy of the local, regional and global projects and initiatives of different actors.

Who acts on whose behalf in guaranteeing the survival, development and welfare of which human community? Unless this point is made clear, no cooperation is possible among the different actors, either domestic or international, in the resolution of military and non-military conflicts. Without a common understanding shared by the parties concerned about what is legitimate or illegitimate, it is impossible to secure the cooperation of the multitude of state and non-state actors in coping with the different global issues in the worsening crisis situation of today's world.[2]

2. THE HEGEMONIC CONTEXT

2.1. The decline of the hegemonic order and its impacts on the West

In the hegemonic context, the decline of the US hegemonic order seems to become an unquestionable reality. In spite of an apparent resurgence of U.S. global military control shown by the overwhelming victory in the Gulf War, this control is characterized by economic reliance on its industrial allies, which is but one manifestation of the destabilizing techno-economic trends described below, i.e. the growing difficulty of the hegemon to pay for the common goods and club goods. Its reliance on its close allies to share the burden, in turn, intensify the crisis of the states which are integrated into that order.

These trends are caused by a general decline in the managerial capacity of the system resulting from the growing need to spend the accumulated surplus to cover expenditures related to different public and club goods. The accumulation of surplus, an essential precondition of the techno-economic development of the world system described below, has to cover not only the distribution of market goods but must also cover a number of costs which are generated by the free market. If no allocations are made by those who control the world surplus, these costs will create conflicts and hamper the sustainability of the system. In recent years, this type of public goods has increased to such an extent that the eco-political stability of the system has been affected.[3]

The reason for the increase in costs related to public goods can be found in the following three emerging trends. Firstly, there is the impact of impoverishment in the peripheral regions exemplified by the international debt crisis. The market mechanism is unable to generate the transfer of funds necessary to cope with this crisis and to trigger the process of industrial development in these regions. Secondly, there is the impact of massive migratory trends, both domestic and international, which lead to urban marginalization and cultural conflicts in the peripheral regions, as well as in the countries of the centre. In this instance, the informal sectors mix with the market economy to generate a black economy and this puts a burden on the public sector, either in terms of social security, or of internal security.

Thirdly, there is the increasingly important cost of environmental deterioration caused by both the over- and the under-development of the different world regions as a consequence of excessive surplus accumulation. The part of this cost which can be internalized by the market is limited and the public goods aspect of sustaining development demands more and more allocation of the surplus. The combined effects of the above tendencies lead to a situation where those who accumulate surplus become less generous in their allocation to cover the public goods costs.

On the world level, several trends have recently emerged as a consequence of the unwillingness of the hegemon and of the major industrial states to assume fully the burden of the public goods. Firstly, the United States feels itself unable to continue to act as the hegemon of the whole world system, as well as the top leader of the 'West'. This is especially so since this bloc is now more' and more forced to take care of the economic stabilization of the 'East'. This is perceived to be a too heavy burden by this superpower which has lost the overwhelming economic supremacy it enjoyed in the 1950s and 1960s. The US is no longer willing to exercise alone its global and regional hegemonic role since this implies shouldering the costs of the public goods formerly associated with the supremacy of the dollar as well as the club goods primarily associated with the nuclear defence of the 'Club West', now transformed into the 'Club North' defended by a larger panoply of high-tech weapons since the Gulf War.

The US prefers to rely on Western Europe and Japan to share the burden of economic aid and defence. The interests of the Trilateral regions require a certain minimum level of stability in the South, especially where oil and other precious resources are produced. Free access to such resources, as well as to the large markets of the Third World, is so crucial for the 'industrial democracies' that they must be ready to shoulder the bill of the carrots (aid) and the stick (police actions) -- this guaranteeing peace and order in the turbulent South where low intensity conflicts call incessantly for such collective operations.

This trend will probably tend more and more to be accompanied by a growing tension among the Trilateral regions, caused by a fundamental difference in the perception of each actor's role. The Americans feel that Europe and Japan have had a free ride for long enough and should now start paying for their share of the public and club goods, while the two partners feel that an increase in their burden-sharing ought to be compensated through more concessions by the declining hegemonic leader.

Another burden sharing trend regards the trans-national corporations (TNCs). Under the new key word 'privatization', a process of deregulation is unfolding as the Trilateral states invite the transnational corporate sector to shoulder part of the bill for the club goods, for example development aid as in the case of the Mini-Marshal Plan to help the Philippines. The trend toward privatization is often presented as a victory of the free-market economy over the state bureaucracy. It is probably more accurate, however, to view this development as a new coalition between the technocrats of the states and the TNCs which allows them to complement each other in achieving their common global objectives.

Whether the coalition will lead to the prosperity of the states at the centre of the world system still remains to be seen. What is already clear is that this process exacerbates the economic and political situation of the peripheral states, and that it is rapidly becoming a major source of insecurity and conflict for the whole world system.

2.2. New developments in Europe and in the Third World

In the Eastern Bloc, the Soviet Union feels that the expense of shouldering the costs of the public and club goods is too high. This has been at least one of the reasons for Gorbachev's perestroika. The Eastern European states have followed the Soviet example, preferring to let the market pay for the goods so far defined as public. While the full impact of this major shift in public policy still remains to be seen, one serious problem which is bound to emerge following the adoption of a free market approach is decreasing welfare allocations by the state. In socialist countries, the expectation of the public has been that the state will provide, through government allocations, for the satisfaction of basic needs. After a honeymoon period with the free market, a time will come when people will ask the state to be more sensitive to the needs of those who cannot take full advantage of the free market. This will raise a serious governance issue; the question of how to avoid ideo-bureaucratic/technocratic governance and yet have public goods, including welfare, covered by the state or any other actor outside of the market. This is a serious governance issue which has to be addressed by all states, not only those in Eastern Europe but also those in the North and in the South.

In this connection, it is interesting to observe another experiment in Europe. The EEC inner market of 1992 will be yet another manifestation of an attempt by the states to cover the costs of public goods in each national society. The impact of European integration on global governance may take any of several different forms and it is difficult to make any predictions at this moment. In addition, the ongoing debate about the future role of the Conference on the Security and Cooperation in Europe (CSCE) system is also an interesting subject, since Europe might wind up careening a large part of the North, from Alaska to Siberia. This is, however just one possibility among many, and everything is uncertain.

What seems clear, though, is that the way Europe deals with issues of public/club goods will influence the internal structure and logic of Trilateral globalism. All will depend on how Europe defines its global role, not only within the Trilateral context, but also in relation to the Third World. Europe faces three possible alternative ways to use the power and influence newly acquired through its unification. One is to concentrate on itself and strengthen the 'fortress Europe'. A second is to play a leading role in the Trilateral club, winning the techno-economic game vis-a-vis North America and Japan. A third alternative is to play a global role using its former colonial ties with different Third World regions as a basis for close cooperation.

It is in this connection that the public goods issue, (i.e. who provides which public goods and get what benefit in return?) plays a key role in determining the basic conditions of North-South relations. Economic and technological redistribution of the surplus accumulated in the centre of the world system constitutes a major part of the transaction of the world public goods. The Trilateral *pax consortis* may attempt, in exchange for cost-sharing, to establish a triumvirate over the Third World, or divide it into regions under the tutelage of the three hegemonic partners; Africa for Europe, Latin America for the United States, and Asia for Japan! Still another scenario, in fact the most gloomy one, foresees an economic system which superimposes a prosperous industrial economy organized by the Trilateral division of labour among Europe, North America and Japan on top of the impoverished and conflict-laden peripheral regions of the Third World.

The hegemons, as well as their clients, have experienced a decline in their capacity to provide public goods. A loss of legitimacy accompanies this failure to meet the expectations of their followers and clients. As a consequence, the hegemons have begun to adopt a more aggressive diplomatic and military stance towards the world outside, while taking stronger techno-bureaucratic and public-safety measures within, in order to compensate for the decline in their power.

The so-called problem of the 'governability of democracies' is but a technocratic legitimization of this kind of 'tough' and 'hawkish' attempt to counteract the decline in their capacity to provide public and club goods. The argument is that the democratic ideal of popular participation in the decision-making processes of the state curtails the capacity of the technocrats to choose optimal solutions to global problems. In fact, what is perceived as global by the technocrats is in reality the club goods of the industrialized countries, and optimality of global 'solutions' is measured against the yardstick of the interests of the industrialized world.

Strangely enough, this pseudo-globalistic problem-solving approach has been adopted by the technocratic elites of the industrialized countries at a moment when world opinion has been alerted by the different popular movements in all the regions of the world, and is searching for a truly global solution based on diverse local-specific realities. It seems that at the present time popular participation in decision-making is more strongly supported in the post-perestroika socialist world than in the post-US-hegemonic Trilateral world. How the former interact with the latter is as yet unclear. It is likely that the socialist world will participate in a complex process of conflict and competition mixed with cooperation and mutual concessions which will develop among the different component units of the centre of the world system.

2.3. The crisis in the centre and in the peripheries

The least we can say about the process of conflict and cooperation developing at the centre of the world system is that it is not heading toward integration. It will rather develop more and more into a conflictual process, full of gaps and contradictions. To begin with, as we saw above, the Trilateral pax consortis has many internal contradictions, and the participation of socialist Eastern Europe in it will not decrease the competition. The centre of the world system, in spite of its apparent prosperity, will thus stay in deep crisis.

This crisis in the centre is likely to worsen in view of the following two factors. There is, as we have already discussed, a growing migratory trend from the peripheral regions to the Trilateral regions which will create internal North-South problems within the countries of the centre. These problems will be compounded by the proliferation of ethnic identity claims, human rights issues, economic and social equity questions, as well as eco-political and the many other problems which plague the 'post-industrial' societies.

These issues will be addressed with less and less success by the states receiving the immigrants, whose institutions are designed to deal with 'well behaved' citizens of an 'orderly' civil society, and hence misread the messages coming from the least integrated sectors of their society. This lack of success by the government is likely to trigger an activation of the civil institutions, to enable the society to respond in a more appropriate manner to the 'voices of the voiceless' coming from the less integrated sectors.

This activation will materialize itself through the development of networks of social movements challenging the legitimacy of technocratic control. The Trilateral hegemonic consortium is thus likely to be plagued by an endemic social crisis. This crisis of the centre of the world system will encourage the emerging competitors from the semi-periphery, especially the NIEs, to claim their right to participate in the pax consortis of the industrialized summit. The South will be divided as the more advanced countries of the semi-periphery seek admittance to the North.

In the semi-periphery, including the NIEs and the former(?) socialist countries of Eastern Europe, in the inner-periphery with so many indebted countries, and in the outer-periphery where the situation keeps worsening, the new international division of labour will create a growing divide between the societies which can hope to follow the NIE model, those who join the ranks of the LLDCs, and those in the outer-periphery.[4]

The LLDCs will continue to be the object of aid cum over-exploitation by the centre. As to the countries trying to join the NIEs, it is not clear whether they can imitate the NIEs whose growth depended on a world market large enough to their products. Now, the limited capacity of the external market does not favour the growth of new NIEs. An alternatives path is to export labour, and this is one of the causes of the growing migratory trends from the aspirant NIEs to the countries of the centre.

The countries which have opted for the NIEs model are faced with many difficult problems. Issues such as how to overcome the gap created by intensive industrial development in the urban sector which has left behind a large traditional rural sector, how to cope with the marginalization and alienation of those who have migrated to the big industrial centres, and how to satisfy the material and non-material needs of the new social strata are just a few examples. In the face of these difficulties, the adoption of an authoritarian development model is a tempting proposition, and this is why we often find the technocrats of the periphery states in alliance with the modernizing military elite.

In the outer-periphery, we find different issues interacting and complicating the already complex situation. In the Pacific, for example, issues regarding maritime nuclear deployment, nuclear and toxic waste dumping, and the equitable and sustainable utilization of marine resources in danger of depletion are combined with issues of independence, sovereignty and ethnic identity.

The crisis in this fringe of the world system may become, if world opinion is alerted through new channels of communication created by a transregional cooperation among social movements now still in an embryonic stage, the locus of counter-trends which oppose technocratic governance and draw the attention of concerned people from the different parts of the world system. The outer-periphery, in a way, externalizes different contradictions latent in the other regions.

In this context, the choice between exogenous and endogenous development is especially difficult for the micro-states of the Pacific. In the northwestern Pacific, for example, it entails a choice between almost total reliance on aid from the United States guaranteeing a decent 'modern' life style in exchange for a renunciation of each nation's autonomy, or keeping one's own ethnic identity and life style and renouncing the luxury of modern societies. In terms of security, exogenous nuclear security is meaningless to the peoples of the island states. These people are seeking a possible alternative in taking an endogenous approach to security, including ecological security from nuclear dumping and nuclear tests, and ethnic security aimed at the maintenance of cultural identity, national independence and sovereignty.

The outer-periphery is the region where the negative surplus of the capital accumulation of the whole world system piles up. Dumping grounds, testing sites, and over-exploitation of the surrounding global commons represent a few examples of this negative accumulation. In spite of its powerlessness, this region gives to its people a considerable nuisance value in view of the special military/economic interest of the hegemon.[5]

Anti-systemic trends in the contemporary world system exist not only in the outer-periphery. Many pockets of negative surplus accumulation can also be found in the semi-periphery, as well as in the centre. Some examples would be the depleted rural regions, the slums of the big urban centres, growing numbers of illicit foreign workers and the different communities where informal and black market economies are dominant. These sectors, which exist in practically all societies in the peripheries as well as in the centre of the world system, are characterized by their resistance to becoming the object of technocratic planning by their respective governments.

3. The Technocratic Context

3.1. Growth and contradictions in the centre

In the previous section, we have seen how the decline of the post-World War II hegemonic order has, among other things, brought about a coalition of state and corporate interests. Let us now examine further the implications of technocratic rule, and the relationship between technocracy and governance (Mushakoji, 1988, pp. 125-42).

At the techno-economic level, the rapid development of high technologies is serving to strengthen the power base of technocratic rule over an increasingly finely diversified and stratified world system, where the surplus is efficiently channelled to feed research and development (R & D) activities in the centre and in the semi-periphery. This development will in turn cause more and more serious global and local problems, alarming an increasing large portion of the educated public, including some of the technocrats themselves. This exemplifies one of the deep causes of the present crisis – the existence of an inherent contradiction in technocratic governance.

Technocrats in governments, international organizations and business all believe in the management of global and local issues through rational planning. According to their common belief, all irrational factors which they cannot control are bound to be eliminated in accordance with the golden rule of the survival of the fittest, i.e. the most rational. Rationality is thus considered to be the deciding factor in determining the course of human progress and development. In truth, this neo-Darwinistic philosophy builds into the world system all kinds of contradictions between the centre where, thanks to technocratic planning and management, everything is made 'rational', and the peripheral regions of the system where the technocrats dispose of everything they consider unmanageable and irrational.

One of the problems with this complete devotion to rationality is that it deprives the system of a mechanism for dealing with irrationality. Rational planning tolerates only one adjustment process – the free market mechanism. This leaves no room for governance which deals with the negative externalities of techno-economic progress. As a result, the development of humankind is left to a selective process which generates inequities and conflicts. The more 'rational' and 'flexible' technocratic management becomes, the more it relies on the invisible hand of the market, and the more it generates inequities and conflicts. For example, while 'regulation' and 'deregulation' are sometimes seen as being opposed to each other, they in fact constitute two sides of the same technocratic project. This is a fundamental contradiction underlying today's crisis.

The contradiction between technocratic management, on the one hand, and conflicts and inequities, on the other, is reflected in the global division of labour in different ways. At the centre of the world system, it destabilizes the political economy through the gaps it generates in the market. The accumulation of surplus by the hegemon, in this 'casino capitalism', is made through speculation and hence widens the gap between the international financial flow and the real productive economy.

The contradiction becomes more acute when it occurs between the financially powerful hegemon (the United States) which is weakening in terms of real production and R & D supremacy, and the competitors in the centre (Japan and Europe) which have a growing techno-productive capacity. This situation has destabilized the domination of the world wide techno-economic order by the American technostructure which has held a predominant position in the world system since the Second World War. It has not, however, led to the emergence of a new hegemon. It has led rather to a Trilateral hegemonic competition full of hidden conflicts and contradictions.

The Trilateral co-hegemony is bound to be unstable, not only because techno-economic competition pits one power against another, but also because the three power bases face a zero-sum situation in terms of the utilization of scarce resources, while they have to reach an agreement on who should pay the public goods, especially in terms of covering the cost of environmental degradation.

The impact of this techno-economic hegemonic crisis appears in three problem areas, each having direct or indirect impact on the global security problematique. Firstly, there is the techno-military dimension of the present R & D supremacy of the United States which complicates the techno-economic competition among the Trilateral regions.

This competition is developing in a world setting where East-West nuclear tensions are decreasing in intensity, and consequently, where the legitimacy of the U.S. nuclear leadership is becoming more and more questionable. How will this new 'detente' process develop, and how will it influence Trilateral governance? This is neither merely an economic question, nor is it only a politico-military problem. In fact, the fields and extent of competition or cooperation between the Trilateral regions influence the global development process. We will come back to this question later. Here we will just stress that the patterns of conflict in the Third World regions will be influenced by the patterns of conflict and cooperation among the Trilateral regions, wherever the latter's interests are at stake in the former.

The above question is directly connected to a second one: What will be the impact of techno-economic development of the North on the countries of the South? We have already seen that ecological security is treated in a pseudo-globalistic context where the club goods of the industrial states area presented as global public goods. This pseudo-globalistic approach to ecological governance and security creates strong resentment in the Third World, where it is felt that the major ecological offenders are the techno-economic activities of the TNCs which exploit and degrade the resources of the Third World. This is why it is important to study the impact of the techno-economic development led by the Trilateral industrial states on the different parts of the Third World. In this context, global governance issues are thus inseparable from the North South problematique.

It is also important to recognize that practically everything related to global or local conflicts and security is related to the impoverishment process already discussed above. Unlike the East-West conflicts where common interest emerged and led to the end of the Cold War, conflicts in the South involve in most cases scarce resources which cannot be shared. Zero-sum relations thus characterize most of the conflicts in the developing regions. Even when the official motives are ethnic or religious, impoverishment is at the root of these conflicts. This was true during the Cold War period when it was feared that local conflicts in the Third World might escalate into a total nuclear war, so that the two super-powers had reached a tacit agreement to 'manage' the crisis, turning the local zero-sum situations into non zero-sum conflicts by the introduction of the danger of a nuclear war, a negative utility for all parties.

Now that the conflicts in the South cannot be easily linked to a danger of nuclear escalation, the zero-sum nature of the conflicts in the developing regions is even more true. No longer is it to prevent a nuclear war, but rather to protect the interests of the 'industrial democracies' that the 'Club West' now transformed into the 'Club North' intervenes and attempts to turn the zero-sum conflicts into positive-sum ones through their powers to both destroy and build up the regional economies. The attempts by regional powers to become regional hegemons are promptly penalised, as in the case of the Gulf War. Even when the conflicting parties are not as strong as Iraq was, the hegemon and its allies are now well prepared to counteract any disturbance of 'law and order' in the South, thanks to their capacity to control 'low intensity conflicts' (LIC).

The term 'low intensity conflict' is used by the military strategists of the industrial powers to single out a specific category of conflicts which employ only limited military means, and stresses the need to develop a 'proper' technique to manage them. This definition shows the lack of understanding of the military experts who are unable to see that while these conflicts are indeed 'LICs', rather than being Low Intensity Conflicts they are in fact 'Legitimacy and Identity Conflicts' which are often impossible to manage by military means, whatever their intensity level.

The third and final question regards the negative impacts of technological development on ecosystems, particularly those in the countries of the periphery, and the social conflicts which accompany any attempts to reduce them. Unless ecological sustainability is guaranteed through a radical reconsideration of the economic growth strategy of the industrial nations of the centre, including their R & D policy, technological development originating in the North will either cause environmental problems or else exacerbate North-South issues, or perhaps both.

This is in a sense the logical consequence of the pseudo-globalistic manner in which ecological questions are treated by the industrial states. We have seen that this conflict is most conspicuous in the outer-periphery, as it is being used as the repository for the negative by-products of the techno-economic and military activities of the industrial states of the centre.

In more general terms, the fact that today's techno-economic development lacks ecological sustainability will inevitably lead to serious security and governance conflicts. These conflicts will focus on the means used to guarantee ecosecurity and will call into question the very legitimacy of the present techno-economic projects of the industrialized Trilateral regions.

3.2. The impact of perestroika
The recent events in the Soviet Union and in Eastern Europe create an interesting situation as far as technocratic world development is concerned. By joining the techno-capitalist world order, the socialist countries create many new possibilities for intensified technological development, thus facilitating the integration of the techno-structures of the former 'Eastern bloc' into the techno-structures of the West. The new cooperation between Eastern and Western Europe seems, for the moment, a positive strengthening factor for the global free market economy. As we have already seen, the disenchantment following the

present euphoria is going to generate conflicts of a different nature. It is to be hoped that other social trends will help to prevent the worst from happening, and in this connection one must not overlook the existence of another important trend linking closely Western and Eastern Europe – the strong popular movements for democracy with equally strong environmental concerns. These movements constitute a powerful countervailing force vis-a-vis technocratic governance in both parts of Europe but especially in Eastern Europe. They may also play a role in limiting the danger of the present rush towards free market economy.

It is quite likely that the West will soon have to learn from the East about how to establish people's control over technocratic power, and we may even say that what is important about Perestroika is not the introduction of market mechanisms, but rather the hopes it create worldwide for stronger participation by the people in checking the power of the technocrats (see for example Kaldor, Holden & Falk, 1989).

The above is obviously a minority point of view. The more widely accepted interpretation of the situation, and that expressed by many journalists, is that the events in the Soviet Union and Eastern Europe are signs of the decline of socialism, and of the victory of world capitalism. In short-run military terms, it is probably true that the retreat of the Soviet Union leaves the United States with a free hand over a considerable part of the Third World. Panama and Iraq are but two examples of the new trends in conflict and conflict management in the post-bipolar world.

It is yet unclear how and to what extent the events in Europe will determine the course of socialism in the Third World. We must, in this context, remember that what we are currently witnessing in Eastern Europe will mean far more to other parts of the world than just the tilting of the scales between socialism and capitalism.

The delegitimization of the technocratic/ideological control of the technostructures in the socialist countries will not necessarily lead to unconditional support of world capitalism in the Third World. It will rather awaken the popular movements which are acquiring, day by day, more legitimacy and greater support from world liberal opinion.

3.3. The NIEs and the others in the Third World

We have already seen how in the semi-periphery, the emergence of the NIEs complicates the picture. They are competitors with the centre, challenging the established order, and at the same time striving for admittance. They also play a role as delegitimizers of the world techno-economic order in view of the fact that the more rapidly they industrialize, the more they cause international frictions and domestic contradictions.

In spite of the above complications, the NIEs draw worldwide attention because of their relative success in keeping a high GNP growth-rate while other developing countries accumulate international debts. In Japan, the centre of the Asia-Pacific region, there is strong optimism about the future development of what the author calls 'the JapaNIEs', which are expected to be followed eventually by the rest of the ASEAN countries plus China.

Thanks to the spill-over effects from the industrial growth of Japan and the NIEs, it is predicted that by the end of the first decade of the twenty-first century, all the NIEs will have become small Japans and all the ASEAN countries new NIEs. This regional development model which we call the 'JapaNIEs model' is supposed to provide a good example for all the 'poor' countries of the Third World as to what one can accomplish if one learns to be as hard-working as the JapaNIEs peoples.[6]

The basic problem with this optimistic view is that it does not take into account the structural and historical circumstances within which the NIEs have been able to industrialize so rapidly. Structurally, in the post-war world, the present-day NIEs were part of a vertical division of labour system with Japan at its top, and during the 1960s-1970s they succeeded in accumulating considerable world surplus.

As we have already seen, now that world market conditions are no longer as propitious as they were in those days, the surplus accumulation process is creating all kinds of frictions with both the North and the non-NIEs South. Historical events, in particular the Korean War for Japan and the Vietnam War for the NIEs, helped the countries to reach take-off. In any event, today international market conditions have changed and just being hard working does not create new NIEs.

In more general terms, only a few countries of the periphery seem to have the potential for joining the high-technology race and becoming NIEs. For the others, the development of a high-technology R & D capacity does not seem possible. These countries thus have to face a dilemma; they can either be on the receiving end of technology transfers from the centre, accepting the concomitant technological domination, or else refuse exogenous technology, resigning themselves to lagging behind other developing nations.

Questions such as whether it would be possible for them to develop an endogenous technology policy selecting only the appropriate high technologies, or whether they will be able to cope with the fact that new R & D may develop alternative products, closing forever the market for their primary products, reflect the fact that the new international technological division of labour generates a major threat to the countries in the periphery.

As we have seen, the outer-periphery is an even more disfavoured part of the world system. All sorts of techno-economic competitions in the centre generate conflicts which are especially acute in the outer-periphery and which have considerable repercussions on public opinion in the centre. These conflicts serve to delegitimize the productivity maximization policy based on the neo-Darwinistic ideology of the technocrats. The legitimacy conflicts which ensue involve not only the development issues regarding exogenous versus endogenous development. They also have a serious impact on international security in terms of the exogenous/endogenous security controversy.

The above review of the techno-economic crisis of today leads us to the following contradictory conclusion. On the one hand, a worldwide trend seems to encourage technocratic governance combined with free competition. This trend is supported by the technocrats of the states in the centre of the world system and of the transnational corporations, generates conflicts and competition in the peripheral regions of the system, and despite the optimism of the technocratics, exogenous security cannot cope with the rise of different types of counter-trends which are deeply rooted in local-specific realities and are gaining popular support owing to their endogenous legitimacy.

4. THE POLITICAL-CULTURAL CONTEXT

4.1. The decline of the hegemonic culture

The above remarks lead us to the third level of our analysis, the political-cultural context. The major question regards the way in which American mass culture should be interpreted. Rock music and blue jeans have been adopted by youth cultures around the world, not only in the West but also in the East and the South. Does this mean that American cultural hegemony will prevail, even after that country's politico-economic decline? The answer is not a straightforward yes, nor an unqualified no. American popular culture is not only hegemonic.

There has been a perceptible decay in the domination of the American hegemonic techno-culture whose message is that the world must adopt the American way of life based on technocratic neo-Darwinism and rationality, combined with a private sector in which prosperity is guaranteed by the free market and mass production/consumption. This cultural trend rejects any kind of communist and/or un-American messages which may put into question this 'American dream'.

In addition to this mainstream message, many different messages are presented by a wide range of American alternative sub-cultures. Like the rock and blue jeans youth culture, many of these are not particularly hegemonic in the sense of the 'American dream' mentioned above. Behind all the alternative messages coming from American counter cultures, we find a common basic message which is fundamentally different from the mainstream message of Empire America. That message is that of the American Republic and of the American Revolution.

The alternative cultures in the United States have had their ups and downs during the two centuries of American history. They have, however, never ceased sending liberating messages to the Old World. The latest messages have included such topics as human rights and democracy, feminism, alternative life styles and ecology, as well as anti-imperialism. These seeds of anti-hegemonic pluralism have been distributed not only in Western and Eastern Europe, but also in all the other regions of the world.

Having said that, we must admit that one of the most striking aspects of the contemporary world crisis is the emergence of a number of anti-systemic cultural trends which question not only American hegemonic culture but also a whole spate of Eurocentric cultural representations. As we saw above, the United States played the hegemonic role by shouldering the costs of technological R & D, plus the cost of a worldwide diffusion of American-generated sciences, modern arts, sports and general consumer life styles. This process of cultural diffusion met with great success in the 1950s and 1960s, but the global domination of Americanism also triggered off a strong countercurrent which rejected the simple imitation of exogenous cultures coming from North America, or more generally from the West. Cultural development, it was felt, presupposes an intellectual creativity which can flourish only through endogenous efforts. Genuine development cannot take place in any dependent culture which regards itself as inferior to the American version of Western civilization. It was strongly felt that all cultures had to build their societies based on values internally developed in resistance to the homogenizing impact of the prevailing hegemonic culture.

4.2. Universal globalism and cultural pluralism

It is interesting to compare the new trends towards pluralism emerging in the Soviet Union and in Eastern Europe with the above-mentioned pluralistic development of alternative subcultures which criticize American hegemonic culture from within. Today, the challengers to American hegemony and their follower states are generating from within their societies the seeds of fundamental cultural change.

The party state is now the target of strong popular critique. It has become more and more clear to the people of the world that ideo-technocratic cultural control by the a party state, achieved through the combined domination by the ideo-bureaucrats of the party and the technocrats of the state, has lost its legitimacy. New cultural movements, fundamentally anti-technocratic and pluralistic, are presently leading the socialist societies into a new cultural adventure. New interest in the so-far forbidden American culture is also manifested by some social groups.

There are also endogenous cultural movements which refer back to their respective cultural and religious traditions, in an attempt to build a society respecting fully the cultural identities of the peoples concerned. Still other trends look into the future in search of more humane cultural values which could help to build a new version of socialism with a human face. We have already discussed the role of Perestroika in delegitimizing ideo-technocratic governance. What is still to be seen is whether these self-organized cultural initiatives will be able to avoid the dangers of chaotic pluralism and continue to exist. In this context, the fundamental question is whether they will be able to build a new order based on a mutual acceptance of plural values in the face of the homogenizing pressures from the top and from the outside.

In the Third World, we find a number of examples of cultural re-awakening. Pre-modern cultural traditions, including the ethnic traditions of indigenous peoples which used to be considered 'primitive' by the 'civilized' Westerners, provide reference points for those struggling to resist the Eurocentric universal culture. Among these are many fundamentalist movements, and we cannot ignore the negative effects of many of these movements on the development of a global identity shared by the whole of humankind, the creation of which is indispensable in the face of so many global problems. It is, however, unrealistic to overlook the critique of modern Western culture presented by the fundamentalists, whose quite pointed questions require answers if we are to find solutions to global problems.

Another problem accompanying cultural re-awakening is that the competition among different ethnic groups, each in search of its own cultural identity, can easily turn into violent conflicts. The weakening of the hegemonic order and the crisis of the state complicate these conflicts, and create the need to develop a new pluralistic world order where different identities can accept each other, not as entities defined within the boundaries of a particular states, but rather by sharing a global identity.[7]

The role played by a a great number of social movements, which are trying to activate the positive traditions contained in their past history while fighting against the feudal authoritarian tendencies of their traditional culture, is more positive. A great number of intellectuals in Third World regions lead these movements, combining a deep interest in the cultural heritage of their nation with a strong identification with the people, especially the poor and the oppressed.

Also noteworthy is the role played in different world regions by religions. Their collaboration with the intellectuals and the popular movements often plays a crucial role in the social processes for democratization and human rights promotion. Such trends are especially conspicuous in the Philippines and the Southern Cone of Latin America. They also exist, with less visibility, yet with comparable dynamism and future potential, in many other countries of the world.

The diverse cultural trends we have reviewed above seem to indicate that the hegemony of a universal techno-culture supporting technocratic governance is now being challenged by a great number of cultural movements and trends. From the Greens in the West to the Gandhian movements in South Asia, they all question the legitimacy of American hegemonic culture in particular and European civilization, especially its neo-Darwinist technocratic tendencies, in general.

Whether the popular movements of the world can build a common cause in the face of the worldwide domination of technocratic globalism is still unclear. However, the most creative elements of humankind are in search of cultural alternatives to the Eurocentric technocratic culture, fundamentally discriminatory and exploitative in both social and ecological terms.

4.3. Technocratic versus democratic governance

We cannot be too optimistic about the possibility that alternative movements will bring about worldwide cultural transformation. Although things may change in the near future, it seems that at the beginning of the 1990s, alternative debates on alternative solutions are no longer as ardent as they were in the 1970s. The overwhelming urgency of a wide range of economic and political problems demanding immediate responses does not help to promote long range reflection. In the 1990s, however, the world is likely to enter into a new phase of the global crisis which will force people to raise again fundamental questions about new values and cultural alternatives (see for example Abdel-Malek, 1986; Mallmann & Nudler, 1986).

Global thinking in the centre often takes the form of a kind of neo-Darwinistic universalism which is, as we have already seen, the dominant technocratic ideology. This globalistic ideology recognizes the need for the technologically advanced Trilateral regions to assume the responsibility for coping with global problems and eventually covering the costs of the public goods. Nevertheless, it refuses to deal with the inequitable distribution of wealth, power and knowledge between the North and the South. This refusal is based on the belief that the unequal development in the world system is the result of a positive competition in which the North has come out victorious, surviving as the fittest among different cultures and societies.

As was mentioned above, in opposition to the globalistic and universalistic trends led by the technocratic globalists, there are a number of counter-currents represented by a growing number of anti-systemic movements and social science paradigms. These sometimes have a very particularistic and parochial world view, but in other cases, they combine the search for identity and endogeneity with locally rooted global concern. This is probably the underlying approach most appropriate for democratic global governance, and the most basic message shared by so many diverse social movements operating on the grassroots level. The essence of that message is that we must counter the abstract rationality of technocratic globalism with a concrete and genuine concern for the living beings, replacing 'survival of the fittest' philosophy of the technocrats with the Gandhian concern for 'the last child'

5. CONCLUSION: A CALL FOR GLOBAL GOVERNANCE

The above comments lead us to a number of tentative conclusions. First of all, the world is in deep crisis today. It is a crisis which forces all actors to reconsider their fundamental premises. What we see today is not, as certain commentators believe, the end of the Cold War with a capitalist victory over socialism. Although the ideo-technocratic version of socialism has lost legitimacy as a result of the emergence of the 'new way of thinking' in the Soviet Union and in Eastern Europe, this does not imply, *ipso facto*, the victory of capitalism under technocratic governance. In fact, at a time when an ever increasing number of public goods need to be allocated outside the market, while the market itself more and more resembles a 'casino', it becomes less and less realistic to hope that capitalism can enable the world to solve its problems satisfactorily. Moreover, the technocratic states are no longer capable of dealing with the plethora of problems emerging throughout the world, concerning everything from global ecology to local identities. The hegemon and its allies in the centre of the world system are in conflict among themselves because none of them are ready to use their surplus accumulation to pay for the public goods. They also quarrel about who has to foot the bill for the club goods.

The difficulty faced by the technocratic states in the Centre of the world system in allocating public goods causes problems for their colleagues in the impoverished states of the peripheral regions where the market economy is in crisis and the so-called informal sectors cover an ever larger proportion of their economy.

True enough, enlightened technocrats try to think globally. They miss their target, however, for a number of reasons. Their neo-Darwinist belief in the survival of the fittest leads them to refuse to see issues from the point of view of the large majority of the people of the world – those who are poor and discriminated against, but full of self-organized initiatives.

This self-imposed blindness means that technocratic top-down management must face many obstacles which are unintelligible to the planners. The technocrats are also prisoners of their unilinear means-end rationality. They cannot think holistically and are therefore unable to comprehend the complex relationships among intertwined cyclic factors, perceiving them only as linear and discrete externalities. They believe that the world they face can be dismantled into manageable parts without damaging the entirety, whereas the deepening crisis of today brings about more and more complex negative interactions among the different issues.

The technocrats, especially those in the centre of the world system, fail to see the growing importance of the self-organized processes involving diverse cultural, political and economic counter-trends which have grown up in opposition to their attempts at rational global management. An increasing number of social movements are emerging as a consequence of the desperation felt by deprived peoples in the face of the ever-worsening process of global impoverishment. The social movements lead a worldwide search for endogenous governance growing out of the self-organized efforts in different societies around the world. The attempts made by the coalition of technocrats in the centre and the peripheries of the world system to manage the globe through exogenous development and security measures are losing legitimacy, while the self-organized counter-trends in Eastern Europe and in the Third World gain momentum. The technocrats of the state, the party and the transnational corporations have combined forces, but their governance is losing legitimacy and efficiency.

Today, the technocrats are no longer able to play the role, proposed by Saint-Simon and others, of an objective group of experts solving the problems arising within a given society, between the state and the society, or between nature and the society. Their 'scientific' approach to the different global and local problems is based on three wrong assumptions.

Firstly, they believe that top-down world management by the hegemon or a hegemonic consortium of the industrial states, without reference to individual and groups, especially in the less privileged regions of the world system, is possible. Secondly, they assume that the free market economy can be regulated through the joint efforts of the technocrats of the states and TNCs in the centre, with the collaboration of their counterparts in the peripheries of the world system. They ignore the worldwide activation of social movements which are gaining legitimacy and popular support. Thirdly, they focus on the global processes of surplus accumulation, refusing to recognize that it is accompanied by an accumulation of negative goods which are detrimental to the cultural and ecological conditions of different communities, and which endanger their sustainability. This is found most clearly in the outer-periphery, the dumping ground of the world system, but one can find many less conspicuous but equally serious cases of technocratic mismanagement of negative surplus in the other world regions.

Global governance involves the creation of a series of mechanisms for regulating market forces, allocating a sufficient part of the world surplus to cover the cost of public goods, stopping the now predominant tendency to present club goods as public goods, and coping with the growth of negative goods, including mechanisms for recycling. Goods must be fairly distributed, and redistributed. This includes the so-called informal sectors of the societies where market forces only help to worsen the impoverishment process. Technocratic institutions are not capable of managing all the above processes. They involve, by definition, different self-organized processes, both natural and social.

The different institutions and regimes in the international system, especially the United Nations, have to deal with all the above processes, and therefore have to avoid becoming an instrument of technocratic globalism, regardless of how universal that claim may appear to be. They must be effective instruments for governance in close touch with the various self-organized initiatives, permitting these self-organized trends to be adequately reflected in global and local governance institutions and processes. This implies refraining from top-down management, and seeking to link the bottom-up trends and movements promoting democratic rather than technocratic governance.

The institutions and regimes have to provide, among other things, a mediating ground for endogenous forces to participate freely in the governance processes along with the exogenous forces. The opposition to the legitimacy of endogenous forces and the power, wealth and technology of exogenous forces will generate conflicts (LICs, for example) unless appropriate institutions and regimes succeed in bridging the different gaps and separate the conflicting trends on the different levels of the international system, from the local to the global.

Governance today cannot be guaranteed by the mere creation of institutions and regimes. It has to deal with the growing contradiction between two opposing trends, one aiming at global governance and the other aiming at a governance approach rooted in local realities. The former is indispensable for the survival of humankind and more broadly, of all living beings, while the latter seeks to guarantee the free expression of endogenous cultural values indispensable for the free expression of endogenous intellectual creativity without which humankind will not be able to cope with the present global crisis.

This is why we must approach global governance issues from concrete human situations, the places where endogeneity is expressed and where self-organized trends, processes and movements sow the seeds of a future order. In these local situations, the voices of the voiceless must be heard, as it is there that the power of the powerless challenges technocratic rationality. In the place of the *civil society* which was, in the modern Western governance model, the indispensable counterpart of the state, the social movements must build a space free from interference by the technocratic forces, in order to permit different bottom-up processes to develop participatory mechanisms as a base for democratic governance. Such participatory processes have to be strengthened by the creation of institutions and regimes from the local to the global levels. Global governance must be based firmly on the realities of local governance, and must respect all the local cultural values and economic-political interests of the different human communities living in specific ecological contexts. Global governance can be effective only if it can reduce all sources of insecurity for the different local human communities. Such sources are diverse, ranging from military to ecological threats. A truly effective governance system must be able to turn the conflicts between human groups, as well as between human groups and nature, into constructive processes which gradually transform chaotic situations into the seeds of a new order.

The present crisis has presented us with a golden opportunity to curb the now predominant power of the technocratic governance trends. The question is now whether global governance will be able to satisfy the above conditions. The time has come for us to shift our perspectives from exogenous top-down governance to endogenous bottom-up governance. We must take as our starting point not technocratic neo-Darwinism which will only exacerbate the present world crisis, but the Ghandian principle of the 'last child', and we must encourage all alternative efforts in search of a new world order, taking stock of all the creative forces in gestation within the present chaos.

The search for global governance must be pursued simultaneously within the three broad contexts as discussed in this chapter – hegemonic, technocratic and political-cultural. It must begin with listening to the many voices being raised throughout the world in opposition to the present hegemonic order. The search must also address the security issues outlined at the start of the chapter.

Some final remarks about conflicts, conflict management and global governance. This article suggests the necessity of looking carefully at a number of conflictual aspects. Firstly, contemporary conflicts involve many actors, not only those states which since the seventeenth century have taken part in a long tradition based on commonly accepted rules of the game. The actors include non-state actors whose identity is not always recognized by the states. Moreover, there is often disagreement regarding the legitimacy of certain activities, like, for example, the taking of hostages. This makes it crucial to find a mechanism through which disputes on legitimacy and identity can be resolved peacefully, especially when different social movements are involved in process.

Secondly, no solutions can be found to the conflicts of today unless endogenous bases for peace and security are guaranteed.

This is why regional institutions must acquire the capacity to help shape a bottom-up process of peaceful change which prevents conflicts from becoming a cause for intervention by major external powers claiming that they have special responsibilities to provide exogenous security guarantees.

Thirdly, special attention should be paid to the self-organized processes which have *bifurcation points* at which conflicts can either escalate or be de-escalated. This means that technocratic concepts regarding crisis-management, and early-warning systems helping such management, must be replaced by more flexible approaches involving conflict transformation from within the self-organized processes.

Finally, conflicts should be seen as part of the process of social transformation, sometimes playing constructive roles by helping the emergence and crystallization of new trends towards a future order. Bearing in mind the above points, conflicts should be understood within the context of the world system, and interpreted according to the politico-economic dynamics and socio-cultural realities they reflect.

NOTES

1. An earlier version of this paper was presented at the Congress of the International Studies Association, April, 1990, Washington DC. The author wishes to thank the colleagues who commented on that version and allowed him to revise and augment it.

2. On governance, the UNU is preparing a new project on Peace and Governance which is coordinated by Drs. Robert Cox and Kumar Rupesinghe. The definition of the concept is based on an unpublished paper presented by him to a planning meeting of this Project in 1989.

3. For a more orthodox discussion on this concept, see for example Baker & Elliott (1990).

4. According to our classification, the LLDCs are found in both the inner- and the outer-periphery. Their definition is based on the scarcity of their resources which force them to rely on external support for their very survival. Such scarcity is sometimes combined with a close integration in the international division of labour based on human and other resources, however scarce they may be. In this case the LLDCs are part of the inner-periphery. The LLDCs may also be related to the world system, only in a non-productive way, as dumping ground or as a point of transfer. In this case, they are part of the outer-periphery. This point of clarification is important, since in the outer- periphery, one does not necessarily find only LLDCs, potential maritime resources, both renewable and non-renewable,

often endow the island micro-states of the pacific. As to the concept of outer-periphery used in contra-distinction to inner-periphery, see Alexander (1989).

5. For example, the nuclear-free constitution of Belau irritates the United States to the point that referendum after referendum is imposed on this small island state by the strongest power in the world, simply because a non-nuclear Belau would create a hole in the seamless fabric of the US nuclear strategic infrastructure of the Pacific.

6. We will not refer to the different authors belonging to a now fashionable school of thought stressing the merits of Confucianist ethic in producing the economic success of Japan and the NIEs.

7. The cultural and civilizational problematique regarding the non-European cultures and their efforts to overcome Eurocentrism has been the object of research in different UNU projects. See for example Chatterjee (1986).

REFERENCES

Abdel-Malek, A., ed., 1986. *Intellectual Creativity in Endogenous Culture*, Tokyo: UNU.

Alexander, Ronni, 1989. *Micro-States and Denuclearization in the Pacific: The Nuclear Free and Independent Pacific Movement and Nuclear Free Initiatives in Belau, Fiji, and Aotearoa/New Zealand*, Ph.D dissertation, Tokyo: Sopphia University.

Baker, S. & C. Elliott, eds, 1990. *Reading Public Sector Economics*, Lexington, Mass.

Chatterjee, P., 1986. *Nationalist Thought and the Colonial World: A Derivative Discourse?*, Tokyo: UNU.

Kaldof, M., G. Holden & R. Falk, eds, 1989. *The New Detente: Rethinking East-West Relations*, Verso and UNU.

Mallmann, C. & O. Nudler, eds, 1986. *Human Development: In its Social Context*, London.

Mushakoji, Kinhide, 1988. *Global Issues and Interparadigmatic Dialogue: Essays on Multipolar Politics*, Torino.

8

Information Aspects of
Humanitarian Early Warning

Hans Thoolen[1]

*'We live in a society full of preventable disorders, preventable
diseases and preventable pain, of harshness and stupid
unpremeditated cruelties.'*

(H.G. Wells, 1866 – 1946)

1. INTRODUCTION

The last decade has seen a surge of interest in 'early warning'
in the humanitarian area, followed by much scholarly writing on
the topic. Starting as military jargon, the term is now widely
used, foremost in the context of natural disasters (climate,
famine)[2] and increasingly with regard to man-made disasters
(war, internal conflict, serious human rights violations, repression of minorities and economic deprivation). Both types
of disasters have commonly led to massive internal and external
displacements of people. For this reason alone, refugee organizations in general and the Office of the High Commissioner
for Refugees in particular have become concerned with early
warning and possible prevention of refugee flows.

Considering the degree to which human life and fundamental rights are at stake in times of violent upheaval and
massive population displacement, it is almost surprising that

early warning did not attract the attention of human rights scholars and activists earlier on. It would probably be helpful for current efforts to devise early warning systems if we could understand why the notion of early warning with regard to human rights violations and refugee flows did not develop sooner in precisely the governmental and non-governmental circles whose prime concern was the protection of human rights. Was the importance or feasibility of early warning simply overlooked, or were there more conscious reasons for not getting involved? Was it the (perceived) inability to develop indicators, or rather the (perceived) inability to (re)act even if the proper information had been generated in time? Was it a lack of technical tools, such as computerized databases and fast and reliable communication channels, or did the information simply not exist? Was it that 'prevention' was seen to be outside the mandates of organizations concerned or rather a lack of priority?

It would seem likely that any combination of the factors mentioned above was at work. Staying within the self-imposed limits of this paper's title, and trying to make a forward-looking contribution to the discussion, the questions could be rephrased as follows: is the situation different now?

• Is there now more appropriate information at hand?

• Are indicators now operational?

• Are there now more and better tools for storage, retrieval and communication?

• Is there now more capacity to act on early information?

• Are there now more resources devoted to early warning?

2. UNHCR'S PARTICULAR ANGLE

Before offering a few reflections on each of these questions, I should explain that I am looking at them from the angle of a refugee organization, without claiming in any way to represent an official UNHCR view. Therefore, a few preliminary remarks with regard to UNHCR's specific interest and role would seem to be in place.

Obviously, an organization such as UNHCR, with a very well-established mandate to find solutions to the refugee problem as well as the problems of refugees, is one of the main organizations in the United Nations system to have an interest in addressing the root causes that lead to forced displacement. Where remedies at the roots fail and exoduses occur, the organization is one of the first in line to have to deal with the consequences. Therefore, it has a heavy operational role in countries of reception, in particular in emergency situations. Although UNHCR has since its creation in 1951 satisfactorily settled in one way or another the situation of an estimated 25 million individual refugees, the magnitude of today's problems (up to 20 million international refugees, and more than that number internally displaced) is such that the traditional solution of (re)settling large numbers of refugees in host countries is no longer a realistic perspective, hence the renewed emphasis placed on voluntary repatriation. UNHCR's total staff and budget have expanded rapidly in the last two decades, but have not been able to keep up with the growth of the problem. Still, with over 2000 international staff members, spread over 100 different duty situations, and an annual budget that has reached the USD 600 million mark, UNHCR remains a key player in any international framework that purports to deal with early warning for humanitarian disasters. Some special features deserve further attention.

Firstly, the UNHCR distinguishes *refugees* from other *migrants*, e.g. purely economic migrants. The latter are not within its mandate, although it cannot be stressed enough that this does not imply any value judgement with regard to the economic migrants' motivation and needs. Large-scale migration from South to North and East to West is likely to be a major feature of an increasingly intertwined world and will continue to put pressure on existing asylum procedures and policies. For this reason alone, the UNHCR cannot escape a broader view and work towards prevention and solutions.

Secondly, the UNHCR's mandate is restricted to refugees who have crossed an international border and can no longer invoke the protection of their own state; it does not encompass those 'internally displaced', although their total number is nowadays estimated at more than the externally displaced. On the other hand, the formal nature of this restriction[3] should not be taken as the final word, as there have been quite a few exceptions – either because a distinction between internally and externally displaced could not be maintained in the day-to-day reality of providing services, or because the United Nations specifically requested the High Commissioner to take care of internally displaced people in a 'good offices' capacity.

Thirdly, the UNHCR's presence in the field is one of the most special features of the organization, distinguishing it – together with the UNDP, the International Committee of the Red Cross and a small number of others – considerably from the remainder of the international organizations. This operational presence on the territory of states is not limited to receiving countries, as the monitoring of return ('voluntary repatriation' to use the proper UNHCR terminology) has become an increasingly important part of the UNHCR's work.[4]

Fourthly, although the UNHCR nowadays places itself squarely within the international human rights movement, the organization remains very much victim-oriented: i.e. protecting the victims will take precedence over imparting blame; still, much of the traditional reluctance towards employing human rights concepts has been overcome in recent years. Finally, it should be clear that the UNHCR's concern with preventing flows of refugees does not mean preventing asylum seekers from leaving their country: by necessity it means addressing the causes and events that force people to leave.

The UNHCR only recently established an in-house Working Group charged with formulating a policy on early warning and following inter-agency developments in this regard. The current High Commissioner Ms S. Ogata – like her predecessor Mr T. Stoltenberg – has made clear from the start of her term that prevention and solution, and in its wake early warning, are among the great challenges for the future of the world's most important refugee organization.[5] This having been stated, there is no illusion that this task is going to be an easy one. The organization is still very much in search of a clear strategy and concrete policy. In fact, the search for a better understanding of the potential and limitations of early warning has led the Office of the High Commissioner to reach out again to the research community and participate more actively in cooperative efforts within and outside the UN system,[6] without committing itself yet to a particular course of action.

All these disclaimers and clarifications are meant to explain why the UNHCR is oriented more towards man-made than natural disasters, more towards forced than voluntary migration, and more towards movements across international borders than within the same country.

2.1. Is there now more appropriate information at hand?

The exponential doubling of the written amount of information per generation since World War II must have had an impact also on information relevant to early warning. The increased attention given to human rights and refugee issues by the media and (inter)governmental as well as non-governmental organizations has certainly more than proportionally broadened the data base (and here I do *not* mean 'database'!) of factual and analytical information – with regard to violations of human rights, the context in which they take place, their escalation and defusing, as well as the consequences with regard to mass flight. Most of these data are, however, of a descriptive nature, and hindsight usually remains the more exact science. The relation between conflict and human rights violations is fairly complex, as is its companion relationship between conflict management and addressing root causes. Moreover, today's information overkill is almost as problematic as the previous paucity. In order to make use of the more generous availability of information, we will have to develop reliable indicators on the one hand, and learn to master the universe of available information on the other. The two issues will be discussed briefly below.

2.2. Are indicators now operational?

The impression is that progress is being made regarding the development and testing of indicators, but perhaps more with regard to the likelihood of armed conflict than of human rights violations. However, an important part of the research has not (yet) been published and may remain unpublished, as much of this kind of prediction is the domain of the intelligence services of governments. Another problem is that preventive action requires a degree of specificity which usually does not flow from the global indicators. In other words, well-tested indicators may help to foretell trouble of the kind that will cause human rights violations, but they will not provide sufficient detail with regard to the kind, scale, time and place of these violations. And even if in some instances it may be possible to 'predict' that, for example, a specific group in the population will soon be subject to arbitrary killings, detention and torture, it does not follow that there will necessarily be a large-scale exodus. The non-governmental Refugee Policy Group (RPG) and the Office for Research and Collection of Information (ORCI) of the United Nations in New York have spent considerable time on the development of indicators, including those relating to massive flows of refugees and the 'triggering events' that are likely to set large populations into motion: but again, results have either not been tested on any large scale or not been made public.

With developments in Eastern Europe fresh in mind, it may no longer be fashionable to think in terms of 'scientific forecasting',[7] but this should not close our eyes to the valuable work that is being undertaken towards developing objective indicators in the area of human rights. Stohl et al. (1986) may well recently have concluded that 'in short, it is still impossible to state with any assurance what variables lead to improvements or retrogressions in a state's human rights behaviour, or to predict when such changes will occur', but this does not mean that the search for agreed and tested indicators is in vain and should be abandoned. The human rights research community has continued its interest in this area;[8] the UN Sub-commission – on the basis of a study prepared by its expert-member Danilo Turk – looked into the theoretical problems of measuring progress concerning social and economic rights,[9] and UNDP has now broadened its assessment of states' performance in economic development with human development and 'freedom' indicators. All this would seem to indicate that the demise of communism and of the ideological cold war is spurring the search for agreed and scientifically tested indicators, rather than bringing measuring and forecasting into disrepute.

2.3. Are there now more and better tools for storage, retrieval and communication?

Computerized information systems have developed extremely rapidly in the past decade. There are now available thousands of databases on-line, as well as hundreds of thousands more which, due to their limited size or partly confidential content, are more of an in-house or personal nature. Telecommunications have improved equally: not only has the telephone network enlarged its reach, but also the carriers of information have improved in type (e.g. data, facsimile) and speed (e.g. satellite, fibre optics). It is probably the combination of electronic data and high-speed transmission which holds the greatest promise for early warning in the long run, as this permits the rapid transfer of large amounts of data at relatively low price (including remote on-line searches of databases).

In the short run, however, there is still a tremendous shortage of electronically available data on which any indicators could be let loose. With the exception of press material in full-text databases and of reference-type information in structured databases,[10] human rights material remains largely outside the scope of databases currently accessible on-line. Even a sustained effort by intergovernmental and non-governmental agencies alike (if such open cooperation could become finally possible) would take several years to yield results.[11]

To make things worse, there is a general dilemma with regard to how to proceed with the creation of databases that could be potentially relevant to early warning. On the one hand, full-text databases are characterized by the absence of a homogeneous data structure; they simply put in a searchable form what otherwise would have existed on paper. The great quantity and diversity of information contained in databases of this kind do not allow the insertion of a structure that could 'foresee' the set of questions to be asked for early warning purposes. On the other hand, the creation of structured databases (including 'fields' representing the indicators mentioned above) is hampered by the unpredictability of the kind of data to be included and, more importantly, by the comparatively high initial cost of tailoring input into structured databases. The cost of professional information staff and the development of tools and terminology constitute the lion's share of the budget of any specially designed database and these costs are generally far greater than those of simply typing or reading text into a full-text information retrieval system.

Thus, for the time being the improved communication will primarily be a speeding up of the transfer of information selected for its early warning relevance by experienced human beings (and, of course, for accelerating the communication of the 'warnings' themselves). This implies that most early-warning information work will have to be executed at the ground level, i.e. at the level of existing organizations with field presence and a relatively strong infrastructure. The importance of databases in early-warning work will certainly increase, but only gradually; and structured databases (such as elaborate references) will continue to be the most important tool despite their shortcomings.[12] Only incrementally will they give way to the more 'intelligent' expert systems or the more open full-text retrieval systems. The most sensible course of action would therefore seem to be to continue the current situation of decentralized data holding, but also to try and harmonize as much as possible the information handling systems in the different organizations. At the same time, efforts should be made to accumulate in shared and easily accessible systems those data that are already in the public domain, and to provide for on-line access to a larger number of users.

2.4. Is there now more capacity to act on early information?

The first thing to understand is that acting on early warning can take place at different stages. Basically, early warning information could be used for prevention, for mitigation or for preparedness. The latter – which could also be described as common-sense readiness to cope with the impact of human disasters that could not be averted – would seem the least problematic in terms of mandate of any international organization. Emergency-preparedness – including the information gathering aspect that goes with it – has thus often formed the starting point for early-warning interest in international organizations, including the UNHCR.[13] For the same reason, early warning is a regular feature in the debate on a new and better coordination of the humanitarian sector of the United Nations.[14] Prevention and mitigation (i.e. stemming the incipient human disaster) are much more controversial, at least among many governments in the UN context. Many hold that international law still lacks an unambiguous basis for such actions without the consent – however reluctantly given – by the state concerned. Even if it is too early to say that there is now a definitely greater capacity in the international community to act in a preventive manner on early-warning information, there are some trends that, taken together, are likely to reinforce this potential:

a) there is diminishing frequency and strength in States' traditional reliance on the principle of non-interference in internal affairs, at least with regard to fundamental human rights, including refugee flows;[15]

b) there is a recently improved standing of the United Nations and its 'authority' to intervene in conflict situations, even if a concept of 'humanitarian intervention' or 'necessity' is far from being universally accepted;[16]

c) there is growing recognition by different UN organs that cooperation and information sharing within the UN system is necessary for effective early-warning work.[17]

This change in attitude, however nascent, is important to the further development of early warning mechanisms. The capacity to act, and to be seen acting, on the basis of early information is a crucial feature for the further development of the early-warning capacity of the United Nations: after all, as information providers will lose interest in feeding information, sometimes collected or communicated at great personal risk, into a non-responsive mechanism. The steady growth in the number and variety of non-governmental actors in the human rights area and their networks, both at the international and the national level and in particular in the South, is a remarkable feature,[18] but will turn out to be of no avail, if these actors perceive their input to be ignored and receive no feedback.

As quite a few humanitarian organizations have tended to stress their 'non-political' character, prevention and early-warning work – which purport to assist in addressing the root causes of human rights violations – have often been considered to fall outside their 'humanitarian mandate'. This reasoning has often been extended, without further reflection, to the systematic collection of such sensitive information and even to its purely internal flow and transfer to other organizations within the UN system. We are now witnessing changes in this attitude, partly under pressure from governmental and non-governmental circles, and the UNHCR at least seems to have embarked on a careful but steady reassessment of its position. As the distinction between 'being knowledgeable' about countries of origin (which requires as an information-efficiency measure that information is shared where possible) and 'taking action' (which could indeed involve the mandate) is increasingly understood, early warning is likely to become more of an accepted activity.

However, the UNHCR will face some particularly difficult questions with regard to the role of its many field offices – which usually were established, in agreement with the host government, with the specific purpose of taking care of refugees coming in from another country. While it would be one thing for the UNHCR to see the refugees more as a possible (additional) source of information, it would be quite different to start using its field presence for reporting on the host country as a possible generator of refugees due to governmental action or inaction concerning human rights. If that reporting is done within the UN system, it may still be acceptable under certain circumstances; but if the results are to be made public, this may require a rethinking and revision of the relationship between the UNHCR and governments concerned.

2.5. Are there now more resources devoted to early warning work?

In repeated resolutions of the General Assembly and the Commission on Human Rights since 1987, it was felt necessary to call for more resources to be devoted to the ORCI, which was specifically set up for early warning work. One can imagine what the situation is in those organizations where early warning has arrived as a recent addition. With information management already not being the UN's strongest point and with non-governmental organizations living in a chronic state of underfunding, there is not much basis for optimism that sufficient resources will be available in the near future. However, this situation has also its advantages, inasmuch as there is no big money to make big mistakes – and here we may note that especially large-scale computerization projects tend to be large-scale failures. Also, the shortage of resources in a single organization may force the main actors to pool resources, in particular with regard to the costly stage of doing research, building up information infrastructures and creating databases. The Joint Inspection Unit's report on the Coordination of Activities Related to Early Warning of Possible Refugee Flows, issued to the General Assembly in 1990,[19] makes abundantly clear that there is a need and scope for cooperation among various UN agencies.

However, the report remains silent with regard to additional resources needed for this work, except for reiterating the recommendation that ORCI needs to be strengthened. As argued above, I believe that the most important and immediate investments concern the capacity of the substantive agencies to revise, modernize and harmonize their own information handling capacity as well as to intensify their cooperation. Coordination by *any* body is most needed and welcome: but one cannot coordinate at higher levels what does not yet exist at ground level.

3. CONCLUSION

In view of the complexity of the subject matter and the fluid nature of the state of international relations at present, these remarks are not intended to provide an overall proposal, even less a marching route, for improved early-warning work in the United Nations. This paper does not do justice to conceptual work and case studies undertaken by the staff of ORCI and independent scholars such as Leon Gordenker and Kumar Rupesinghe (1986; 1989a; 1989b). It pays enough attention neither to earlier UN efforts by Sadruddin Aga Khan in 1981[20] nor to the proposals of the Group of Governmental Experts in 1986,[21] and it certainly does not refer sufficiently to recent developments in the UNHCR's EXCOM Working Group on Protection and Solutions.[22] The discussion which was started in ECOSOC concerning the role of the United Nations with regard to refugees, returnees and (internally) displaced persons has in the meantime moved to the General Assembly. It is still too early to say what the outcome will be. Rather than trying to predict the future of early-warning work in the humanitarian sector, this paper is intended to solicit discussion and reflection on where we stand and where we are going with regard to the information aspects of early-warning work concerning human rights and refugees.

If any conclusion is called for, it would be that the following aspects need to be addressed with greater vigour in the current debate on improving early warning of human disasters and refugee flows:

• Information handling is the key

• Computerized databases and electronic communication are (indispensable) tools

• Harmonization and compatibility of information systems are preconditions

• Cooperation is a must

• Coordination of early-warning systems within the UN will have to wait until there exists systems that are functioning.

NOTES

1. This paper does not necessarily reflect the views of the UNHCR.

2. Operational early-warning systems include the FAO (GIEWS – Global Information and Early Warning System), UNEP (GEMS – Global Environment Monitoring System; however, still in an early stage) and UNESCO (ITWS – International Tsunami Warning System). In the mid-1980s the UNU developed GEWS (Global Early Warning System for Displaced Persons) as a first computer-based model for forecasting, but this seems not to have been pursued beyond a single test case.

3. See art. 6 of the UNHCR's Statute and art. 1(A) of the 1951 Convention relating to the Status of Refugees.

4. Major recent repatriation cases in which the UNHCR is involved, in varying degrees, include: Namibia, Viet Nam, South Africa, Western Sahara and Central America, the latter in the context of an also otherwise interesting comprehensive regional approach called CIREFCA. For more information on CIREFCA, see inter alia: Wollny (1989), Lamb et al. (1989) and Gros Espiell et al. (1990).

5. Ms Sadako Ogata made the following statement upon arriving in Geneva: 'An effective and humanitarian approach to the refugee issue must focus on causes as much as effects (...) We must reinforce our efforts to prevent and resolve [destabilizing population movements].' (Press Release REF/1666, 18 February 1991). In addition, lecturing at Georgetown University, 25 June 1991, she said: '... Now let me turn to the political aspects of promoting a preventive and solution-oriented approach. As the analysis of the underlying causes clearly shows, the refugee problem is multi-faceted and cannot be resolved in isolation from the major political and economic challenges facing the international community. Therefore, the refugee issue must not be seen

only as a matter for humanitarian agencies of the UN but also as a political problem which must be placed in the mainstream of the international agenda as a potential threat to international peace and security.'

6. Including meetings since 1987 organized by the International Peace Research Institute, Oslo (PRIO), International Alert, the International Peace Research Association (IPRA), the Centre for Refugees Studies at York. For meetings in the UN context, see note 17 below.

7. e.g., Leon Trotsky in 1931, as quoted by William Pfaff in the *International Herald Tribune* for 30 August 1991, stated: 'Only the study of the anatomy of a society and of its physiology makes possible a reaction to events that is based on scientific forecasts rather than the conjectures of dilettantes.'

8. The journal *Human Rights Quarterly* devoted a special issue to the theme 'Human Rights and Statistics' which contained several other interesting contributions. An elaborate interdisciplinary research project for the root causes of human rights violations (with the rather idiosyncratic acronym P.I.O.O.M.) was started at Leiden University in 1988. It issues an occasional bulletin with progress notes.

9. E/CN.4/Sub.2/1990/19.

10. In the area of human rights and refugees these databases contain mostly bibliographic references, case law and sometimes the full text of international instruments and national legislations For more detailed description of the state of affairs in the refugee area see Toth (1991) and Thoolen (1989).

11. The most relevant efforts have come from the HURIDOCS network (Human Rights Information and Documentation System), which has tried since 1982 to develop and introduce a coherent set of standard formats and other tools for use in a large variety of organizations; the more recent International Refugee Documentation Network (IRDN) has taken over these tools and developed in addition an international thesaurus of refugee terminology, now widely used in refugee work.

12. It should be added that even if the more 'static' type of databases do not provide immediate and operational information of an analytical nature to be used in early warning, they do contribute greatly to information efficiency by reducing the time and effort needed to locate existing ('old') information, thus freeing time and energy for reading, analyzing and understanding 'old' and 'new' information alike.

13. The comprehensive doctoral thesis by Louise Druke (1990) illustrates how the UNHCR's interest evolved from internal contingency planning to broader response mechanisms in times of mass influxes; when it touches on prevention, this book usually does so in the context of other UN actors.

14. Jacques Cuénod prepared, as an independent consultant, a study which was discussed at the July 1991 session of ECOSOC, under the title Report on Refugees, Displaced Persons and Returnees.(Geneva : United Nations, 27 June 1991.- 51 p. : annexes.- E/1991/109/Add.1.) In this study and the ensuing debate, emergency preparedness and disaster coordination are strongly linked to (material) assistance after the events, while prevention and mitigation are much less brought to the fore.

15. See, inter alia Akhavan & Bergsmo (1989). It is also interesting to note that in the latest Report of the Secretary-General on the Work of the Organization (UN Doc. A/46/1, September 1991), J. Perez de Cuellar states: 'It is now increasingly felt that the principle of non-interference with the essential domestic jurisdiction of states cannot be regarded as a protective barrier behind which human rights could be massively or systematically violated with impunity.' He goes on to say that '[territorial integrity and independence of states] would only be weakened if it were to carry the implication that sovereignty, even in this day and age, includes the rights of mass slaughter or of launching systematic campaigns of decimation or forced exodus of civilian populations in the name of controlling civil strife or insurrection.'

16. It should be noted that the famous Security Council Resolution 688 (S/RES/688(1991)) did not pave the way for humanitarian intervention as such, but did so specifically in the context of the more 'traditional' peace mandate of the United Nations. It is also noteworthy that several third world countries voted against or abstained on this resolution. However, several influential persons have long taken the position of considering that there should be, at least in the 'humanitarian framework', a moral and legal underpinning of the 'right to interfere', or a least the recognition of a State's obligation to accept and facilitate humanitarian assistance to victims of natural and man-made disasters. See inter alia Bettati & Kouchner (1987), Jokovljevic (1987), Kalshoven (1989) and Macallister-Smith (1988).

17. JIU/REP/90/2, issued as General Assembly document A/45/649; on the basis of recommendations of this study as well as GA Resolution 45/153, the ACC created in 1991 an Inter-agency Working Group on Early Warning (ACC/1991/DEC/9), which was to report back to the ACC in the second half of 1992.

18. See, inter alia, Thoolen (1990).

19. see note 17

20. E/CN.4/1503.

21. A/41/324 (13 May 1986).

22. The first Report of the Working Group on Solutions and Protection was to be submitted to the 42nd session of the Executive Committee of the High Commissioner's Programme, 12 August 1991.- 22 pp. .- EC/SCP/64. It should become available to a wider audience after the meeting.

REFERENCES

Akhavan, P. & M. Bergsmo, 1989. 'The Application of the Doctrine of State Responsibility to Refugee Creating States', *Nordic Journal of International Law*, vol. 58, no. 3/4, pp. 243-56.

Bettati, M. & B. Kouchner, eds, 1987. *Le Devoir d' Ingérence: Peut-on les Laisser Mourir?*, Paris: Editions Denoël, 300 pp. :annexes

Druke, Louise, 1990. *Preventive Action for Refugee Producing Situations*, Frankfurt am Main: Peter Lang, 271 pp. :annexes, European University Studies: Ser. 31, *Political Science*; vol. 151

Gros Espiell, H. et al., 1990. Principles and Criteria for the Protection of and Assistance to Central American Refugees, Returnees and Displaced Persons in Central America', *International Journal of Refugee Law*, vol. 2, no.1, January 1990, pp. 83-117.

Jakovljevic, B., 1987. 'Le Droit à l'Assistance Humanitaire – Aspects Juridiques', *Revue Internationale de la Croix-Rouge*, no. 767, October 1987, Genève: Comité International de la Croix-Rouge, pp. 490-506.

Kalshoven, F., ed., 1989. *Assisting the Victims of Armed Conflict and Other Disasters*, Dordrecht (Netherlands) :Martinus Nijhoff, 258 pp. :annexes.

Lamb, S. et al., 1989. 'CIREFCA: International Conference on Central American Refugees: An Essential Step forward', *Refugees*, no. 62, March 1989, pp. 19-37 : ill., maps

Macallister-Smith, P., 1988. 'The Right to Humanitarian Assistance in International Law', *Revue de droit international, de Sciences Diplomatiques et Politiques*, vol. 66, no. 3, September 1988, Geneva, pp. 211-33.

Rupesinghe, Kumar, 1986. 'The Quest for a Disaster Early Warning System. Giving a Voice to the Vulnerable', *Bulletin of Peace Proposals*, vol. 18, no. 2.

Rupesinghe, Kumar, 1989a. 'Early Warning and Conflict Resolution', in *Prio Report*, no 4.

Rupesinghe, Kumar, 1989b. 'Some Conceptual Problems with Early Warnings', *Bulletin of Peace Proposals*, no. 2.

Stohl et al., 1986. 'State Violation of Human Rights: Issues and Problems of Measurement', *Human Rights Quarterly*, vol., 8 no. 4, November 1986, pp. 592-606.

Thoolen, Hans, 1989. 'The Development of Legal Databases in Refugee Work', *International Journal of Refugee Law*, vol. 1, no. 1, pp. 89-100.

Thoolen, Hans, 1990. 'Information and Training in an Expanding Human Rights Movement', *Journal Society for International Development*, no. 2, pp. 86-7.

Toth, Tibor, 1991. *Refugee Abstracts*, vol. 10, no. 2, July 1991, foreword.

Wollny, H., 1989. 'CIREFCA – Internazionale Konferenz über Zentralamerikanische Flüchtlinge: Neue Lösungsansätze auf dem Amerikanischen Kontinent' ('CIREFCA – International Conference on Central American Refugees: New Openings for Solutions on the American Continent'), *Zeitschrift für Ausländerrecht und Ausländerpolitik*, vol. 8, no. 3, 15 September 1989, pp. 116-24.

9

Early Warning in United Nations Grand Strategy

Gangapersand Ramcharan[1]

1. INTRODUCTION

There are growing demands upon the United Nations to operate systems of early warning and take action to prevent problems and to avoid human suffering. Early warning will, without a doubt, be one of the main areas of endeavour of the United Nations system in the future. Early warning, however, cannot be seen in isolation. To attempt to address early warning issues without placing them within the context of broader policies and strategies of the United Nations could lead to problems. Besides, not locating early warning activities within the context of a United Nations grand strategy could lead to difficulties or to disappointments in the performance of early warning and preventive systems.

But is there such a thing as a grand strategy at the United Nations? Grand strategy, as the term is traditionally used by historians, political scientists, and strategists refers mainly to the key strategies of Great Powers, such as the United States and the USSR – as they jostle for advantages; as they seek to defend and advance their vital interests; as they seek to maintain a balance of power. Recently, for example, there has been much discussion of American grand strategy for the coming period (Huntington, 1991; Chase, 1988). In the aftermath of the recent Gulf War and in the wake of President Bush's advocacy of a new world order, there have been those, such as former Secretary of State Kissinger, who have argued that only a balance-of-power approach can maintain stability in the world (Kissinger, 1991). There are others who would like to believe in the vision of the new world order but ask to see how it can be made a reality. There are others still who see great dangers for the United Nations in the aftermath of the Gulf War. Questions which are raised include the following: Apart from a genuine United Nations interest in repelling aggression, was the United Nations idea really at work at all stages in the handling of the crisis? How does the United Nations come out as an institution in the aftermath of the crisis, and where is the United Nations to go henceforth?[2]

These are very serious questions. The United Nations is, first and foremost, its Member States, which vary in power and influence. The United Nations is, secondly, its peoples – 'the peoples of the United Nations'. But the influence of the peoples of the United Nations is still rather limited. Thirdly, the United Nations is its Secretariat – a Secretariat expecting a new sense of direction following the election of a new Secretary-General in the autumn of 1991.

The aftermath of the Gulf War sees the Secretary-General reportedly feeling that somehow he and the United Nations had been somewhat marginalized. The aftermath of the Gulf War reveals the existence of a unipolar world at the politico-military level and a multipolar world at the economic level. The aftermath of the Gulf War reveals questions about the future role of the Security Council and about the place in the Council of new economic powers, such as Germany and Japan.

The aftermath of the Gulf War makes the question inevitable: Who will shape the future of the United Nations – the dominant powers acting in concert, or the emergence of neutral United Nations actors not controlled by the major powers but, rather, bringing the influence of the United Nations idea to bear upon all States, including the major powers? The key strategic issue for the future of the United Nations is thus posed – namely, shall the future of the United Nations be one of a quest to validate and implement the Purposes and Principles of the Charter, or shall the future of the United Nations be placed in the custody – and hence at the whims – of the major powers? Upon the answer to this question will depend many things, including the future of early warning systems at the United Nations, which has to be situated within the context of a much-needed grand strategy for the Organization.

2. THE NEED FOR A UNITED NATIONS GRAND STRATEGY

It will follow from what we have said so far that we believe there is a case for the United Nations idea to be picked up and to be placed in contention against self-interested interpretations of that idea. For this to happen, leadership will be critical. That leadership will have to come from each of the three United Nations constituencies – namely, among Member States from the middle and smaller powers; from among 'the peoples' as mentioned in the Preamble of the Charter and from non-governmental organizations and concerned individuals; and, in the Secretariat, from the Secretary-General of the United Nations.

The leadership of the Secretary-General could well be the most vital (Urquhart & Childers, 1990). There is evidence of efforts to provide such leadership but so much goes on at the United Nations that it has been difficult, so far, to focus on defining issues or on defining strategies so as to give the United Nations *forward momentum*. Only with Secretary-General Hammarskjold could it be said that there was a grand strategy at the United Nations. For him, the Principles of the Charter were sacred; the role of the middle and the smaller powers was crucial; preventive diplomacy through peacekeeping was of great importance; and the role of helping the underdeveloped countries of Asia, Africa, and Latin America was where he saw great potential for the United Nations. Since Secretary-General Hammarskjold, there has not been a grand strategy at the United Nations. If the United Nations is to be given the opportunity to succeed in the coming period, the development of such a grand strategy will be among the highest order of priorities at the world organization.

3. ELEMENTS OF A UNITED NATIONS GRAND STRATEGY

If a United Nations grand strategy is needed, as we have suggested, of what should it consist? Before attempting to answer this question, let us be clear: by making the case for a United Nations grand strategy, we are not arguing for the replacement of current United Nations activities. We are, rather, arguing that in the midst of those activities certain defining areas should stand out prominently and help to integrate to the rest. In our submission, a United Nations grand strategy should consist of the following components:

3.1. Promoting the United Nations ethic globally and helping the United Nations idea to take root in all parts of the world

The power of the United Nations idea is the only power that the Organization has to match the raw power of its major Member States – or indeed of any Member State, for that matter. It must, therefore, follow that the most important battle that the United Nations has to win is the battle for the human mind. People and organizations everywhere must be persuaded that the United Nations way is the only way forward – namely, the principle of toleration and good neighbourliness; the principles of the rule of law and the peaceful settlement of disputes; the principle of respect for human rights and fundamental freedoms; and the principle of international co-operation and solidarity for the common welfare. Unless the United Nations succeeds in communicating its basic messages globally and getting people to call upon their governments to act in accordance with the Purposes and Principles of the Charter of the United Nations, the Organization will never be able to break anyway from the clutches of the major powers or a system based on the balance of power. It will be evident, then, that the ability to communicate and to convey its message will be one of the most important requirements at the United Nations. The United Nations needs its *'Great Communicator'* – and who can this be other than the Secretary-General of the United Nations?

3.2. The domestic application of the United Nations Charter

Closely related to, and as a logical extension of, its efforts to communicate the United Nations idea, is the question of the introduction and the application of the United Nations Charter within the national orders of its Member States. The United Nations would need to encourage each of its Member States to ask the following questions:

• Should not the United Nations Charter be reflected in the constitutional orders of Member States?

• Are there regular parliamentary debates on issues at the United Nations?

• Is there in each national parliament a committee on the United Nations?

• Is instruction on the United Nations a regular part of the curricula in schools and universities?

• How is the Charter of the United Nations being disseminated within the country?

• What support can be given to national United Nations Associations?

The Charter of the United Nations must be made to count, and must be *seen* to count, within Member States. Only then will the United Nations idea have a chance of prevailing globally.

3.3. Strengthen the international rule of law

Without a doubt, a key to the vindication of the United Nations idea is the international rule of law and the peaceful settlement of disputes. The successive generations of thinkers who sought to promote international organizations to reduce the risks of war and to avoid human suffering pinned their hopes on the development of the international rule of law. It could not, therefore, have been more timely that the United Nations decided to designate the 1990s as the Decade for International Law with the following objectives:

a) To promote acceptance of and respect for the principles of international law;

b) To promote means and methods for the peaceful settlement of disputes between States, including resort to and full respect for the International Court of Justice;

c) To encourage the progressive development of international law and its codification;

d) To encourage the teaching, study, dissemination and wider appreciation of international law.

3.4. Promotion and protection of human rights, including democracy and the rule of law

If a situation could come about in the world in which governments were chosen democratically, the rule of law prevailed and human rights were respected, the risks of conflict would certainly be considerably diminished. Indeed, one could say that a key to prevention would lie in universal respect for human rights and fundamental freedoms. In the future, it will be necessary to develop further standards for the protection of minorities and also to develop international procedures which minorities can use to air their grievances and to seek redress for their problems. It will also be important to elaborate further the content of the right of self-determination and guidelines for the application of this right particularly in independent States.

3.5. The maintenance of a comprehensive global watch

The international community is well launched on the process of developing a global watch with components in the environmental, political, economic, social, humanitarian, and nuclear sectors. Impressive early warning arrangements already exist within such institutions as the International Atomic Energy Agency (IAEA), the Food and Agriculture Organization (FAO), the United Nations High Commissioner for Refugees (UNCHR), the United Nations Disaster Relief Coordinator (UNDRO), the United Nations Environment Programme (UNEP), the World Health Organization (WHO), and the recently established Office for Research and the Collection of Information. The efforts have, so far, developed in an independent manner and one of the challenges for the future, as we shall discuss later, will be to provide opportunities for them to share information and experience at periodic consultations.

3.6. Protection of children and other vulnerable groups

UNICEF has already captured the imagination of the world in its efforts to protect children and to promote their welfare. The recent entry into force of the International Convention on the Rights of the Child should help in this process. It makes eminent good sense that the United Nations should continue to place in high esteem on its activities for the protection of children. Not only does this correspond to sentiments of decency and humanitarianism but it is also a good way of offering future generations a better opportunity in the world. Attention should also be paid to other vulnerable groups, especially indigenous populations.

3.7. Technical assistance, education and training

In its efforts, since its establishment, to promote global development, the United Nations has tried a variety of approaches,
including: technical assistance programmes; strategies for four
development decades; defining the economic rights and duties of
States; efforts to establish a new international economic order;
North-South negotiations; and now, more recently, human
resource development. Of all of these ideas, only the technical
assistance approach has rendered much tangible benefit in the
past. The United Nations should be realistic in its assessment
of what it can offer the world in the development sector. Along-
side technical assistance, it should in the future, in co-operation
with UNESCO, place emphasis on programmes of training and
education. The rationale here is simple but well-known. Better
training can help people to help themselves.

3.8. The alleviation of poverty

The United Nations has to count for people. Unless it meets this
test, it will never be successful. Too many people in the world
suffer from the consequences of crippling poverty. The United
Nations should seek to co-ordinate international mobilisation for
poverty reduction in all countries.

4. EARLY WARNING AND PREVENTION AS PART OF A UNITED NATIONS GRAND STRATEGY

If one keeps in mind that the United Nations will have, in the
coming period, to get its act together and to fashion useful roles
for itself in a world dominated by powerful states, one can
readily see that schemes for the operation of early warning and
preventive systems would have to be carefully designed in order
to be effective. Early warning is still a fairly new idea in the
United Nations. It took several years for the notion of peace-
keeping to take root. Similarly, it has taken quite a while to
develop arrangements for the international protection of human
rights. Early warning strategies and arrangements will have to
be built up step-by-step over a period of time.

One of the problems in the development of an integrated
early warning system is that there is still no central forum
where the constituency for early warning can marshall its
resources and stimulate policies and strategies. In the case of
peace-keeping for example, there is the Special Committee on

Peace-keeping Operations and the Special Political Committee of the United Nations General Assembly. In the case of human rights, there is a Commission on Human Rights, various human rights organs and the Third Committee of the United Nations General Assembly. While there are some specialized fora that deal with specific aspects of early warning, there is no general forum where the efforts of member states, non-governmental organizations and the Secretariat can come together in a creative manner for the nurturing of early warning and preventive arrangements.

For the time being, the task, especially in the political and humanitarian sectors, is left to the Secretary-General of the United Nations, although it may change after the possible creation of a senior post of the coordinator for humanitarian affairs. It is, however, not sufficiently realized that usually the Secretary-General may have only one shot to fire by way of early warning. The Secretary-General may alert the government(s) concerned, he may call the attention of the members of the Security Council to a potential problem, or he may choose to express his concern publicly. Once the Secretary-General has done so, however, the power of action usually passes to other actors, i.e., to member states acting individually or collectively, to United Nations organs, to non-governmental organizations perhaps or, conceivably, to the international media.

To forget the limitations upon the United Nations Secretary-General, or upon the United Nations Secretariat, in providing early warning or in taking follow-up action would be a mistake on the part of those seeking to develop early warning arrangements. Let it be clear what we are saying. The Secretary-General and the United Nations Secretariat should have the best possible system for gathering and analyzing information and for making the results of these analyses available to those in a position to act so as to avert potential problems. There is, however, a distinction between communicating information and analysis and being in a position to obtain action or results based on the information or analysis.

If these are inherent limitations upon the Secretary-General and the United Nations Secretariat, where can action emanate from? What can we expect, for example, on the part of the Security Council? The Council, as far as is known, still has no regular review of the situation in the different regions of the world; still has no arrangement for receiving and evaluating information from the Secretary-General or the Secretariat; has not yet clarified its thinking on how to approach the handling of internal conflicts; and is still caught in the throes of consensus-based procedures built largely around the need to secure agreement among its five Permanent Members.

There is no gainsaying the fact that, unless and until the Security Council develops some arrangements for reviewing the global situation systematically, and for acting on information presented to it by the Secretary-General, the Security Council would really not be in a position to offer much for the time being in the form of early warning and preventive action to deal with potential conflicts or humanitarian emergencies. Here one would do well to recall the following suggestion made by Secretary-General Perez de Cuellar in his 1990 Annual Report on the Work of the Organization:

'I believe that the peace-making capacity of the United Nations would be considerably strengthened if the Security Council had a peace agenda that is not confined to items formally inscribed at the requests of Member States, and if it held periodic meetings to survey the political scene and identify points of danger at which preventive or anticipatory diplomacy is required. Since the proceedings of such meetings need not necessarily be published, they would encourage candid discussions without making parties to disputes harden their positions. Nor would the reports of the Secretary-General to such meetings amount to an invocation by him of Article 99 of the Charter. There is little use in encumbering the peace effort with formal procedures when such procedures are not likely to lead to results conducive to peace. Other ways to strengthen the Council's role in dealing with incipient disputes lie in improving fact-finding arrangements, in establishing a United Nations presence in unstable areas and in instituting subsidiary bodies, where appropriate, for preventive diplomacy.

In this context, it needs to be stressed again that the means at present at the disposal of the Secretary-General for gathering the timely, accurate and unbiased information that is necessary for averting violent conflicts are inadequate. I made suggestions in this regard in my report last year and I would urge Member States to consider afresh ways of enabling the Secretariat to monitor potential conflict situations from a clearly impartial standpoint. The strategy of peace must reflect a better regard for timing than has been the case so far. The Organization's mediatory or investigative capacity should not be kept in reserve until it is too late to avert hostilities.' (United Nations Document)

If there are inherent limitations on what the Secretary-General of the United Nations can do by way of early warning and preventive action and if the Security Council is not yet in a position to offer much in this area, where should one make investments in early warning and preventive strategies? There is need here for more clarity of thought. Perhaps one should think about co-existing networks of early warning tailored to the needs for early warning in different areas. On environmental issues, for example, the early warning network will necessarily be specialized. The same will be the case with early warning on food supplies, on potential health problems, and about potential nuclear accidents (Ramcharan, 1991). These are all highly specialized areas and it is probably much better that they be tended to by specialized networks – which could still take account of one another's experience.

If one accepts the desirability of specialized early warning networks, a question that would arise for discussion is how they can be encouraged to share experiences and, to the extent desirable or possible, to co-ordinate their activities. In the human rights sector these days, there is an annual meeting of the chairpersons of the different human rights organs operating within the United Nations. One could see the case for an annual consultative meeting of the representatives of different early warning networks operating within the United Nations system.

The participants in early warning networks must necessarily be drawn from different constituencies: from governmental representatives; from non-governmental organizations; from scientific institutions and think tanks; from the United Nations Secretariat; and from the media. Only such an approach to early warning networks can have any chance of operating successfully. Any idea that early warning can be limited to the secretariats of international organizations would be rather short-sighted. In fact, the net should be drawn as widely as possible. The information analyzed would then be of greatest value.

Not only should the network and the sources of information in early warning be widely based, but the targets for action on early warning should be similarly broad. In some instances, of course, the Secretary-General of the United Nations may wish to approach governments or United Nations organs. Invariably, the Secretary-General would have to do so very discreetly. But there will be, undoubtedly, numerous occasions when it will be necessary to sound the alarm publicly and urgently. The media, non-governmental organizations, expert groups or member states may be in a much better position to obtain preventive or remedial action than the Secretary-General or even the Security Council. The United Nations was established as a centre to harmonise international activities for the attainment of common ends. It was never meant to become the exclusive actor or the exclusive forum. Responsibility for early warning and preventive action therefore has to be widely shared if any system is to be successful.

Pursuing the analysis further, should early warning have in view only the identification of situations of potential conflict or emergency or should one also have in mind the development of preventive strategies generally. In other words, should one address early warning and preventive action both in their specific and in their generic dimensions? So far, one has the impression that attention has been focused on the identification of specific situations to the detriment of broader preventive strategies. In the United Nations Human Rights programme, it has been found that one way of tackling a thorny problem occurring in different parts of the world may be to launch a global study. By gathering information and sharing experiences on the nature and characteristics of the problem generally, one may devise strategies and make recommendations for preventing the problem in the future. Excesses committed during states of emergency for example, led to studies on human rights during states of emergency and to the establishment of a procedure for monitoring compliance with international human rights norms during times of emergency.[3]

In like manner, there would seem to be need for a series of studies to be undertaken by those interested in early warning and preventive action on more general issues such as: strategies for the prevention of internal conflicts; strategies for the prevention of ethnic or religious conflicts; strategies for the prevention of gross violations of human rights; strategies for the avoidance of massive outflows of refugees or massive internal displacements. The list could be added to significantly. One thing is becoming more and more clear however: while attempting to establish arrangements to detect and act on potential problems, one would also need to undertake systematic studies, research and consultations on preventive strategies that can be pursued for tackling the kinds of situations that are nowadays generating conflicts and emergencies in the world. In short, one would have to deal with the *symptoms* of problems as well as their underlying root causes. And it may well be that the approach that would have most to offer in the long term would be the approach that seeks to deal with the root causes of conflicts or emergencies.

5. CONCLUDING OBSERVATIONS

In this essay we have deliberately sought to distance ourselves from details regarding the establishment and operation of early warning arrangements. Instead we must view those arrangements, particularly in the political sector involving the Secretary-General, against the background of the current state of the United Nations and a grand strategy for the United Nations if it is to succeed in the world. We have also taken into account some general policy propositions which we believe cannot be avoided if early warning procedures in the political and humanitarian sectors are to develop effectively in the future. Three observations may be emphasized to conclude this essay. First, the need for multi-pronged approaches and multiple actors in the early warning effort; second, the need for the best possible system for research and the collection of information in the United Nations Secretariat; and, third, the paramount need for the development of procedures and arrangements within the Security Council so that the Council, the Secretary-General, and the Secretariat can work in partnership in a cause that unites the people of the world – namely, the prevention of conflicts, crises, and emergencies.

NOTES

1. The views expressed are those of the author in his personal capacity.

2. See for example, Mouat (1991). See also, 'The Dangers of the UN Gulf Myth', *The Sunday Telegraph* (London, 10 March 1991).

3. See, e.g., E/CN.4/Sub. 2/1989/30/Rev. 1: Third Annual Report and List of States which... have proclaimed, extended or terminated a state of emergency.

REFERENCES

Chace, J., 1988. 'A New Grand Strategy', *70 Foreign Policy*, pp. 3-25.

Huntington S., 1991. 'America's Changing Strategic Interests', *Survival*, January/February, pp. 3-17.

Kissinger H., 1991. 'America Cannot Police The World Forever', *The Times*, London, March 12.

Mouat, L., 1991. 'The World From the United Nations', *Christian Science Monitor*, March 26, p. 3.

Ramcharan, B. G., 1991. *International Law of Early Warning and Preventive Diplomacy: The Emerging Global Watch*, The Hague: Martinus Nijhoff.

United Nations document, A/45/1.

Urquhart,B. & E. Childers, 1990. *A World in Need of Leadership*, New York: Ford Foundation and Stanley Foundation.

10

Socio-political Indicators for Early Warning Purposes

Jürgen Dedring[1]

1. INTRODUCTION

The study of internal conflicts and of ways and means of their resolution has gained recently in prominence, as the world has witnessed more and more violent disturbances in a wide range of communities in Europe, Africa, Asia and the Americas. The frequency and severity of these occurrences has led to a search by political leaders as well as scholarly experts for methods of managing and resolving these social crises.

In recent years, the international political scene has become the target of endeavours to anticipate the possible outbreak of international conflicts and thereby take measures to bring them to an early end before major violence erupts.[2] The fledgling attempts at competent early warning going beyond normal diplomatic prognostic assessments are still in need of thorough professionalism applying latest available tools and methods including computerized data management,[3] but it has become clear that while the borderline between international and internal conflicts is indeed disappearing (Rupesinghe, 1990), early warning regarding the two types of conflict must be clearly differentiated. What is salient in international affairs may be completely irrelevant for domestic conditions.

While there is still uncertainty whether early warning can be made to work in either of the two domains of interaction, it is reasonable to restrict the following argument to the domestic realm only, making of course allowances for factors on the outside affecting an internal situation.

The following pages constitute an exploratory essay about such socio-political indicators which are assumed to be indicative for conflictual action within states and about important theoretical and practical questions as regards the suggested measures for tension and conflict in societies. Little research has been done on such early warning indicators for internal conflict. The emphasis in this conceptual examination will be on those factors and events that are judged to be relevant for the realm of social conflict and that allow proper monitoring and specific analysis.

The principal part of this chapter consists of a rather detailed review of factors that have been identified as indicators for potential or incipient internal conflict. In this connection, the criterion of whether and to what extent these indicators can be made operational in real life conditions will be of special significance. These considerations may be of some help as researchers and practitioners continue their search for effective early warning.

2. THE NATURE OF INTERNAL CONFLICTS

If we accept Galtung's definition of conflict as the situation where an action system has two incompatible goals (Galtung, 1965), it is clear that this conception applies to any social system including the global international system. The focus on internal conflicts is primarily a strictly definitional one which delineates intra-state from inter-state situations. But in terms of early warning, the emphasis is not so much on terminological aspects, but on substantive issues that allow the observer to draw certain conclusions about the attitudes and likely actions of social actors.

International conflict is governed by other behavioral principles than internal conflict; the autonomy of the state actors is especially important. While the international community lacks an overarching executive authority that maintains order and has the ability to coerce compliance, the normal modern state is characterized by a functioning government whose rule represents the law of the land. While the incompatibility of goals is frequent and reflects the diversity of aims and policies shaping the behaviour of the different members of the international system, a certain amount of agreement and homogeneity is assumed in a functioning national community. The divergence and incompatibility of the respective political agendas espoused by various state actors are systemic features of the international community. The governmental fiat within the self-contained state community equally must be seen as systemic in quality. This principal distinction gives rise to significant differences in the approach to early warning for each of these situations. It is self-evident that there are always deviations from that basic distinction, but their occurrence should not lead us to believe that international and internal conflicts are no longer to be seen as conceptually and empirically apart.[4]

When emergent international conflicts are observed, logic demands that internal factors must be carefully monitored in that frequently foreign policy decisions of the government are affected or caused by domestic conditions. As many states have become more transparent and less authoritarian, the observer can find out so much more about internal processes, other than governmental action, which were inaccessible less than a century ago. Taking the case of a closed society, Iraq's aggression against Kuwait is not explained by the pattern of interstate relations in the Gulf region, but is largely due to powerful pressures within Iraq after its long and costly war against Iran. Thus, even highly authoritarian communities are nowadays open, at least to a certain degree, to international monitoring.

With regard to internal conflicts, we do not depend on international conditions or factors as explanatory devices for what is likely to happen in domestic political and social behaviour. Again, there are occasional instances where the decisions or intentions of government leaders are based on phenomena or events in the international realm, but the main evidence is to be sought and found within the particular community. In terms of identifying or anticipating the emergence of incompatible goals in a society, the internal scene will be sufficient most of the time.[5] Hence, for this exploration, it is suggested that only internal factors be listed and examined as early warning indicators regarding domestic conflicts.

As Galtung's basic definition shows, the search is for those elements that reveal a high level of disturbance or disequilibrium in the social system. Since the range of unrest and upheaval is quite wide, more factors should be taken into consideration than just conditions of civil war or violent confrontation. Dissatisfaction, peaceful protest and other less destabilizing incidents must be included in the monitoring framework. We can stipulate a more detailed list of socio-political indicators once it has become clear what they should indicate specifically.

3. THE SEARCH FOR INDICATORS

What gives rise to social tensions and confrontations? The question itself and possible answers make clear that in view of the intricate web of social relations in established political communities there are many factors that could be seen as responsible for social disorder or system collapse. The wave of mass demonstrations across Eastern Europe in 1989, the small trickle of East Germans escaping from the GDR via Czechoslovakia or Hungary, the lack of basic foods or the feeling of hopelessness, these and many others must be noted as elements that permit a causal analysis of these momentous events leading to a total reversal of the social and political conditions in those countries.

Any manageable set of indicators needs to be selective, clear and salient. In addition to those criteria, availability and reliability of the material required to match the stipulations implied in the language and specificity of the indicators must also be ensured.[6]

What kind of internal conflict is to be anticipated from the indicators? Shall we restrict it to those turbulences that are likely to result in a radical restructuring of the political and social order, or should we include cases of popular unrest that disrupt the social peace without affecting the stability of the government? Is low-level criticism by small groups to be monitored on a permanent basis, or does that only begin at a higher level of social dissent? Should the observation of relevant events and conditions extend to early signs of socio-economic shortfall and failure, e.g. the protests of Soviet miners over increasing shortages and inadequate wages?

An effective set of sociopolitical indicators must try to be comprehensive in covering the wide field of organized social and political relations and actions, but also including inchoate perceptions of social change, disequilibrium or impatience – all of which may lead to collective movements. The main concern that arises in this connection is whether such a wide range of indicators can be monitored regularly and reliably. Moreover, a more basic issue needs clarification: Going for a broad-based indicator set, how salient or relevant are the situations and events to be observed for the incidence of internal conflicts? While there is no preordained certainty as to what is, or is not, salient, any serious early warning approach must endeavour to arrive at such a determination, even if it is merely for heuristic or methodological reasons. Only the actual process of monitoring and validation will provide empirical evidence with regard to the prognostic strength of the sociopolitical indicators. The degree of uncertainty in this undertaking can be illustrated by the Romanian case, where direct suppression of a member of the clergy from the Hungarian minority in a provincial town gave rise to a rapidly escalating wave of popular protest and defiance, to the point where the dictatorial regime collapsed. The swiftness of this and other peaceful revolutions against overbearing authoritarian governments reminds the observer and analyst that the path and speed of sociopolitical change are highly irregular and unpredictable.

Thus, whatever is put forth as suitable frameworks and indicators for early warning about internal conflicts must be seen as tentative and preliminary until practical application gives reliable insights. Practical considerations regarding the volume of data, the scope of analysis and the timeliness and reliability of accessible information need to be taken up once a list of seemingly viable indicators has been drawn up and reviewed.

4. SOCIOPOLITICAL INDICATORS REVIEWED

Leon Gordenker, in his important monograph on *Refugees in International Politics* (Gordenker, 1987), lists, when discussing causal elements in internal turbulence giving rise to refugee flows, a number of conditions and situations which could be seen as feasible indicators for emergent internal conflict. While the study by Gordenker does not envisage such causal links, the factors lend themselves easily to such an examination in the context of domestic unrest.

Under the heading of 'insurrectionary social structures' the extreme social stratification based on racial separation in South

Africa is mentioned (Gordenker, 1987, p.71). Enforcement of the unjust rules to maintain the *apartheid* system leads to violent responses in the affected groups of the South African population. Depending on how the repression of human rights is carried out, the reactions by the victimized strata of society range from unspoken fear and hatred to open protest and violent disturbances. This kind of volatile social situation is unquestionably found in cases other than the South African society and constitutes a meaningful yardstick for societal stability/instability.

Another indicator for social conflict is the division of national groups and allocation of parts of them to different states (Gordenker, 1987, p.72). The fate of the Kurds comes to mind, as they have so far failed to be joined together in one separate community. As long as this separate and disparate existence prevails, it seems likely that the volatility of such situations reflecting the more or less inchoate yearnings of the Kurds for their separate national unity will not diminish, regardless of how much repression is applied.

Even if no irredentist or separatist desires exist, one related condition is the persecution of, or discrimination against, minorities (Gordenker, 1987, pp.72-3). Evidence for such situations is abundantly available. It should be noted that the methods of direct or indirect persecution or discrimination are manifold and that the reactions by the victims, individually as well as collectively, also cover a wide spectrum of attitudes and actions. However, this pattern of deprivation and denial against minority groups and their response is so close to a state of internal conflict that such evidence would no longer allow for enough lead time to be useful for proper early warning.

Another major dimension for early warning is what Gordenker has labelled brutal government (Gordenker, 1987, pp.74-5). Dictatorial and authoritarian regimes are still abundant in the current international system. Oppressive and repressive practices are welcome tools for the rulers to enslave their populations and to control their lives including their minds. Although numerous subjects try to escape from oppression and flee the country, the overwhelming majority does not have that option and is condemned to suffer. If such regimes manage to seal their borders hermetically and turn into closed societies, it is usually very difficult to obtain detailed and precise information about the real conditions in those dictatorships and, more importantly, the rulers also succeed to a considerable extent in isolating their citizens from the outside media and communications and feed them only with their own 'truths'. Nevertheless, these conditions seem especially important for the detection of signs that anger is rising and that the victims are attempting to organize a protest or even an uprising, disregarding the risk to their lives. How reliable is the information that can be gathered under such forbidding circumstances?

Gordenker mentions in particular the wholesale denial of human rights as a means of controlling the subjects of an oppressive regime (Gordenker, 1987, pp.74-5). A lot of thinking has gone into the identification of human rights violations and the preparation of standards to monitor the widely divergent abuse of individual and group rights by the authorities.[7] The instigation of human rights violations against special groups in society, such as the persecution committed by Idi Amin against Asians in Uganda, is a subspecies of the evil practice of human rights abuse. The insidious and often hidden manner in which such abuses are committed renders it difficult to gather reliable information about these occurrences in a systematic fashion.

Another interesting category proposed by Gordenker is that of incompetent government, which is defined as 'a government that is incapable of making or implementing decisions or of controlling its administrative apparatus' (Gordenker, 1987, pp.76-7). This conception can actually be somewhat expanded to include in a more general form the phenomenon of governments increasingly falling short in their ability to deliver the expected goods and services to the citizens and residents, either due to fatigue after too many years in power or because the governing elite views its authority as an opportunity to enrich the people at the top at the expense of the general population. Thereby we broaden the category suggested by Gordenker into a wider spectrum of governmental performance covering inept behaviour as well as deteriorating standing and corrupt exploitative conduct.[8] From this description it is immediately apparent that the monitoring of these government-related phenomena is bound to be delicate and difficult, with the governing elites watching suspiciously any indication that their privileged situation has become precarious.

If the pattern of governmental inadequacy worsens, it is quite likely that popular dissatisfaction and social unrest will ensue. Protests, strikes and riots are likely to occur first in isolated instances, but if the malaise continues, social disturbances will spread and draw larger crowds. The reaction by the government plays a most important role as far as the growth of popular disquiet and protest is concerned. Much of this social movement deserves detailed observation because it rates as a principal causal factor for the outbreak of both non-violent and violent internal conflict which may be directed against the government in office or may be unfocused. Yet another consequence of widespread dissatisfaction among the general public may be hostile behaviour among different groups in society. This will be taken up further below.

Among other related suggestions by Gordenker, mention should be made of 'deliberately undertaken change of social structures' (Gordenker, 1987, pp.77-82) involving violent as well as legitimate replacement of socio-political elites or the decline of certain groups in society due to economic obsolescence. Examples for these categories can be found quite easily. In varying degrees, all of them are certain to affect the stability of the political and social order negatively. But only concrete monitoring can establish a higher degree of validation as to what the repercussions of specific circumstances are in terms of covert or overt social strife.

If we take the case of the overthrow of the Allende Government in Chile in 1973, the turbulence which resulted did indeed involve a wide-ranging replacement of elites, and major internal conflict was long contained through systematic repression by the military regime. One wonders, however, whether the military rulers were at last removed because many people had never abandoned their strong opposition to the Pinochet regime throughout the years until 1989.

The legitimate replacement of elites through elections or other established procedures rarely gives rise to public unrest including protests by those losing their privileged status in society. Nevertheless, it deserves to be watched carefully as the potential for social instability is present.

Recent demonstrations by miners in certain areas illustrate the issue of economic obsolescence: the mining of coal has for several decades been on the decline in some parts of the world. Therefore, economic satisfaction and social status diminish. Recurrent waves of erratic protest and strikes demonstrate the volatility which is generated thereby. Careful observation and assessment of these and similar symptoms of social change are therefore also advisable for early warning purposes.

A very different perspective on society and its dynamics is the one chosen by the research team of the Peruvian Peace Research Association (Associación Peruana de Estudios e Investigación para la Paz) in its basic study on Structural Violence in Peru (APEP, 1989). As the Head of the Association, Padre Felipe McGregor, made clear in the early phase of the project, the focus of this recent investigation was the presence of deep-seated characteristics in Peruvian history and society that have been the cause of patterns of violence in that community. The term 'structural violence' is, of course, taken from Johan Galtung's early peace and conflict research writings (Galtung, 1969, pp.167-92). But it should be added that the use of this notion for the Peruvian situation resulted from thorough knowledge of Galtung's thinking on the matter and from a deliberate decision to measure social and political practices in contemporary Peru with this conceptual rod.

The comprehensive approach to Peruvian society in its totality encompasses the question of the individual and how he is affected by the dynamics and shortcomings of his community. The twelve spheres stipulated by the research team, namely the rights of each human being, the individuality of human beings, the family, social discrimination in its various facets, social silence, the means of communication, democracy, social class and racism, authoritarianism, male chauvinism ('machismo'), aggressiveness, and individual and social progress, are the realms in which the main social factors related to structural violence are located; they also provide the chances of achieving social pacification (APEP, 1989, conclusions).

The list of principal social factors reveals considerable attention to the level of the individual in society. For a thorough examination of any social system the role of the individual cannot be overlooked. The Peruvian study has produced a series of close-up photos of the social organism at the level of individual aims, expectations, concerns and fears and at the next higher level of small groups including the family. The conclusion of the team as a whole that Peruvian society reveals a pervasive strong strain of structural violence cannot be taken lightly. If their judgement is empirically sound, the probability of social and political turbulence must be rated quite high. This perception astounds the outside observer since there are no signs that the political system tends towards authoritarianism. The best-known sign of danger for Peru is the growth of the Shining Path movement and its ability to terrorize the Government and the administrative services and to coerce simple peasants into submission in the high mountain regions. Is there an even greater menace to a stable and peaceful Peru? From the vantage point of the study on structural violence, one might well decide that in the long term structural violence presents a greater danger and that it may have contributed to the rise of the Shining Path movement.

The discussion of all twelve social factors in the Peru study exceeds the scope of this essay. But a few should be described and evaluated in order to judge their utility as socio-political indicators for potential internal conflicts. Serious shortcomings are reported, for instance, in the availability and fair application of human rights in Peru. The effect of such inequities is severe as they exacerbate the gap between the haves and have-nots, pushing the latter to violence in their revenge against a social and political system that fails to meet their material or spiritual needs.

The family in Peruvian society is described as a unit accustomed to violence; there is evidence of maltreatment of the wife by the husband, and an authoritarian, e.g. hierarchical, structure and distance between parents and children together with physical punishment in education. These features are deeply ingrained in many social groups and add to the level of violence in society.

The research team also concludes that discrimination against the poor and against women is pervasive and that race frequently plays a role in whether one succeeds in job-hunting. These findings are related to the presence of racism and ethnocentrism in Peru: the characteristics and potential of people are assessed on the basis of the colour of their skin, although this practice is suppressed in social behaviour through 'social silence'. Authoritarianism, male chauvinism and aggressiveness are all listed as adding in various configurations to the way in which Peru is afflicted by structural violence.

This brief description and summary cannot do justice to the sophisticated in-depth analysis produced by the Peruvian peace research team. The case is of such great interest because the canvas of Peruvian social and political conditions that has been explored offers no simplistic condemnation of the society as violent and close to disaster. Instead, the reader is given the impression that much of the violence-promoting heritage and sociopolitical culture afflicts the dynamics of modern Peru in subcutaneous and inchoate ways. Whether, when and in what form a major sociopolitical crisis might shake the foundations of that society remains a wide open question. What has been provided is like an x-ray picture of the Peruvian social system revealing aspects that normally remain hidden to the uninitiated outside observer and that are also unknown to most Peruvians. As such, the information flowing from that study is most valuable in the search for viable indicators regarding potential internal conflicts. Does that huge study, however, offer a model to be emulated? How many scientists would be able to replicate the rich findings of the Peru project?[9]

In this review of possible indicators, a digression may be allowed to take up briefly the topic of the ORCI global data base. This consists *inter alia* of country profiles, and has already been constructed, but needs further conceptual and programming work to reach completion. As is known, the purpose of that data system is to provide the Secretary-General on a continuous basis with reliable and up-to-date information regarding potential conflicts and crises that might endanger international peace and security. With the establishment of ORCI in 1987,[10] the issues of how its early warning function would be carried out and what kind of system had to be set up needed to be resolved. Early on, it was decided that the search for early warning indicators should be comprehensive in view of the indeterminacy of most indicators as regards possible political outcomes.

With the decision to select many indicators relating to the countries of the contemporary international system, the gates were so to speak opened for factors and connections that *a priori* have little bearing on international conflictual behaviour. The underlying argument was and is that many international disturbances can arise out of strictly domestic developments or considerations. The Falkland war, for example, was caused by powerful internal priorities of the troubled military junta in Argentina, and the British decision to respond militarily has also been ascribed to the hard-pressed domestic situation of the Conservative Government.

As the result of these basic determinations,[11] ORCI adopted a long list of indicators for its early warning data system, among them quite a few that relate to the present probe into early warning of internal conflict. Without looking at the total set of indicators, it is proposed to consider briefly those factors that appear salient as regards internal political and social behaviour.

Several indicators in ORCI's system focus on ethnic, religious and linguistic groups, their demographic growth, their size, and how they are connected with identical groups across the border. Important corollary factors include the oppression or persecution of social groups, the size of internal security forces, the occurrence of domestic hostilities and conflicts, the governmental policy towards such hostilities or tensions, also the existence of separatist groups in the various countries.

Standard data on demonstrations, strikes and riots are also collected. With basic government and defense data, the ability of the analyst to arrive at certain assessments about the proclivity of a social system toward unrest and violent disruptions will depend on reliable factual information. Due to the global scope of the data system, little more can be done than scratch the surface of the internal conditions that might give rise to disquiet, unrest, repression or social strife.

To supplement the above-mentioned information the ORCI database also seeks to obtain material on land ownership, on population growth and density, on basic food and health statistics, on employment and unemployment conditions, on refugees and displaced persons and on distribution of wealth as well as income, also per-capita and GDP figures and inflation rates, to name a few secondary factors which, nevertheless, in the total picture are certain to have an impact on the prognosis.

It can be seen that the indicators chosen for the ORCI system are by necessity somewhat disparate and do not permit anything approaching comprehensive coverage for internal situations. It should also be noted at this point that the Office is restricted to publicly available data, which further diminishes its capacity to detect and to forewarn. Nevertheless, the ORCI case adds to the impression that we have arrived at in this brief review of some lists of socio-political indicators, namely that a certain confluence or convergence seems to emerge. If that is indeed the case, we can anticipate some progress in the search for suitable terms and concepts allowing for early warning regarding intra-state conflicts.

5. GOVERNMENT AND SOCIETY – SOURCES OF CONFLICT

A systematic assessment and attempt at conceptualization should help to bring out those features that promise to be of lasting usefulness in the task of alerting about emergent internal conflict situations. Whatever is suggested here is still preliminary, but it may assist in sketching out the route of further more detailed explorations. The review of analytical schemes by Gordenker, by the Peruvian peace researchers and by ORCI – which are closely related – allows us to set out categories and linkages making up the envisaged early warning approach.

A first cluster of indicators can be identified as revolving around the characteristics and behaviour of governments. The discussion above has focused on the phenomena of instability, oppressiveness and incompetence to show what the main sources for potentially conflictual developments might be. Weak political systems or executives are bound to generate troublesome reactions in a more and more disillusioned citizenry either because they fail to make available in an equitable fashion the benefits expected from the ruling establishment or because they fall short in providing security and stability for the community. A government that is steadily in danger of losing its political base is unlikely to be decisive in articulating the basic beliefs and aims of society and will soon be exposed as a failure in meeting the daily needs and in planning for the future.

Incompetent governments show similar characteristics in an exacerbated manner: the proven inability to deliver the expected services is bound to give rise to rapid disenchantment among the strata and groups in society. Available alternatives are not easily found – this in itself will speed up patterns of social disintegration because everybody will seek to help himself. Examples of this effect of incompetent leadership can be cited from many historical and contemporary cases. As group egoism takes hold, the distribution of benefits, especially in conditions of scarcity, is certain to create tensions and possible confrontations. Nevertheless, the degree of social unrest is likely to be still manageable even when the incompetent leadership has been ousted or overthrown, although there might be severe disturbances under such conditions.

The explosive quality of oppressive regimes marks them clearly as indicators for the outbreak of internal conflicts. The crucial variable to be regarded is the quality of oppression exercised by the ruling elite. The tighter the system of control and the more threatening the surveillance by the police state, the less likely is the generation of oppositional activities. In the long run the search for lessening the burden of suppression and for the removal of the dictatorship will intensify and violent means will be employed in order to ensure the overthrow of the regime. Even if the desire for liberation from the authoritarian yoke is not fulfilled, the covert struggle between the public authorities and the suffering populace will produce enough tension and disturbance that can be detected by observers within the country and on the outside.

The phenomena of instability, incompetence and oppression can be refined into variables for inclusion in a systematic and detailed indicator list for steady monitoring. It would appear that a considerable amount of basic information about the political system and the social structure would need to be surveyed and assessed in order to detect early on and reliably evidence for the destabilization of a particular socio-political entity. Such examination goes beyond the scope of this initial exploration.

The other side of the coin in internal conflict has to do with the societal component: here we refer once again to what was reviewed above, namely the incidence of demonstrations, strikes and riots as indicators of internal friction. The terms subsumed under the category of social unrest constitute key symptoms of a restless community in which people either protest publicly and visibly against lagging delivery of social goods and services or they profess principles and ideas that diverge from the ideological orientation of the government in power or of other social groups. The incendiary quality of such collective utterances is well-known, and the escalating dynamic of such public disturbance must also be pointed out.

In this connection, an earlier remark about the impact of social groups competing with each other must be taken up. The confrontation is frequently not so much a clash between government and society as a case of nonviolent and occasionally violent rivalry between different groups in society. Recent attempts to widen social equity in India through the inclusion of lower social strata, by granting certain privileges with regard to access to education and well-paid secure civil service positions, demonstrates the underlying social conflict where governmental remedial measure can have only a limited expression. The government acted in this case as the voice of those lower strata that so far have complained of being discriminated against and shut out. What appears to the outsider as a clash between government and society is really the outward expression of a deep-seated social antagonism.

Many social and socio-economic data need to be gathered and analyzed to gain sufficient understanding of the fundamental forces shaping and moving social bodies. The Peruvian study shows in this connection the required depth and breadth of documentation. This enables the outside observer to trace the structural and procedural elements and to distil from the mass of material those facts shedding light on the web of social interaction that is potentially disruptive or explosive.

A related matter not requiring extensive treatment is the issue of human rights violations. The severity of these infringements on the human and civil rights of every human being has been well documented in recent years. The international community has launched big campaigns to expose current practices of such infringement wherever they occur. The grass-root oriented documentation network HURIDOCS has made a major contribution in developing standard formats for recording human rights violations. The emphasis on common or compatible information systems to implement the work with the standard formats is well-founded. The formats and the information load to be gained from their application are directly relevant in the approach to emergent internal conflicts as the human rights question comes into play in most unstable and turbulent intrastate situations. Detecting human rights violations is a first phase in the identification of societal conditions that are volatile, tense and conflict-prone. The need for detailed close-up information presents a challenge, yet the achievement of solid reliable early warning data depends on that material becoming available.

Attention to what is commonly referred to as 'ethnic conflict' is also relevant for early detection of probable internal conflict. Much has recently been said and written about the resurgence of ethnic strife within states and affecting inter-state relations.[12] The direct impact of ethnically based tension and strife on the well-being of a society as a whole needs no validation, as evidence abounds. Clearly, ethnic conflict afflicts international politics, too, but the main damage is felt in cases that affect mainly states and their internal situation. What we have learned in recent years is that ethnicity in itself must be perceived as a potentially conflictual factor, especially nowadays when more and more people identify with, and seek emotional fulfilment in, ethnically defined groups below or outside the nation state. This trend toward sub-national affective links has caused numerous difficulties in regions and states, in particular when emotional attachment is connected with strong long-standing socio-economic or political grievances – usually complaints about discrimination in education, employment, income, and services. Even relatively peaceful ethnic entities constitute a potential factor for initiating social conflict since their separateness, real or alleged, is seen as a challenge by the other members of the larger community.

As in the other cases discussed so far, the monitoring scheme for ethnic conflict unquestionably requires a comprehensive and at the same discreet approach to the gathering of relevant information and to the assessment in terms of open conflict potential. Such a wide scope and delicate nature of monitoring adds to the difficulty of launching a suitable early warning operation.

Another major source of conflict that has become an issue of growing public concern is the ecological situation. The depletion of resources and the damage to the environment have alarmed governments and populations worldwide.[13] If we take a longer term view of the matter, resource scarcity can easily lead to the mass movement of people in search of alternate sources of food, energy, etc. Also, severely damaged land might force the inhabitants to flee to more hospitable regions which would in all likelihood not be empty unsettled spaces. These would either begin to suffer from overpopulation or become the object of fighting, with far-reaching consequences for all sides concerned. Some of the current North-South tensions seem to be at least partly due to environmental exigencies that have resulted in major flows of people. The effect of the 1986 Chernobyl disaster with regard to displacement and mass flight is not an isolated case, as recent news about other instances of massive environmental degradation document.

Ecological reasons for potential internal conflicts have not yet been studied very closely. The next few years will move this complex issue into wide public awareness. Decision-makers and researchers will delve deeply into possible indicators for such occurrences and enlarge the base from which these matters will be examined. The imminent crises regarding water resources in the Middle East, firewood in the Third World and food production in many parts of the world illustrate the rapidly growing probability of internal as well as international conflict. Much must be done to arrive at a finely tuned set of investigative tools to probe knowledgeably and reliably the antecedents of ecology-related confrontations. It will require the pooling of available expertise from ecologists, sociologists, political scientists and futurists to match the challenge posed by this novel causal element of conflictual behaviour within and among states.

6. CONCLUSION: THE SEARCH FOR OPERATIONAL INDICATORS

In summing up the tentative argumentation of the previous pages, one big issue is looming through it all: How good are the chosen indicators? Are they operational? Have they been made operational? This query is highly theoretical, yet of direct relevance for any real effort at early warning regarding internal conflict. The intimate introspective focus of the Peru study, the very precarious perspective underlying the HURIDOCS Standard Formats for Recording Human Rights Violations, and attempts to probe embarrassing incompetence or brutal oppression by governments in power all erect barriers against successful monitoring. Instead of open access, the early warning observer is likely to encounter obstruction or at the least obfuscation. There are no easy ways to overcome this impediment, but in spite of these obstacles the search for a feasible system of effective observation and data-gathering must be carried on.

Other difficulties have arisen, as the earlier discussion already pointed out. First among these is the access to data: although much is available in published form, essential sources may either be withheld or possibly distorted. Seeking truthful, precise and reliable information is frequently a dangerous business, because those who harbour ill intentions – whether it deals with political power or economic wealth – will want to hide illicit dealings from their rivals and the general public. If the observer is watching the society from the outside, his access to privileged materials is doubtful anyway, as the stranger will not easily be taken into confidence. Often, those who are willing to make information available may do so at great risk and will therefore not divulge their own sources nor allow their names to be used. This diminishes both objectivity and reliability in the attempt at early warning.

Is it enough to utilize only publicly available data? While the shortcomings deriving from such a restriction are already apparent in early warning about probable international conflicts, it is of much greater consequences for internal conflicts because communications in closed communities go far beyond the published paper or document. Verbal communications are as important, if not more so, as written material. Therefore, a serious early warning approach to internal disturbances could not do without general access to all people and all types of communication.

A matter of considerable importance is connected with the issue of the contextual relevance of particular indicators. While computerized data files and operational indicators will unquestionably enhance monitoring and early warning in the future, the analyst's awareness of the historical, social, economic and 'ideological' contexts in which particular indicators affect sociopolitical processes is of paramount importance in the eventually successful implementation of a comprehensive monitoring approach to internal conflicts.

In view of this and related determinants of early warning of conflict situations it appears necessary that an attempt be made to combine model-based anticipatory estimates of socio-politically pertinent trouble with the insight and circumspection of the so-called expert, i.e. of case specialists whose judgement is based on comparative historical and contemporary knowledge.

Having said this, we should take the next step and acknowledge that the task is of urgency and cannot be postponed even though the information will not be fully available nor will it always be timely. The likely disruption of social harmony, and the distant but serious danger that some societies may disintegrate and fall apart, make it imperative to launch a comprehensive early warning operation using socio-political and socio-economic indicators that seem to capture the key dimensions of societal disturbances and conflicts. The long years it took before ORCI was established with a focus on internationally relevant conflicts prove that it may still take some time before a credible monitoring system can be instituted to alert the communities about emergent societal conflicts. The search for that early warning monitor must continue until its successful completion.[14]

NOTES

1. The views expressed in this article are those of the author and do not necessarily reflect the views of the United Nations.

2. One of the first major voices was that of UN Secretary-General Perez de Cuellar in his report to the General Assembly. See document A/37/1, dated 7 September 1982.

3. For a basic expose regarding the ORCI early warning approach see Dmitrichev (1990).

4. The distinction between international and internal conflicts is both legal/normative *and* factual/empirical. Of course the connections between the two spheres are numerous and close, but to abolish the distinction would neither serve a heuristic purpose nor add anything to our practical understanding of either of these phenomena.

5. This is not meant to disregard important academic work on economically oriented global models, global geographies of social conflict, or the North-South dimensions of world conflict patterns. These contribute much to our understanding of what binds the international and intrastate realms together. Nevertheless, a large portion of what goes on within a state is caused by predominantly internal factors and processes.

6. For a very insightful view on indicators see Marcus, no date. Unfortunately, other papers and studies by Marcus were not available to the author for this essay.

7. Special reference is made here to the pioneering work done by HURI-DOCS. Its work on the standard formats for recording human rights violations and in particular its conference in Utrecht in July 1989 are described in *HURIDOCS News*, n. 9 (special issue). Rupesinghe, Thoolen and others have been principal collaborators in this undertaking and have articulated the conception, methodology and aim of that approach.

8. For some further elaboration of this monitoring category, see below. Hayward Alker has appropriately drawn this author's attention to the enormous complexity of the definition and measurement of 'governmental inadequacy'. Yet, the factor seems to be centrally important for the understanding and forecasting of internal conflicts.

9. Only a very close examination of the long study (in the original Spanish) will bring out the heuristic, theoretical and methodological foundations of the project and the scientific validity and salience of their findings. This author has not been able to carry out such a close review of the full study.

10. See the Secretary-General's Bulletin (ST/SGB/225) dated 1 March 1987 for the structure and functions of ORCI.

11. These considerations are based on working papers prepared by this author and others in ORCI. The views expressed here are, however, personal opinions and do not necessarily reflect the position of the UN.

12. Among many, see here Rupesinghe (1988a, 1992); also Stephen Ryan (1990). See also Jakob Roesel (1989). The growing number of special studies including work by Ted Gurr, Ed Azar and others justifies the brief reference in this paper to the question of ethnic conflict.

13. For an ecological perspective, see Rupesinghe (1992); also Okwudiba Nnoli (1990) and M.A. Mohamed Salih (1990). See also Richard Swift (1990). The ongoing work of Tad Homer-Dixon at the University of Toronto should be mentioned here as reflecting the new wave of serious academic research on this pressing issue.

14. In revising the first draft, the author has benefited greatly from criticism and suggestions by the two referees who were asked to review the original text. While this paper falls short in empirical content, it is intended subsequently to build on the conceptual-analytical foundation and to take up specific aspects of early warning and monitoring involving a more historical-empirical approach.

REFERENCES

APEP, 1989. *Violencia Estructural en el Peru*, Lima: Asociación Peruana de Estudios e Investigación para la Paz.

Dmitrichev, Timour, 1990. 'Conceptual Approaches to Early Warning: a UN view', paper submitted to the IPRA Conference in Groningen.

Galtung, Johan, 1965. 'Institutionalized Conflict Resolution: A Theoretical Paradigm', *Journal of Peace Research*, vol.2, no. 3.

Galtung, Johan, 1969. 'Violence, Peace and Peace Research', *Journal of Peace Research*, vol.6, no. 3.

Gordenker, L., 1987. *Refugees in International Politics*, New York: Columbia University Press.

HURIDOCS News, no. 9, February 1990, Special issue: 'Human Rights Violations and Standard Formats: Towards Compatibility in Recording and Transferring Information'.

Marcus, S., 'The Semiotics of Social Indicators: A Methodological Framework', unpublished manuscript, no date.

Millan, V. & M. A. Morris, 1990. 'Conflicts in Latin America: Democratic Alternatives in the 1990s', *Conflict Studies*, vol. 230, London.

Nnoli, O., 1990. 'Desertification, Refugees and Regional Conflict in West Africa', *Disasters*, vol. 14, no. 2, pp. 132-8.

Roesel, J., 1989. 'Ethnische Konflikte in den Staaten der Dritten Welt', *Verfassung und Recht in Uebersee*, vol. 22, no. 3, pp. 285-311.

Rupesinghe, Kumar, 1990. 'The Disappearing Boundaries Between Internal and External Conflicts', Paper submitted to the IPRA Conference in Groningen, July 1990. Revised version in Kumar Rupesinghe, ed., 1992, *Internal Conflicts and Governance*, London: Macmillan.

Rupesinghe, Kumar, 1988a. 'The Quest for a Disaster Early Warning System', *PRIO Report*, no. 2, 1988.

Rupesinghe, Kumar, 1988b. 'Theories of Conflict Resolution and Protracted Ethnic Conflict', *PRIO Report*, no. 1, 1988.

Ryan, S., 1990. 'Ethnic Conflict and the United Nations', *Ethnic and Racial Studies*, vol. 13, no. 1, pp. 25-49.

Salih, M.A. Mohamed, 1990. 'Ecological Stress and Political Coercion in West Africa', *Disasters*, vol. 14, no. 2, pp.125-31.

Swift, R., 1990. 'Is Any Development Sustainable?', *Ploughshares Monitor*, June, pp.15-17.

Wilkenfeld, J.H., W. Gerald & P.J. Rossa, 1979. 'Socio-political Indicators of Conflict and Cooperation', in Singer, J. David & Michael D. Wallace, eds, *To Augur Well. Early Warning Indicators in World Politics*, pp.109-51, Beverly Hills and London: Sage.

11

Early Warning Capacity of the United Nations System: Prospects for the Future

Michiko Kuroda[1]

1. INTRODUCTION

The end of the Cold War seemed to give some hope for lasting peace without further escalation of the arms race, nuclear threats or ideological battles. However, today's society is threatened, not only by armed conflicts or physical violence, but also by a whole range of other factors: social upheaval, increasing ethnic and religious conflict, economic and environmental degradation, social problems (drugs, AIDS, etc.), increasing gaps between the poor and the rich, violation of human rights, and so on. There is a growing danger of conflicts of various types in many regions, subregions, countries, and among groups of people.

The recent developments that have led to humanitarian disasters and tragedies – among the Kurds, or in Bangladesh or the Horn of Africa – represent an opportunity to highlight the role of the United Nations in international conflicts, especially with regard to humanitarian assistance. Many of these tragedies could have been avoided or at least minimized. One of the purposes of the United Nations, under Article 1 of the Charter, is to remove and prevent the threat to international peace and security. The political Declaration of the Group of Seven made in July 1991 at the London Economic Summit indicated various measures for strengthening the United Nations – specifically mentioning 'the early warning capacity of the United Nations.'

In this context, it is indeed timely to reconsider the capacity of the United Nations with regard to early warning. Has, in fact, the United Nations a substantial capacity for early warning? And how might it be used?

Here I will take a practical, managerial approach, because firmly established early warning is a solid management tool for preparedness, prevention and mitigation. Advance knowledge through systematic monitoring of root causes of developing situations could better prepare the concerned agencies of the UN system to take appropriate, timely action aimed at mitigation, negotiation or prevention. Good managers within the organization will need to incorporate the component of early warning into their policy planning process.

2.   PRACTICAL APPROACH TO EARLY WARNING

In one sense, 'early warning' seems clear enough – meaning an action of notifying beforehand. However, it has taken on different connotations and concepts, depending upon the specific context. Thus, the concept of early warning will need to be redefined for practical and managerial purposes.

2.1.   Nature and concept of early warning

Early warning should be viewed as a useful *management tool* (action-oriented although requiring extensive research work) as well as an *ongoing learning process* of developing situations. The component of early warning should form a part of a management cycle of early warning, preparedness, action, and post-action evaluation. All of these processes should be handled in a systematic way. 'Early' suggests advance or prior to events. Warnings can be useful if they give adequate time to respond, so the specific time reference ('how early?') will depend on the particular case. This does not preclude, however, the continuation of monitoring also after the events. Early 'warning' is an alert function, not merely a forecasting or projection endeavour. Warnings should identify the risks and provide possible scenarios of developing situations. Since every event and developing situation has a cause, early warning exercises will necessarily address 'root causes.' These would permit us to grasp the situations, its possible developments, the conditions for resolution and guidance to better settlement, and ways of forestalling or alleviating the worst effects – including early intervention so as to transform or resolve conflicts. Examining root causes will lead us to identify and focus on 'the vulnerable' – always the first and the most seriously affected. This suggests that early warning should have a close link with developmental and poverty issues.

Despite their keen interest in early warning, Member States of the United Nations have not yet given due consideration to the many methodologies of early warning. These range from historical survey and analysis of events, content analysis of documents and reports, comparative analysis of relevant information, physical inspections and field visits, statistical sampling and inference, operations research techniques, economic or econometric analysis, modelling and simulation to remote sensing techniques.[2]

2.2. Purposes of early warning

The purpose of early warning is not to threaten the target group or the international community. Early warning should not be an end in itself: it is only a tool for preparedness, prevention and mitigation with regard to disasters, emergencies and conflict situations, whether short or long-term ones. From a managerial point of view such a system will necessarily depend on the efficiency and effectiveness of the organizational work – particularly if these phenomena are to be tackled *before* the worst occurs, at a lower cost to human lives and financial resources. The real issue is not detecting the developing situation, but reacting to it. This will guide us to a reflection on two major efforts on early warning.

Prevention

Prevention of natural disasters is not possible. With regard to man-made disasters, however, early warning exercises can guide the entities to take action for prevention through solid understanding of causes and situation. Such actions could be of a very political nature and meet strong resistance from governments. Article 2(7) of the Charter, on non-inference in the 'domestic jurisdiction' of States, has been cited as a strong argument against it. However, many disasters – whether man-made or natural – are interlinked, and disaster-prone regions, countries or groups of people are vulnerable to any kind of disasters.

Prevention will definitely imply peace-keeping – involving physical military intervention – as well as peace-making – comprising efforts for political settlements through mediators, good offices or other diplomatic negotiations. However, early warning for prevention will also suggest that UN organizations should make efforts for 'peace-building' as proposed in Galtung's approaches to peace[3] (see Chapter 6). Peace-building would entail all the attempts to alter destructive attitudes – through encouraging contact between the ordinary people on all sides of the conflicts, and including such areas as: economic development, confidence building measures, education for mutual understanding, technical assistance and cooperation and promotional activities. Many UN agencies are in fact well placed to play a role in this process. Of course, it is not possible to eliminate all the causes of developing conflicts. However, through this process, at least the risks of their evolving and escalating could be reduced.

Preparedness
While many disastrous situations cannot be prevented, early warning could provide a solid basis for preparedness in providing assistance. Once events have erupted, different bodies and organizations will provide relief measures or assistance. The United Nations agencies act at the request of the governments by making appeals, fund-raising, gathering materials and equipment, as well as finding experts. Cannot this, however, be planned in advance as contingency planning? Certainly, yes. In fact, many agencies did attempt to do contingency planning – even after the invasion of Kuwait and before the mass flood of Kurds. These contingency plans were not very accurate, however, and proved useless. This should show that better, more solid and systematic early warning is urgently needed.

2.3. Information management for early warning purposes
As early warning necessarily deals with and consists of information, it falls under information management. The reception of data does not in itself constitute early warning. Only when data-gathering is systematized, classified and organized for retrieval and analysis, can it constitute the rudiments of early warning.[4]

Types of information required

Any indication of developing situations represents information relevant to early warning. Thus, information should be provided on each indicator, rather than on effects only. A specific piece of information on an event may have a value as early information, but this should be distinguished from early warning. Information may take different forms: raw or analyzed data, a given event or its historical background. Before transmitting it to the monitoring office, officials should consult with colleagues or other offices in the same country or region and even with their respective headquarters in order to verify its relevance and significance. They should make a primary assessment and comment on the information (see Chapter 8).

Management of data

Presenting the evaluated information to decision-makers, together with the processed and relevant information, would necessitate the establishment and management of appropriate databases by the competent personnel. Data would have to be retrievable at any time. As the situation develops, such data should be updated, stored and transmitted.

2.4. Actors and destinees

Various networks with institutions operating at different levels of specialization should work out efficient ways of sharing information. There are various possible components – such as entities of the UN system, individual officials, groups of people and non-governmental organizations (NGOs). Whatever the field they are involved in, and wherever they are located, all these can play an active role. All of them should be trained to be aware of the importance of indicators. They should be provided by the monitoring office with criteria for assessment, specific indicators, the types and formats of the information required, etc. Further, they may be consulted when developing indicators. The information obtained should then be processed and analyzed by expert personnel to evaluate to what extent the situation may involve warning signs. The immediate destinee of early warning is the UN Secretary-General, who can then bring matters to the attention of the members of the Security Council, as provided for in Article 99. On the other hand, this Article does not exclude the possibility of other destinees – such as decision-makers of legislative organs and executive heads of specialized agencies, or indeed the whole international community. The question of destinees, however, should be treated with prudence. In some cases, early warnings could yield negative consequences and worsen the situation. Moreover, destinees will need to take very seriously the warnings given; otherwise they may be of little value. Situations may develop rapidly, so one must make the best use of early warning.

3. POLICY FRAMEWORK FOR EARLY WARNING AT THE UN

According to Article 99 of the Charter of the United Nations, 'the Secretary-General may bring to the attention of the Security Council any matter which in his opinion may threaten the maintenance of international peace and security.' This short text provides the right – but not the obligation – for the Secretary-General to assume functions related to early warning within the framework of the maintenance of international security.[5]

The Secretary-General has, therefore, the discretionary power to convene the Council to inform its members when, in his judgement, any matter 'may threaten' the maintenance of international peace and security. To this end, the Secretary-General should be kept informed of developing situations, including anticipatory information and analysis. This can provide a basis for the preventive role and early warning function as required. The article will not attempt to define what is meant by 'any matter': this can be interpreted in an expanded sense, covering a wide range of political, economic, social, humanitarian and environmental factors, all of which could indeed threaten international peace and security.

Within the framework of Article 99, former Secretary-General Dag Hammarskjöld developed a broad scope for early warning of with information gathering purposes. He developed the concept of 'UN presence' in terms of some on-the-spot arrangements by the United Nations, and for keeping UN Headquarters informed. Further, he created the concept of 'preventive diplomacy,' the competence of which belongs to the

Secretary-General. However, Hammarskjöld's innovative action related to preventive diplomacy was, during the Congo crisis, critically challenged as a political overstep. In practice, the United Nations has not been expected to take an initiative in conflict prevention or early warning; and to date the Security Council has not been convened for early warning purposes. The rules and procedures of the Security Council are such that no active measures could be taken against the political will of its Permanent Members. There is doubtless great scope for further utilizing the Security Council to discuss potential conflicts in developments, thereby linking early warning and prevention – particularly now, with political climate and conditions so different from the Cold War epoch of Hammarskjöld. Such a broader approach to the interpretation of Article 99 could guide the United Nations and its organs to take steps towards reducing root causes and preventing disaster situations.

Reflecting the changes of political power in the USSR, a remarkable achievement was made as early as in 1988 when the UN General Assembly adopted resolution 43/51 on 'Declaration on the Prevention and Removal of Disputes and Situations which may Threaten International Peace and Security and on the Role of the United Nations in this Field.' This recognizes and reaffirms the central role of the United Nations and its organs in preventing international disputes and situations which may lead to international friction. It has also encouraged the Secretary-General to consider using, at an early stage if he deems it appropriate, the right accorded to him under Article 99.

The new Secretary-General, Mr. Boutros-Ghali, is specifically interested in 'preventive diplomacy.' The Summit Meeting of the Security Council in January 1992 – the first meeting of this kind – marks a distinctive development in this regard. Heads of states and governments have demonstrated keen interest in strengthening the effectiveness of UN commitments to the maintenance of peace and security. Indeed, the members of the Security Council requested the Secretary-General to prepare 'his analysis and recommendations on ways of strengthening and making more effi-cient within the framework and provisions of the Charter the capacity of the United Nations for preventive diplomacy, for peace-making and for peace-keeping.'[6]

4. EXISTING EARLY WARNING CAPACITY OF THE UN
    - POTENTIAL AND WEAKNESS

The previous Secretary-General, Mr. Péres de Cuéllar, showed a keen interest in developing the capacity of the United Nations to serve as an early warning centre, and took several measures to this effect. His annual reports on the Work of the Organization always commented on this aspect. In his annual report, he acknowledged that in order 'to avoid the Secretary-General from becoming involved too late in critical situations, it may well be that the Secretary-General should play a more forthright role in bringing potentially dangerous situations to the attention of the Council within the general framework of Article 99 of the Charter.'[7] More concretely, he created the Office for Research and the Collection of Information (ORCI)[8] with the specific mandate of providing early warning of developing situations requiring the Secretary-General's attention, of monitoring factors of possible refugee outflows and comparable emergencies and of carrying out ad hoc research and assessments for the immediate needs of the Secretary-General.[9]

Recognizing that 'information and communication, properly used, are key instruments,'[10] Mr de Cuéllar admits that more refined information is required in order to increase the Organization's preparedness for emergencies and enable it to act surely and swiftly.

The Special Rapporteur to the Commission on Human Rights has made interesting suggestions for spelling out basics for early warning:[11]

> *In order to give birth to an 'early warning system,' it would be necessary to gather, on an ongoing basis, impartial information from proven sources such as governments, the United Nations presence in the countries concerned (whether the UNDP resident representative, specialized agencies, UNIC or other) and further informed parties in order to gain an understanding of the background and all the facets of a situation, including the ethnic, economic, political and social aspects. Of necessity, there would be visits to the field. After assessing all available data, an appreciation to include a number of possible scenarios for the future development of the situation would be given to the Secretary-General of the United Nations and to the competent intergovernmental organs.*

With a view to finding a way of improving international cooperation to avert new massive flows of refugees, the Group of

Governmental Experts on International Cooperation to Avert New Flows of Refugees has examined the existing machinery and practices for dealing with refugee questions. It concludes that improved international cooperation is needed at all levels, in particular within the framework of the United Nations.[12]

Aware of the necessity to activate the potential, the Secretary-General mentioned in his annual report on the Work of the Organization in 1989 the following:[13]

> *The United Nations needs to demonstrate its capacity to function as guardian of the world's security. Neither any alterations in the structure of the Organization nor in the distribution of competence among its respective organs are needed for that purpose. What is needed is an improvement of existing mechanisms and capabilities in the light of the demands of the unfolding international situation.*

What is needed is to develop a conceptual framework that can define and develop a clear, consistent link with the legal basis and information management by the Secretary-General or other institutional authorities.

To determine the capacity of organizations for early warning, we need to examine the extent to which they are involved in monitoring activities (not necessarily early warning as such), and the methodologies they use. Also organizations that have not developed any of these may still potential for early warning in the future.

In this regard, we should note the findings of the Joint Inspection Unit (JIU) report on 'The Coordination of Activities Related to Early Warning of Refugee Flows'.[14] It has stressed that causes of mass movements of people are multiple and complex – a point pertinent to other types of conflicts and disasters as well. The United Nations and its organs have related activities within their own fields of competence, whether directly or indirectly involved in the root causes. Given this extensive involvement, combined with geographical coverage through regional or field offices, the UN system has an immense potential for early warning and could constitute a well-developed network, if only the necessary positive measures are taken.

Recent discussion at the United Nations, particularly in the Economic and Social Council and in the General Assembly, related to the coordination of humanitarian assistance has revealed a growing recognition of the importance of early warning activities.[15] In the General Assembly, discussions on strengthening international response to humanitarian emergencies have lead to the creation of a high post of an Emergency Relief Coordinator, by resolution 46/182 of 19 December 1991.[16] One of the main concerns of the Member States has been the lack of mandate. Many people who are vulnerable or suffering from conflicts or emergency situations do not fall under the mandates of the United Nations and its organs. Under the present structure, they do not enjoy sufficient protection – the most serious examples being displaced persons, who are far more numerous than refugees.

Deliberations at the 46th session of the General Assembly, on the other hand, illustrated a certain apprehension and reserve felt by many developing countries with regard to early warning of conflicts, particularly concerning political factors. By contrast, industrialized countries tended to be very supportive to the idea. Those Member States which are reluctant about early warning cite the claim for 'domestic jurisdiction' of States under Article 2(7) of the UN Charter. However, early warning of developing situations, whether political or not, should by no means imply intervention into the domestic jurisdiction or internal affairs of sovereign States. Only for preparedness and efficient humanitarian assistance or for eventual prevention should the United Nations conduct early-warning related activities. This needs to be made clear.

5. FUTURE PROSPECTS

The review of several offices and organizations has demonstrated that the capacity for early warning certainly, or at least available information, exists – albeit in varying forms – within many UN fora. This capacity can and should be further utilized and even reactivated in order to serve as a useful management tool. The effectiveness of the good use of early warning capacity will largely depend on active involvement of organizations already operating early warning systems or monitoring their fields of activity. Some certainly overlap, but they can also be complementary.

The tendency towards fragmentation of work, with lack of co-operation and coordination, has been a stumbling block. Despite the immense potential and existing capacity, there has been no entity responsible for system-wide coordination of early warning – apart from the ACC Task Force on Long-term Objectives, mainly oriented towards economic forecasting. Now ORCI has been designated as a system-wide central focal point for coordinating early warning of refugees and displaced persons.[17] ORCI has already convened meetings of an Inter-Agency Working Group on Early Warning of New Flows of Refugees and Displaced Persons to work out practical measures for cooperation. Through this working group, strategies, methodologies and procedures will be established for developing steps towards providing early warning as a system-wide input.

The usefulness of early warning depends on how the entities concerned react to it. Therefore a strengthened structure for coordinating mechanisms in humanitarian emergencies would certainly extend the role of early warning. At the same time, early warning would in turn assist the strengthening of international response, where the UN should play an essential role. In adopting resolution 46/182, the General Assembly has stressed the importance of early warning and newly appointed Emergency Relief Co-ordinator will have to highlight the role of early warning in practical terms. However, capacity itself will remain the same, unless positive or proactive measures can be taken to mobilize necessary resources. Urgently needed is further coordination and good management policy planning among the organizations for early warning purposes (see Chapter 2).

The widespread field representation of the UN system suggests that contributions from its field offices to early warning would be of paramount importance. That most of these field offices are located in developing countries and are familiar with local conditions adds to their importance, because underdevelopment is a major element in compounding the vulnerability of the populations. UN field officers also have close contacts with NGOs which can provide them with useful information. Since field-office activities differ in mandate and scope, the exchange and share of information and intersectoral consultations at the field level would of course be crucial. Great scope remains for developing regular and systematic field-level co-operation for early warning purposes. The problem of co-ordination is not insurmountable as long as the objectives and procedures are clearly defined. The managerial approach to early warning will the UN and its organs with a good opportunity to take concerted action for such an important task.

With regard to the gap in the UN mandate, it may be necessary to develop additional legal instruments and acceptable practices which could cover the wide scope for protecting the humanitarian aspect of mankind. Future prospects for developing the early warning concept within the United Nations are not necessarily pessimistic. Deficiencies within the UN system could be offset and supplemented by the activities and competences of other bodies such as NGOs, research communities and governments.

A major step to reactivate, build up and make use of the capacity for early warning is to have the will. Indeed, it would appear that there is a determination on the part of the UN Member States to prevent and reduce many conflicts and their attendant damages. Now that the priority is given to early warning, the United Nations will have to take concrete measures to move ahead swiftly. This can become reality if managers of the organizations take the initiative to introduce such efforts as a regular component of their work. In the end, it is all a matter of transforming strategic thinking into management policy for peace.

NOTES

1 The views expressed in this article are personal and do not necessarily reflect those of the Joint Inspection Unit or the United Nations.

2 'Remote sensing' means the observation of a target (object) by means of a device (sensor) which is separated from the target by a certain distance. A technical definition is given in the International Convention on the Delivery and use of Data from Remote Sensing of the Earth from Outer Space (signed on 19 May 1978).

3 Galtung, J. 1976. 'Three approaches to peace: peace-keeping, peace-making and peace-building', in J.Galtung, *Essays in Peace Research*, Vol.2. Copenhagen.

4 K. Rupesinghe, '*The Quest for a Disaster Early Warning System Giving a Voice to the Vulnerable, Bulletin of Peace Proposals*', vol. 18, no. 2, 1987, p. 218.

5 For further discussion, see Boudreau, Thomas E., 1991. *The U.N. Secretary-General and the Prevention of International Conflict*, New York – Westport, CT – London: Greenwood Press; see also Cot, F.J.P. and Pellet eds, 1985. *La Charte des Nations Unies*, Paris and Brussels, Economic and Bruylant; Gordenker, Leon, 1967. *The U.N. Secretary-General and the Maintenance of Peace*, New York: Columbia University Press, p. 138.

6 S/23500 of 31 January 1992.

7 A/37/1.

8 ST/SGB/225, 1 March 1987. This office will be a part of a new Department of Political Affairs. See A/46/882 of 21 February 1992.

9 ST/SGB/225, 1 March 1987.

10 See A/42/314.

11 E/CN.4/1503, para. 131, p. 59.

12 A/41/324, paras. 51 – 64.

13 A/44/1, p. 11.

14 JIU/REP/90/2, submitted to the 44th session of the General Assembly as A/45/649.

15 See documents A/46/568, *Report of the Secretary-General* on the review of the capacity, experience and coordination arrangements in the United Nations system for humanitarian assistance. E/1991/109/Add.1, *Report on Refugees, Displaced Persons and Returnees*, prepared by Mr. Jacques Cuenod, Consultant.

16 Among the various documents circulated for the discussion, see particularly a study by Urquhart & Childers on '*Strengthening International Response to Humanitarian Emergencies*,' October 1991.

17. As referred to in note 8, the ORCI does no longer exist as such. It will instead be incorporated into a new department which will take over ORCI's old functions. A new post of Emergency Relief Coordinator, and a new office called the Department of Humanitarian assistance may take over some of the functions of ORCI related to early warning. However, the role of the Inter-Agency Working Group and the role of ORCI as convenor and focal point will continue to exist.

Index

Selected Bibliography

Aga Khan, Sadruddin, 1981. Report to the Commission on Human Rights. Question of the Violation of Human Rights and Fundamental Freedoms in Any Part of the World, with Particular Reference to Colonial and Other Dependent Countries and Territories: Study on Human Rights and Massive Exoduses. United Nations, E/CN.4/1503, Geneva: United Nations.

Aga Khan, Sadruddin, 1984. 'Human Rights and Mass Exodus: Developing an International Conscience', in *Minorities: A Question of Human Rights*, Whitaker B., ed., Oxford, United Kingdom: Pergamon Press, pp. 119-27.

Andriole, Stephen & Robert A. Young, 1977. 'Toward the Development of an Integrated Crisis Warning System', *International Studies Quarterly*, vol. 21, no. 1, pp. 107ff.

Beyer, Gregg A, 1990. 'Monitoring Root Causes of Refugee Flows and Early Warning: A Need for Substance'. *International Journal of Refugee Law*, Special Issue.

Boudrean, Thomas E., 1991. *Sheathing the Sword. The United Nations Secretary-General and the Prevention of International Conflict*, New York, Wesport, Connecticut, London: Greenwood Press.

Clark, Lance, n.d. 'Early Warning of Refugee Mass Influx Emergencies', Washington, D.C.: Refugee Policy Group (RPG).

Clark, Lance, 1986. 'Early Warning Case Study: The 1984-85 Influx of Tigrayans into Eastern Sudan', working paper # 2, Washington, D.C.: Refugee Policy Group.

Clark, Lance, 1988. 'Early Warning of Refugee Flows', Washington, D.C.: Refugee Policy Group, June.

Clark, Lance, 1988. 'Selected Constraints on Early Warning Actions by UNHCR (And What to Do About Them)', Washington D.C.: Refugee Policy Group.

Clark, Lance, 1988. 'Recommended Next Steps for UNHCR Regarding Early Warning', Washington, D.C.: Refugee Policy Group.

Clark, Lance, 1988. 'Famine in Ethiopia and the International Response', opening remarks, conference at Harvard, 11 May.

Claude, Inis. 'Preventive Diplomacy as an Approach to Peace', *Swords into Plowshares*, 4th ed. 1971, pp. 312-48.

Clay, Jason W. & Bonnie K. Holcomb, 1986. 'Politics and the Ethiopian Famine, 1984-1985', *Cultural Survival Report 20*, rev. ed.

Clay, Jason W., Sandra Steingraber, & Peter Niggli, 1988. 'The Spoils of Famine, Ethiopian Famine and Peasant Agriculture', *Cultural Survival Report 25*, Cambridge, Mass.

Coles, G.J.L., 1982. 'Pre-Flow Aspects of the Refugee Phenomen', background paper prepared for the International Institute for Humanitarian Law, San Remo, Italy.

Coles, G.J.L., 1982. 'Report of the Round Table on Pre-Flow Aspects of the Refugee Phenomen', San Remo: International Institute of Humanitarian Law.

Coles, G.J.L., 1986. 'A United Nations Early Warning System and the Role of UNHCR', Memorandum, 21 January.

Drüke, Luise, 1988. 'Causes of Refugee Problems and the International Response', in Alan Nash, ed., *Human Rights and the Protection of Refugees under International Law*, Montreal: Canadian Human Rights Foundation and the Institute for Research on Public Policy.

Drüke, Luise, 1990. *Preventive Action for Refugee Producing Situations*, Frankfurt am Main: Peter Lang.

Franck, Thomas M., 1985. *Nation Against Nation*, New York: Oxford University Press.

Gordenker, Leon, 1986. 'Early Warning of Disastrous Population Movement', *International Migration Review*, vol. 20, no. 2.

Gordenker, Leon, 1987. *Refugees in International Politics*, New York: Columbia University Press.

Gordenker, Leon, 1989. 'Early Warning of Refugee Incidents: Potentials and Obstacles', in Loescher, Gil & Leila Monahan, eds, *Refugees and International Relations*, New York: Oxford University Press.

Gordenker, Leon, 1989. 'Refugees in International Politics', in de Jong, Deny & Alex Voet, eds, *Refugees in the World: the European Community's Response*, Amsterdam and Utrecht: Dutch Refugee Council and Netherlands Institute of Human Rights.

Haüsermann, J., 1986. 'Root Causes of Displacement: The Legal Framework for International Concern and Action', London: Rights and Humanity, p. 31.

Jonah, James O.C., 1989. 'The Monitoring of Factors Related to Possible Refugee Outflows and Comparable Emergencies', statement made to United Nations Commission on Human Rights, New York.

Kanninen, Tapio, 1987. 'New Prospects at the United Nations to Utilize Research and Technology Related to Data on International Relations', background paper for participants at the Conference on New Technologies for the Codification, Storage, Retrieval and Analysis of International Events Data, 13-15 November at the Center for International Studies, M.I.T., Cambridge.

Kanninen, Tapio, 1990. 'Early Warning of Forced Migration in the United Nations: Conceptual and Practical Issues', paper presented at Seminar on Development Strategies on Forced Migration in the Third World, The Hague: Institute of Social Studies, 27-29 August.

Kaufmann, Johan & Schrijver, Nico, 1990. *Changing Global Needs: Expanding Roles for the United Nations System*, Hanover, N.H.: Academic Council on the United Nations System.

Lanphier, C. Michael, 1988. 'Bureaucratization and Political Commitment: Challenges for NGO Refugee Assistance', in Bramwell, Anna C., *Refugees in the Age of Total War*, London: Unwin Hyman.

Lamb, K, 1985. *An Information and Warning System to Improve Information Management in the Refugee Field: An Evaluation of the Concept*, Harvard University, Cambridge.

Lee, Luke T., 1984. 'The United Nations Group of Governmental Experts on International Co-operation to Avert New Flows of Refugees'. *American Journal of International Law*, vol. 78, pp. 480-4.

Lee, Luke T., 1987. 'The United Nations Group of Governmental Experts on International Co-operation to Avert New Flows of Refugees: Part II', *American Journal of International Law*, vol. 81, pp. 442-4.

Lee, Luke T., 1986. 'The Right to Compensation: Refugees and Countries of Asylum'. *American Journal of International Law*, vol. 80, pp. 532-67.

Lee, Luke T., 1987. 'Toward a World Without Refugees: The United Nations Group of Governmental Experts on International Co-operation to Avert New Flows of Refugees', *The British Yearbook of International Law*, 1986, rpt, Oxford: Clarendon Press.

Macalister-Smith, Peter, 1985. 'International Humanitarian Assistance: Disaster Relief Actions in International Law and Organizations', Dordrecht: Martinus Nijhoff Publishers.

Maynard, P.D., 1982. 'The Legal Competence of the UNHCR', *International and Comparative Law Quarterly*, vol. 31, pp. 415-425.

Mazur, Robert, 1986. 'Linking Popular Initiative and Aid Agencies: The Case of Refugees'. British Refugee Council/Queen Elizabeth House working paper 3, no. 2.

Nnoli, Okwudiba, 1990. 'Desertification, Refugees and Regional Conflict in West Africa', *Disasters*, vol. 14, no. 2, pp. 132-8.

Onishi, Akira, 1987. 'Global Early Warning System for Displaced Persons: Interlinkages of Environment, Development, Peace and Human Rights', in *Technical Forecasting and Social Change* 31, pp. 269-99.

Pitterman, Shelly, 1987. 'Determinants of International Refugee Policy: A Comparative Study of UNHCR Material Assistance to Refugees in Africa, 1963-1981', in Rogge, John R., ed., *Refugees: A Third World Dilemma*, Totawa, N.J.: Rowman and Littlefield.

Puchala, Donald J. & Roger A. Coate, 1988. *The State of the United Nations*, Hanover, N.J.: Academic Council on the UN System.

Puchala, Donald J. & Roger A. Coate, 1989. *The Challenge of Relevance: the United Nations in a Changing World Environment*, Hanover, N.H.: Academic Council on the United Nations System.

Ramcharan, B.G., 1989. 'Early Warning at the United Nations: First Experiment', *International Journal of Refugee Law*, Oxford University Press, vol. 1(3).

Refugee Policy Group, 1983. 'Early Warning of Mass Refugee Flows', Washington, D.C.

Refugee Policy Group, 1984. 'Emergency Preparedness and Response Capacities: Notes from a Meeting on Early Warning', Washington, D.C.: Refugee Policy Group.

Refugee Policy Group, 1983. 'Early Warning: An analysis of Approaches to Improving International Responses to Refugee Crises', mimeographed paper, Washington, D.C.: Refugee Policy Group.

Refugee Policy Group, 1983. 'Refugee Issues: Current Status and Directions for the Future', Washington, D.C.: Refugee Policy Group.

Refugee Policy Group, 1985. 'Early Warning of Refugee Influx Emergencies', paper prepared for the UNHCR Emergency Training Seminar at the University of Wisconsin.

Refugee Policy Group, 1988. 'Selected Constraints on Early Warning Actions by UNHCR (And What to Do About Them)', Washington, D.C.: Refugee Policy Group.

Roesel, Jakob, 1989. 'Ethnische Konflikte in den Staaten der Dritten Welt', *Verfassung und Recht in Uebersee*, vol. 22, no. 3, pp. 285-311.

Rupesinghe, Kumar, 1990. 'The Disappearing Boundaries Between Internal and External Conflicts', paper submitted to the IPRA Conference in Groningen, July, revised version in Rupesinghe, Kumar, ed., 1992. *Internal Conflicts and Governance*, London, Macmillan.

Rupesinghe, Kumar, 1989. 'Some Conceptual Problems with Early Warning', *Bulletin of Peace Proposals*, no. 2.

Rupesinghe, Kumar, ed., 1989. 'Building Peace after Military Withdrawals', *Bulletin of Peace Proposals*, special issue, no. 3, also published as book by Sage, London.

Rupesinghe, Kumar, ed., 1987. 'Ethnic Conflict and Human Rights. A comparative Perspective', *Bulletin of Peace Proposals*, special issue, vol. 18, no. 4, also published as bood by United Nations University and the Norwegian University Press, Tokyo/Oslo, 1988.

Rupesinghe, Kumar, 1988. 'Ethnic Violence, Human Rights and Early Warning', *UNESCO Yearbook for Peace and Conflict Studies*, Westport: Greenwood Press. Also PRIO Paper 05/86.

Rupesinghe, Kumar, 1987. 'The Quest for a Disaster Early Warning System. Giving a Voice to the Vulnerable', *PRIO Paper*, 15/86, and *PRIO Report*, 2/88. Also published in *Bulletin of Peace Proposals*, vol. 18, no. 2.

Rupesinghe, Kumar, 1987. 'Theories of Conflict Resolution and their Applicability to Protracted Ethnic Conflicts', Bulletin of Peace Proposals, vol. 18, no. 4. Also published as *PRIO Report*, no. 1, April, 1988.

Rupesinghe, Kumar, 1989. 'Early Warning and Conflict Resolution', a discussion paper presented at a seminar on Early Warning and Conflict Resolution, Oslo, 24-25 April, in *PRIO Report* no. 4.

Rupesinghe, Kumar, 1989. 'Report of the Proceedings of the Early Warning and Conflict Resolution seminar in Oslo 24-25 April, in *PRIO Inform*, no. 3.

Ruru, Sharon, 1990. 'The Role of the Collector in Early Warning'. *International Journal of Refugee Law*, special issue, vol. 2, Oxford University Press, pp. 65-70.

Russett, Bruce, 1974. *Power and Community in World Politics*, San Francisco: Freeman, esp.ch. 3: 'Indicators for America's Linkages with the Changing World Environment'.

Ryan, Stephen, 1990. 'Ethnic Conflict and the United Nations', *Ethnic and Racial Studies*, vol. 13, no. 1, January, pp. 25-49.

Salih, M.A. Mohamed, 1990. 'Ecological Stress and Political Coercion in West Africa', *Disasters*, vol. 14, no. 2, pp. 125-31.

Singer, J. David, ed., 1968. *Quantitative International Politics. Insights and Evidence,* New York: Free Press, 1968, esp. the contributions by Rummel, Rudolph J. 'The Relationship Between National Attributes and Foreign Conflict Behavious' and Russett, Bruce M. 'Delineating International Regions'.

Singer, J. David & Richard J. Stoll, eds, 1984. *Quantitative Indicators in World Politics, Timely Assurance and Early Warning,* New York: Praeger.

Singer, J. David & Michael D. Wallace, eds, 1979. *To Augur Well. Early Warning Indicators in World Politics,* Beverly Hills - London: Sage.

Swift, Richard, 1990. 'Is Any Development Sustainable?', *Ploughshares Monitor*, June, pp. 15-17.

Taylor, C.L., ed., *Aggregate Data Analysis. Political and Social Indicators in Cross-National Research*, Paris - The Hague: Mouton & Co.

United Nations Group of Governmental Experts on International Co-operation to Avert New Flows of Refugees, 1984. A/35/PV.1-33. Official Records of the General Assembly, Thirty-Fifth Session, Plenary Meetings, vol. 1, New York: United Nations.

United Nations Group of Governmental Experts on International Co-operation to Avert New Flows of Refugees, 1988. United Nations Document ST/SGB/Organization: ORCI, 3 October, Organization Manual: 'A Description of the Functions and Organization of the Office for Research and the Collection of Information'.

United Nations Group of Governmental Experts on International Co-operation to Avert New Flows of Refugees, 1986. Supplement No. 49, A/41/49, New York, Report of the Group of 18, General Assembly, 41st session.

United Nations, Joint Inspection Unit, 1990. 'The Co-ordination of Activities Related to Early Warning of Possible Refugee Flows', United Nations Document A/45/649, Geneva.

United Nations, 1991. E/1991/109/Add.1. 'Report on Refugees, Displaced Persons and Returnees', prepared by Mr. Jacques Cuenod, Consultant, 27 June.

Wilkenfeld, Jonathan, Hopple, Gerald W. & Paul J. Rossa, 1979. 'Sociopolitical Indicators of Conflict and Cooperation', in: To Augur Well, *Early Warning Indicators in World Politics*, edited by Singer, J. David, & Wallace, Michael D., Beverly Hills-London: Sage, pp. 109-51.

Williams, Douglas, 1987. *The Specialized Agencies and the United Nations*, London, Hurst & Co.

Zolberg, Aristide, Suhrke, Astri & Sergio Aguayo, 1986. 'International Factors in the Formation of Refugee Movements'. *International Migration Review*, vol. 20, no. 2, Summer.

Zolberg, Aristide, Suhrke, Astri & Sergio Aguayo, 1989. *Escape from Violence: Conflict and the Refugee Crisis in the Developing World*, New York: Oxford University Press.